W9-AVZ-204

RED SKY in the Morning

BILL Bright
&
JOHN N. Damoose

Red Sky in the Morning: How You Can Help Prevent America's Gathering Storms

Published by
New*Life* Publications
A ministry of Campus Crusade for Christ
P.O. Box 593684
Orlando, FL 32859-3684

Design and production by Genesis Publications.

Cover by Koechel-Peterson Design.

Printed in the United States of America.

Library of Congress Cataloging-in-Publication Data
Bright, Bill.
Red sky in the morning : how you can help prevent America's gathering storms / by Bill Bright and John N. Damoose.
p. cm.
Includes bibliographical references and index.
ISBN 1-56399-095-4 (hc.)
1. Christianity—United States. 2. United States—Moral conditions.
I. Damoose, John N., 1972– . II. Title.
BR526.B754 1998
277.3—dc21
98-24200
CIP

For more information, write:

L.I.F.E., Campus Crusade for Christ—P.O. Box 40, Flemington Markets, NSW 2129, Australia.

Campus Crusade for Christ of Canada—Box 529, Sumas, WA 98295

Campus Crusade for Christ—Fairgate House, King's Road, Tyseley, Birmingham, B11 2AA, United Kingdom

Lay Institute for Evangelism, Campus Crusade for Christ—P.O. Box 8786, Auckland, 1035, New Zealand

Campus Crusade for Christ—9 Lock Road #3-03, Paccan Centre, Singapore 108937

Great Commission Movement of Nigeria—P.O. Box 500, Jos, Plateau State, Nigeria, West Africa

Campus Crusade for Christ International—P.O. Box 593684, Orlando, FL 32859-3684, USA

Contents

Part III: An Appeal to the Church

Part IV: A Plan for Spiritual Renewal

Appendices

Urgent Personal Letter

My dear fellow Americans:

It is with burning hearts and a great sense of urgency that John N. Damoose and I have written this book, *Red Sky in the Morning.*

We are writing to encourage all concerned citizens in our beloved country to join us in a crucial endeavor to help bring about a moral and spiritual rebirth in America. We are also writing to all followers of Jesus Christ, urging you to pray, fast, and work for a revival in our churches and for a mighty spiritual awakening across our land.

Our concern is great because, according to most social indicators, we as a nation are in danger of losing our soul. Our Lord's warning to individuals also applies to nations: "What does it profit a man if he gains the whole world and loses his own soul?" (Matthew 16:26). The problems facing America are severe. Solving these problems is to us a matter of life and death for our beloved country.

Some time ago, I sat next to a stranger on an airplane en route from Los Angeles to Orlando. He was lamenting what is happening to our nation—the skyrocketing drug use, widespread crime, rampant immorality, unwise judicial decisions, and national political infighting. I listened for a few minutes, then asked, "Would you like to know why we are having these problems?"

He asked, "Do you know why?"

"Yes, I do," I said. "Here, read this." I handed him my Bible and directed him to Deuteronomy chapters 8 and 28, which describe God's promise of blessings on Israel if they obeyed Him, or curses if they disobeyed Him. These principles applied not only to Israel then, but to all nations today, especially America.

He read it. He read it again. He seemed deeply moved, as though a light had come on in his understanding. "Now I understand," he said soberly as he handed the Bible back to me.

The same God who spoke to Abraham, Isaac, and Jacob concerning His plans for their descendants also spoke to our Founding Fathers, such as George Washington, although certainly not in words that would become holy Scripture. Washington's love for and dedication to our Lord Jesus Christ were demonstrated by his daily spiritual walk, including at least one hour each morning and evening reading his Bible and praying on his knees.

My dear friends, please read the above-mentioned passages from Deuteronomy as well as 2 Chronicles 7, especially God's promise to King Solomon recorded in verse 14:

> "If my people, who are called by my name, will humble themselves and pray and seek my face and turn from their wicked ways, then will I hear from heaven and will forgive their sin and will heal their land."

When you fully recognize the relevancy and the urgency of these passages, you will understand why I have fasted and prayed for forty days each year since 1994, claiming by faith an awakening and revival for America and the world, which would result in the fulfillment of the Great Commission. No other spiritual discipline meets the conditions of that great promise of God's healing like personal and corporate fasting and prayer.

Furthermore, when our Lord gave the Great Commission to His disciples, He admonished them to teach the new disciples what He had taught them. One of the most important instructions He taught them by personal example was the need for fasting and prayer. As our model and mentor, Jesus set the example for our need to fast and pray as preparation for spiritual ministry.

Only God can help us find solutions to this present crisis, the greatest our nation has ever faced. Unless He sovereignly and supernaturally intervenes, our nation shall lose its own soul, and the consequences will be worse than Russia's revolution under

Lenin and Stalin or Germany's under Hitler.

In *Red Sky in the Morning,* five main points form the core of our concerns for this nation. We invite you to join us on a fascinating journey exploring these areas to rediscover our nation's purpose:

- The circumstances surrounding the *birth* of the greatest nation on earth
- The *beliefs* of those who contributed to its birth
- The reasons America has received God's *blessings* as no other nation in history
- The factors leading to the *breakdown* of the moral and spiritual values that form the fiber of our nation
- The way in which our beloved country can experience a *rebirth* of God's favor and blessing

Before you read further, let me explain how John Damoose and I have handled the difficult aspects of dual authorship. Both of us were writing a book on our nation's Christian heritage and its moral and spiritual decline. Upon learning that God had given each of us a burden to share this message, I asked John to join me in this effort. For clarity, we have presented the book from my viewpoint. This was only to make the book easier to read and in no way minimizes the importance of John's contribution to this book.

Many of you may have little or no knowledge of the biblical foundation upon which our Founding Fathers built this great nation; others may already be familiar with our country's godly heritage. In either case, please begin by taking a few moments to read the following sections containing quotations and stories of the many sacrifices made to give *birth* to this nation. As you read this book, ask God what He wants you to do to help bring about a moral and spiritual *rebirth* in our beloved country.

Sincerely,

Bill Bright

Dr. Bill Bright, Founder and President
Campus Crusade for Christ International

They Spoke of Their Faith

Quotations From Our Founding Fathers and Other National Leaders

George Washington, *"Father of Our Country," 1st President of the U.S.:*

"Bless O Lord the whole race of mankind, and let the world be filled with the knowledge of Thee and Thy Son, Jesus Christ."[1]

"It is impossible to rightly govern the world without God and the Bible."[2]

"Of all the habits which lead to political prosperity, religion and morality are indispensable supports... Reason and experience both forbid us to expect that national morality can prevail in exclusion of religious principle."[3] *(in his Farewell Speech, 1796)*

Patrick Henry, *American Revolutionary Leader:*

"It cannot be emphasized too strongly or too often that this great nation was founded, not by religionists, but by Christians; not on religions, but on the Gospel of Jesus Christ."[4]

Thomas Jefferson, *3rd President of the United States:*

"God who gave us life gave us liberty. And can the liberties of a nation be thought secure when we have removed their only firm basis, a conviction in the minds of the people that these liberties are a gift from God? That they are not to be violated but with His wrath? Indeed I tremble for my country when I reflect that God is just, and that His justice cannot sleep forever."[5] *(excerpts are inscribed on the walls of the Jefferson Memorial in the nation's capital)*

Benjamin Franklin, *signer of the Declaration of Independence:*

"Whoever shall introduce into public affairs the principles of primitive Christianity will change the face of the world."[6]

John Adams, *2nd President of the United States:*

"We have no government armed with power capable of contending with human passions unbridled by morality and religion. Avarice, ambition, revenge, or gallantry would break the strongest cords of our Constitution as a whale goes through a net. Our Constitution was made only for a moral and religious people. It is wholly inadequate to the government of any other."[7]

James Madison, *known as the "Chief Architect of the Constitution":*

"[A] watchful eye must be kept on ourselves lest, while we are building ideal monuments of renown and bliss here, we neglect to have our names enrolled in the Annals of Heaven."[8]

"To the same Divine Author of every good and perfect gift we are indebted for all those privileges and advantages, religious as well as civil, which are so richly enjoyed in this favored land."[9]

Continental Congress, *1778*:

"Whereas true religion and good morals are the only solid foundations of public liberty and happiness…it is hereby earnestly recommended to the several States to take the most effectual measures for the encouragement thereof."[10]

Samuel Adams, *signer of the Declaration of Independence:*

"May every citizen in the army and in the country have a proper sense of the Deity upon his mind and an impression of the declaration recorded in the Bible, "Him that honoreth me I will honor, but he that despiseth me shall be lightly esteemed [1 Samuel 2:30]."[11]

"The Supreme Ruler of the Universe, having been pleased in the course of His providence to establish the independence of the United States of America…we ought to be led by religious feelings of gratitude and to walk before Him in all humility according to His most holy law…That with true repentance and contrition of heart we may unitedly implore the forgiveness of our sins through the merits of Jesus Christ and humbly supplicate our heavenly Father."[12] *(in proclaiming a Day of Public Fasting, Humiliation, and Prayer, 1795)*

John Jay, *1st Chief Justice of the U.S. Supreme Court:*

"I... recommend a general and public return of praise and thanksgiving to Him from whose goodness these blessings descend. The most effectual means of securing the continuance of our civil and religious liberties, is always to remember with reverence and gratitude the source from which they flow."[13]

"Providence has given to our people the choice of their rulers, and it is the duty, as well as the privilege and interest of our Christian nation to select and prefer Christians for their rulers."[14]

Benjamin Rush, *signer of the Declaration of Independence:*

"I do not believe that the Constitution was the offspring of inspiration, but I am as perfectly satisfied that the Union of the States in its form and adoption is as much the work of a Divine Providence as any of the miracles recorded in the Old and New Testament."[15]

Charles Carroll, *signer of the Declaration of Independence:*

"[W]ithout morals a republic cannot subsist any length of time; they therefore who are decrying the Christian religion, whose morality is so sublime and pure... are undermining the solid foundation of morals, the best security for the duration of free governments."[16]

Daniel Webster, *statesman, congressman*

"If the power of the Gospel is not felt throughout the length and breadth of the land, anarchy and misrule, degradation and misery, corruption and darkness will reign without mitigation or end."[17]

Noah Webster, *statesman, lexicographer:*

"In my view, the Christian religion is the most important and one of the first things in which all children, under a free government ought to be instructed... No truth is more evident to my mind than that the Christian religion must be the basis of any government intended to secure the rights and privileges of a free people."[18]

John Witherspoon, *signer of the Declaration of Independence:*

"He is the best friend to American liberty, who is most sincere and active in promoting true and undefiled religion, and who sets himself with the greatest firmness to bear down profanity and immorality of every kind. Whoever is an avowed enemy of God, I scruple not [do not hesitate] to call him an enemy of his country."[19]

Andrew Jackson, *7th President of the United States, referring to the Bible:*

"That book, Sir, is the Rock upon which our republic rests."[20]

House Judiciary Committee, *1854*

"The great vital and conservative element in our system is the belief of our people in the pure doctrines and divine truths of the gospel of Jesus Christ."[21]

Abraham Lincoln, *16th President of the United States:*

"It is the duty of nations as well as of men to own their dependence upon the overruling power of God, to confess their sins and transgressions in humble sorrow...and to recognize the sublime truth, announced in the Holy Scriptures and proven by all history: that those nations only are blessed whose God is the Lord."[22]

"We have been the recipients of the choicest bounties of Heaven. We have been preserved these many years in peace and prosperity. We have grown in numbers, wealth and power as no other nation has ever grown. But we have forgotten God. We have forgotten the gracious Hand which preserved us in peace, and multiplied and enriched and strengthened us; and we have vainly imagined, in the deceitfulness of our hearts, that all these blessings were produced by some superior wisdom and virtue of our own. Intoxicated with unbroken success, we have become too self-sufficient to feel the necessity of redeeming and preserving grace, too proud to pray to the God that made us! It behooves us then to humble ourselves before the offended Power, to confess our national sins and to pray for clemency and forgiveness."[23] *(in proclaiming a National Fast Day, March 30, 1863)*

U.S. Supreme Court, *Church of the Holy Trinity v. United States (1892):*

"Our laws and our institutions must necessarily be based upon and embody the teachings of the Redeemer of mankind. It is impossible that it should be otherwise; and in this sense and to this extent our civilization and our institutions are emphatically Christian."[24]

They Pledged Their All

Whatever Happened to the Signers of the Declaration of Independence?

On July 4, 1776, delegates to the Continental Congress voted to accept the Declaration of Independence in Philadelphia's Independence Hall. On August 2, fifty-six men signed their names to this historic document, giving birth to a new nation as they declared their independence from Great Britain.

If General George Washington's ragged, outnumbered army could not drive back the British troops, every signer, upon capture, would be tried for treason against the British Crown under penalty of death. Their signatures could, win or lose, mean that their homes would be looted and burned. If Washington surrendered in defeat, their farms, businesses, and properties would be confiscated or destroyed. Fifty-six men knew—when they signed—that they were risking everything, including their lives.

Yet, to a man, the desire for freedom drove them to sign and make this pledge: "For the support of this declaration, with a firm reliance on the protection of Divine Providence, we mutually pledge to each other our lives, our fortunes, and our sacred honor."

Who were these "superpatriots"? Most were well-educated, prosperous businessmen and professionals. Two dozen were lawyers or judges; nine were farmers or plantation owners; eleven were merchants. Among them were also physicians, politicians, educators, and a minister; several were sons of pastors.

Have you ever wondered what happened to the men who

signed the Declaration of Independence, pledging all that they possessed so that this nation, under God, would not perish from the earth? What price fell upon the heads of those courageous patriots?

Here is the documented fate of that gallant fifty-six.

Carter Braxton of Virginia, wealthy planter and trader, saw his ships swept from the seas by the British Navy. To pay his debts, he lost his home and all of his properties, and died in poverty.

Thomas Lynch, Jr., an aristocratic plantation owner, was a third-generation rice grower. After he signed, his health failed. With his wife he set out for France to regain his declining health. Their ship never reached France, and he was never heard from again.

Thomas McKean of Delaware was so harassed by the enemy that he and his family were forced into hiding, moving five times during the war. He served in Congress without pay. Poverty was his reward.

Vandals and enemy soldiers looted the properties of Bartlett, Ellery, Clymer, Hall, Gwinnet, Walton, Heyward, Rutledge, and Middleton; the latter four were captured and imprisoned.

Thomas Nelson, Jr., of Virginia, raised $2 million to supply our French allies by offering his property as collateral. Because he was never reimbursed by the struggling new government, he was unable to repay the note when it came due—wiping out his entire estate. In the final battle for Yorktown, Nelson urged General Washington to fire on his home as it was occupied by British General Cornwallis. Nelson's home was destroyed, leaving him bankrupt when he died.

The British seized the home of Francis Hopkinson of New Jersey, and for seven years occupied the home of William Floyd of New York.

Francis Lewis had his home and everything in it destroyed, and his wife imprisoned. She later died from the brutal treatment she had received.

After signing the Declaration, Richard Stockton, a State Supreme Court Justice, rushed back to his estate near Princeton in an effort to save his wife and children. Although he and his family found refuge with friends, a Tory betrayed them. Judge Stockton was pulled from bed in the night and beaten by British soldiers. Then he was jailed and deliberately starved. After his release, with his home burned and all of his possessions destroyed, he and his family were forced to live off charity.

John Hart was driven from his dying wife's bedside. Their thirteen children scattered in all directions as they fled for their lives. His fields and grist mills were laid waste. For more than a year he lived in forests and caves and returned home after the war to find his wife dead, his children gone, his properties all destroyed. He died a few weeks later of exhaustion and a broken heart without ever seeing a member of his family again.

Lewis Morris and Philip Livingston suffered fates similar to Hart's.

John Hancock was known for more than his large, sweeping signature. One of the wealthiest men in New England, he stood outside Boston one terrible night of the war and said, "Burn, Boston, though it makes John Hancock a beggar, if the public good requires it." He lost most of his fortune during the war, having given over $100,000 to the cause of freedom.

They fulfilled that PLEDGE. They paid their PRICE. And FREEDOM was born.

Caesar Rodney, Delaware statesman, was gravely ill with facial cancer. Unless he returned to England for treatment, his life would end. Yet Rodney sealed his fate by signing the Declaration of Independence. He was one of several who fulfilled their pledge with their lives.

Nathan Hale also laid down his life for our nation. As a captain in the Continental Army, Hale volunteered to penetrate enemy lines to spy for the American cause. He was captured by the British. On the day of his execution by hanging in September 1776, Hale spoke these last words: "I only regret that I have but one life to lose for my country."

In all, five of the fifty-six were captured by the British and tortured. Twelve had their homes ransacked, looted, confiscated by the enemy, or burned to the ground. Seventeen lost their fortunes. Two lost their sons in the army; another had two sons captured.

Nine of the fifty-six lost their lives in the war, from wounds or hardships inflicted by the enemy.

These were only a few examples of the sacrifices made by those fifty-six courageous men who boldly pledged their all to support the Declaration of Independence. Of those who took the pledge to defend the sovereignty of their nation and the liberty of its people, many were forced to pay a heavy price before that bold vision could be realized.

It is important to remember this about them: Despite the hardships they encountered—regardless of the heavy price exacted by that pledge—not a single one of them defected or failed to honor his pledge! These men of means, prosperity, and security, who enjoyed much ease and luxury in their personal living, considered liberty to be so much more important than security that they pledged their lives, their fortunes, and their sacred honor. And they fulfilled that pledge. They paid their price. And freedom was born.

I have often wondered, *Why would a loving God allow those deeply dedicated Founding Fathers of our beloved country to suffer such tremendous personal hardship?* Then one day, the obvious answer occurred to me.

God sent His one and only Son to die on the cross to pay the penalty for our sins, to liberate us from the darkness of Satan's kingdom and set us free to enjoy life in all its fullness. In much the same way, He provided godly, dedicated men to pay a great price to bring liberty to this nation so that we can experience a freedom unparalleled by any country in history. These examples show us that great success does not come without great sacrifice.

Today, 265 million Americans enjoy freedoms unknown to the rest of the world. Our Founding Fathers undertook an "experiment" unprecedented in history to build a great nation based on biblical principles for the glory of God. Their willingness to sacrifice inspires us to put aside the anxieties keeping us from advancing the kingdom of God. We too should be prepared to give up our comforts, material wealth, and perhaps our lives, if necessary, to help spark a spiritual rebirth of this nation whose Founding Fathers sacrificed at great personal cost to birth over two hundred years ago.

Foreword

By Chuck Colson

Just as the apostle Paul exhorts believers not to be conformed to this world but to be transformed by the renewing of our minds, so too does *Red Sky in the Morning* compellingly call us to think and care about the culture around us in a Christian way. This book, written by my dear friend Bill Bright and the very talented John N. Damoose, is a clarion call to the Church and right-thinking citizens throughout our nation.

No one is more able to issue this kind of challenge than Bill Bright. He has long been recognized as a great visionary for the cause of Christ in our age. His leadership earned worldwide recognition in 1996 when he was awarded the prestigious Templeton Prize for progress in religion. I have known Bill Bright personally for twenty-two years, and rarely have I met a more selfless, more godly man. I have never known him to say or do anything except in obedience to the leading of the Holy Spirit. So when he speaks, as he does so eloquently in these pages, all Christians should listen and pay heed. In *Red Sky in the Morning*, Bill Bright and John Damoose help us to escape our own limited, myopic view of the world and will call us to the heroic effort our faith demands.

The task that these men lay before us is a daunting one. Americans have been blessed beyond any other nation in history. And yet, as another recipient of the Templeton Prize, Alexander Solzhenitsyn, once trenchantly declared, "Men have forgotten God." Ours is a land that has abandoned its own heritage.

That heritage is rooted firmly in the Christian faith. Our Founders pledged their lives, their fortunes, and their sacred honor to undertake this noble experiment in ordered liberty. They firmly believed that human freedom could be guaranteed only as long as the people exercised their civic duty, as long as virtue was exalted. A growing government can be curbed only when the people can dependably govern themselves. But this presupposes a people with a deep and abiding religious faith. John Adams, one of the most influential of the Founding Fathers, put it succinctly: "Our Constitution was made only for a moral and religious people. It is wholly inadequate to the government of any other."[1]

But are Americans still a religious people? To be sure, many contemporary Americans love the Lord; church attendance remains about forty-five percent. More Christian missions are supported by America than by all the other nations of the world combined.

Yet the religiously informed moral consensus undergirding our free institutions has been eroded by the cultural upheaval of the sixties, by rampant materialism, by the mocking of honor and virtue, by a rejection of moral truth by the majority of Americans. It can no longer be said that America is a Christian nation; instead, it has become post-Christian in its values, attitude, outlook, and worldview.

The loss of a Christian consensus poses a grave peril to our political system. There exist only two restraints on the sinful human disposition: the internal restraint of conscience and the external force of law and the state. As statesman Robert Winthrop warned 150 years ago, the weaker the internal restraint, the stronger the external restraint must be. Take away a nation's Bible and you'd better polish up its bayonets. Ultimately, the collapse of moral restraints—the death of conscience—must lead to the loss of freedom. Swiss theologian Francis Schaeffer used to say that as truth retreats, tyranny advances.

This process is well underway in America today. As moral standards have withered, the courts have stepped in to fill the void. Since *Roe v. Wade*, the courts have been taking upon themselves more and more power, denying to the people the right to govern themselves through their own elected representatives. This is what Thomas Jefferson warned could happen: the judiciary would become a despotic branch.

The trend toward judicial usurpation, i.e., the courts' overruling of democratically enacted laws, brought together several Christian leaders in 1996 for a much-publicized symposium called *The End of Democracy?* This led to a remarkable statement titled "We Hold These Truths," signed by forty-two leaders—Catholic, Protestant, and Orthodox—among them both Bill Bright and myself. The paper, released on July 4, 1997, called the courts to account and urged all Americans to protect the instruments of self-government, especially to renew and refresh that moral consensus that makes self-government possible.

Bill Bright and John Damoose understand the contemporary crisis. They know that the greatest threat to America is her moral decline. They also understand where the answers will be found: among people of faith who are aware of the problem and prepared to act courageously. This is the case that these men set forth so powerfully in the pages that follow.

America's spiritual recovery is no small challenge to meet, but is it any greater than the one that confronted the Pilgrims or the settlers of Jamestown? They faced a dangerous journey and the arduous work of establishing a new way of life, and they found God's grace sufficient. What of George Washington and the Continental Army? Confronted with the most highly trained and powerful foe in the world, they too found God's grace sufficient. And in circumstances of spiritual decay not unlike our own, Jonathan Edwards and the other evangelists who led the Great Awakening found that God's grace lent efficacy to their preaching. Today our land stands in great need of another spiritual renewal, and men like Bill Bright and John Damoose are leading the effort to awaken us. We ignore their call at great peril.

Thankfully, we are not called to struggle in our own strength, for we strive not against flesh and blood but against a spiritual foe. As Luther wrote in his great hymn, "on earth is not his equal." The victory we seek, the victory we know is ultimately already won, is not one that will come of our own power. For years I have kept on my desk a plaque of the wonderful phrase by Mother Theresa: "Faithfulness Not Success." Success belongs to Christ; ours is not to win the battle but to be faithful. This has been Bill Bright's great mission—to call the Church to faithfulness. *Red Sky in the Morning* is just that—a clear and compelling call to be faithful men and women of God in our world today.

I have read dozens of books on America's spiritual history. None have done a better and more balanced job than this. Both Bill Bright and John Damoose have devoted years to studying the history of our republic. This is a brilliant work. Read on. You are in for a rich experience; you will not only learn, you will be moved.

As I write, it is only a matter of months before we mark the beginning of the third millennium since the birth of Christ. Modern history began with His birth; it will end with His return. But in the fading days of this millennium, as we approach the dawn of the new one, let it not be said that Christians were faint-hearted, nor that they failed to do their duty. Rather, let it be said that they were at their posts, faithfully bringing God's righteousness to fruition in all of His creation.

Charles W. Colson
Chairman
Prison Fellowship Ministries

CHAPTER 1

A Red Sky Is Rising

As society enters the third millennium since the birth of Christ, we find America in the midst of a grave internal crisis that poses a threat to our existence. A "red sky" is rising in our nation, warning all who read the signs that we are indeed on the verge of moral and spiritual collapse. Gathering spiritual and moral storms threaten to destroy all the blessings God has given us over the years.

These warning signs are given to us for our benefit—that by understanding them we may take action. That is what we hope to achieve through this book, which takes its title from an old weather proverb:

Red sky in the morning, sailor take warning.
Red sky at night, sailor's delight.

Many people are surprised to learn that the origin of this proverb is Jesus' own words:

> One day the Pharisees and Sadducees came to test Jesus' claim of being the Messiah by asking him to show them some great demonstrations in the skies. He replied, "You are good at reading the weather signs of the skies—red sky tonight means fair weather tomorrow; red sky in the morning means foul weather all day—

but you can't read the obvious signs of the times!" (Matthew 16:1–3, TLB).

Jesus scolded Jewish leaders for their inability to recognize the signs around them. Today we see signs all around us of the storms afflicting our land. Read any newspaper, listen to radio programming, view television, or surf the Internet, and you will find abundant evidence of the growing problems we face as a nation and the sin that threatens to destroy our society. Like the men of Issachar, "who understood the times and knew what Israel should do" (1 Chronicles 12:32), so too should we discern the times in which we live. Yet like the Pharisees and Sadducees, many people today do not recognize God reaching out to them, nor do they discover the truth of God's Word and the simple solutions needed to turn our situation around. Most tragically, they do not foresee their own inevitable destruction because they have rejected God's personal warnings.

Yet as followers of Christ, we can be almost as blind to the consequences of ignoring God's standards as those who do not know our Lord. By doing so, we neglect our serious responsibility to lead America back to God.

Today we stand on the brink of decision. We must heed God's warning recorded in 2 Chronicles 7:19,20:

> "If you turn away and forsake My statutes and My commandments which I have set before you and shall go and serve other gods and worship them, then I will uproot you from My land which I have given you, and this house which I have consecrated for My name I will cast out of My sight, and I will make it a proverb and a byword among all peoples" (NASB).

Although this warning was written to the people of Israel should they turn a national deaf ear to God, the principle still applies today. Those nations that heed God's call are blessed; those that deny and turn from God are led by their own sin into God's judgment—and to destruction.

But God never gives a warning without describing a way out, even a blessing. Verse 14 of that same chapter contains God's promise to us. Although it was mentioned earlier, it bears repeating:

> "If my people, who are called by my name, will humble themselves and pray and seek my face and turn from their wicked ways, then will I hear from heaven and will forgive their sin and will heal their land."

Today, America has only two choices: continue on its ungodly path to destruction, or respond to God's call for repentance. John and I thoroughly believe that with a genuine revival of righteousness and a renewed biblical commitment to God, He will restore our nation even at this late hour.

Reestablishing National Righteousness

We readily admit that America has never been perfect, nor will it ever be—only God is completely holy and righteous. But as our nation has turned to God in the past in the midst of deep crises, He has given us amazing success. We can do that again. God wants to help us, and He is more powerful and creative than any enemies we will ever face. He can provide victory through the power of His Holy Spirit and the wisdom of His Word!

John and I earnestly pray that through reading this book you will be impressed by our Lord to join with us in paying any price necessary to bring a spiritual revival to America. We trust that this book will inflame your desire to help reestablish our national morality and righteousness.

We have a fourfold purpose for writing this book. First, *we want to help you understand why God created America.* We believe our purpose as a nation is to provide the freedom to establish and practice the Christian faith and to share with every person on earth the message of God's love and forgiveness available in our Lord Jesus Christ.

Second, *we want you to see how far we have already traveled down the broad road to destruction.* Forces are working to topple this great society. But believers must recognize that we ourselves are a major part of the problem. We have not faithfully obeyed God's command to be the salt of the earth, preserving our godly heritage and preventing moral and spiritual decay.

Third, *we want you to prayerfully consider a practical plan of action (given at the end of this book) for personal spiritual renewal.* This plan will help you equip yourself to become part of the solution. Then comes the critical step.

Fourth, *you will have an opportunity to commit yourself to the task of helping restore America and reaching the world for Christ* as you join with others to implement a national plan for the rebirth of America. As we consider the signs around us, let us number ourselves among those who understand the times and know what they should do.

To give you a basis for understanding the future of our nation, let me explain how reaching the world for Christ fits into God's purpose for America.

The Greatest Mission

One of the most essential concepts in Scripture is the Great Commission. It has a deep significance to us as Christ's followers. Just before Jesus ascended into heaven, He told His disciples:

> "All authority in heaven and on earth has been given to me. Therefore go and make disciples of all nations, baptizing them in the name of the Father and of the Son and of the Holy Spirit, and teaching them to obey everything I have commanded you. And surely I am with you always, to the very end of the age" (Matthew 28:18–20).

These instructions have been known throughout Church history as the *Great Commission*. In other words, Christ commissioned His disciples and all who would receive Him throughout the centuries to continue His ministry of "seeking and saving the lost" (Luke 19:10). This is the primary reason He came to earth. Our Lord has called us to share His message of eternal salvation with the entire world. This is the greatest mission in which any person can possibly participate. Imagine! God has chosen to speak through us to a lost world, giving us the privilege of helping introduce others to His Son, Jesus Christ, the living Lord and Savior! Because of the Great Commission's central place in God's eternal plan, I have committed my life to helping fulfill it in our generation. As a result, I have found more joy and fulfillment, professionally and personally, than I could ever have dreamed. The greatest joy in life is seeing someone become a new member of the family of God as he or she receives Christ as Savior and Lord.

Yet, to some, the words "Great Commission" have almost become a cliché. To others, the concept is completely unfamiliar. Surveys indicate the sad truth that most Christians today have no understanding of Christ's mandate to His followers. In fact, a recent survey conducted by George Barna sadly revealed that a mere 9 percent of those polled recognized that this command was given by Jesus. Perhaps even more shocking, among those who consider themselves "born again," only 14 percent accurately understood the Great Commission. Eighty percent of those who claim to be born again cannot even guess what it is![1]

This revelation is more startling when you consider that Christ's instructions represent a mandate for *each* of our lives. The fact that the vast body of believers has little comprehension of this biblical principle shows a major failure on the part of the American Church. (We will address this issue in Part III.) But even more important, if true followers of Christ in America have little understanding of the Great Commission, we have largely lost sight of the purpose for Christ's visit to earth—to die for our sins and restore our relationship with God. No wonder fewer and fewer people are aware that the Great Commission is a pillar upon which this nation was founded.

Surveys indicate the sad truth that most Christians today have NO UNDERSTANDING of Christ's mandate to His followers.

As we will see in Part I, the earliest Americans clearly understood the Great Commission and committed themselves to helping fulfill it. The settlers stated many times that their reason for coming to this land was to bring the gospel to those who had never heard the good news. Therefore, the Great Commission was essential to the founding of America. It is likewise essential not only to our understanding of America's original direction, but also to understanding where we believe our nation is currently headed.

What Is On the Horizon?

What lies ahead for America is difficult to predict. Will we heed the ominous warning of the red sky on our horizon? Or will we ignore the signs and reap the consequences?

John and I are confident that through God's power we can conquer *all* the forces of darkness unleashed against us in these times of crisis. Together with you, we can be instruments in God's hands to help restore our country to its biblical foundation. After all, what we do today to reverse this evil tide will set an example of courage and forthrightness that all who come after us can follow. May they find us faithful, as our Founding Fathers have been. Our heartfelt prayer is that we will commit ourselves to be a greater influence for our dear Lord for the benefit of many more generations to come—or until Jesus returns.

God has undoubtedly blessed our nation. With only 6 percent of the world's population, America owns more than 50 percent of its wealth. What is there about our history that has brought us so many blessings—both spiritual and material? Does God really work on a national scope with a purpose in mind? In the next chapter, we will look at these questions and how the answers affect our daily lives.

CHAPTER 2

The Next American Century

A massive party raged in Babylon the night the mighty empire toppled. Belshazzar, ruler of the most powerful kingdom on earth, used the sacred golden vessels taken from God's temple in Jerusalem to host a drunken party. In front of a thousand people, Belshazzar and his men drank wine from the holy cups; while holding vessels of the God of heaven and earth, they praised the gods of gold, silver, and bronze.

Although he had no doubt heard the stories of God's intervention during Nebuchadnezzar's earlier reign, Belshazzar refused to acknowledge God. He was too entrenched in his materialistic, hedonistic lifestyle.

Suddenly the drunken revelers sobered as fingers of a human hand appeared and wrote on the wall of the royal palace. The mysterious phrase was in a language no one could read. With his face white and his knees knocking, the king called for his astrologers and fortunetellers. But these "wise" men could not decipher a single word of the supernatural writing on the wall.

Then King Belshazzar called for Daniel, the prophet who had interpreted dreams for Nebuchadnezzar years ago. He offered the old prophet gifts and power if he could translate the writing. Although Daniel did not want the king's wealth or favor, he read the inscription, giving credit to the God of heaven and earth. Staggering, King Belshazzar listened as Daniel interpreted the writing:

> "*Mene:* God has numbered the days of your reign and brought it to an end. *Tekel:* You have been weighed on the scales and found wanting" (Daniel 5:26,27).

God's judgment was swiftly carried out. By the next morning, Belshazzar, once the most powerful ruler in the world, was dead and his kingdom lay in the hands of invaders.

Like Belshazzar, many people today deliberately defy almighty God. Their arrogance and independence, often backed with desires of the sinful nature, lead them down the same road to destruction that others before them have taken.

History is filled with many such cases. As with Babylon, nations that took years, even centuries, to build collapse in a furious firestorm. This pattern of national calamity continues today. Empires are built, then fall into ruin. Recent examples are Hitler's Nazi Germany, Lenin's and Stalin's Russia, and Pol Pot's regime in Cambodia.

God's Power Over History

The Bible is clear about God's role in history. He is completely sovereign. He controls everything. God taught this fact to Nebuchadnezzar through a series of events that humbled the proud king. After years of insanity in which he ate grass like an animal, Nebuchadnezzar himself testified:

> "At the end of that time, I, Nebuchadnezzar, raised my eyes toward heaven, and my sanity was restored. Then I praised the Most High; I honored and glorified him who lives forever.
>
> "His dominion is an eternal dominion; his kingdom endures from generation to generation. All the peoples of the earth are regarded as nothing. He does as he pleases with the powers of heaven and the peoples of the earth. No one can hold back his hand or say to him: 'What have you done?'" (Daniel 4:34,35).

The prophet Daniel recognized God's total power over history: "He changes times and seasons; he sets up kings and deposes them" (Daniel 2:21). In his warning to Belshazzar, Daniel stated:

> "The Most High God is sovereign over the kingdoms of men and sets over them anyone he wishes.. But you did not honor the God who holds in his hand your life and all your ways" (Daniel 5:21,23).

Most of us realize that God works in our personal lives, blessing us when we love, trust, and obey Him, and judging us who defy Him and spurn His laws. This principle applies just as surely to nations. King David writes:

> Arise, O Lord, let not man triumph; let the nations be judged in your presence. Strike them with terror, O Lord; let the nations know they are but men (Psalm 9:19,20).

George Mason, known as the Father of the Bill of Rights, also recognized this biblical principle of national accountability. He stated:

> As nations cannot be rewarded or punished in the next world, they must be in this. By an inevitable chain of causes and effects, Providence punishes national sins by national calamities.[1]

One clear example of God's intervention in national affairs is when Moses led God's people out of Egypt. When Joseph, an Israelite, reigned as second in command under Pharaoh four centuries earlier, the Egyptians treated the Israelites with special favor. Later, a pharaoh rose to power who did not remember Joseph and oppressed the Israelites. As a result, the Israelites cried out to God, and God raised up Moses to lead His people out of the land. God would give the Israelites their own nation, and all ties to Egypt would be broken.

You recall the story. Pharaoh would not let the people go until God sent numerous plagues that devastated the land. Finally, after the death of all the firstborn Egyptian males, Pharaoh expelled the Israelites.

As soon as the great multitude left, Pharaoh changed his mind. After all, how could he let his slave labor go—especially now that Egypt faced severe economic hardship from the devastating plagues? He sent his mighty army thundering after the people to bring them back. But God miraculously parted the Red Sea under Moses' hand. The Israelites crossed safely, then the sea closed over Pharaoh's army hot in pursuit.

God orchestrated the events that freed the Israelites and formed their nation. The Scripture declares that God is the same yesterday, today, and forever (Hebrews 13:8). Just as He was actively working in the nation of Israel, He works in nations today.

Divine Involvement

Was God involved in the forming of the United States of America? George Washington certainly thought so:

> May the same wonder-working Deity, who long since delivering the Hebrews from their Egyptian oppressors planted them in the promised land—whose providential agency has lately been conspicuous in establishing these United States as an independent nation—still continue to water them with the dews of Heaven...[2]

A sermon delivered by Reverend S. W. Foljambe in Boston on January 5, 1876, describes how God orchestrates history and offers insight into why America may have been created. One key excerpt reads:

> Observe the hand of God in the wise and beneficent timing of events in the dawn of our history. The events of history are not accidents. There are no accidents in the lives of men or nations. We may go back to the underlying cause of every event, and discover in each God's overruling and intervening wisdom. It has been said that history is a biography of communities; in another, and profounder sense, it is the autobiography of him "who worketh all things after the counsel of his own will" (Ephesians 1:11), and who is graciously timing all events in the interests of his Christ, and the kingdom of God on earth.[3]

Known as the Father of Our Country, George Washington more than anyone else was responsible for our nation's freedom from England. He and his compatriots shared a deep conviction that each person has a mission from God. Washington wrote in his own handwriting:

> Bless O Lord the whole race of mankind, and let the world be filled with the knowledge of Thee and Thy Son, Jesus Christ.[4]

Along with the other great men and women who founded this

nation, Washington understood that America was uniquely called of God to touch the world with the love of Jesus Christ. As a result, these individuals were willing to pay an extraordinary price to follow the Savior. Earlier, we read about the faithfulness of our Founding Fathers in their effort to birth the United States. They sacrificed their lives, their fortunes, and their sacred honor to create this wonderful country. Their commitment led to the unprecedented blessings of God that we experience today. From their examples, we can understand our urgent need to have that same measure of devotion for the rebirth of America, the land of purpose and destiny.

A Blessed Nation

After more than 500 years of history, the United States of America is a kingdom among nations. Today our country is recognized as the world's economic, political, and military leader. As Americans, our influence has never been greater; our worldwide impact is undeniable. For example, a boatload of Asian refugees picked up in the Pacific Ocean en route to America spoke one phrase of English: "MTV." Young protesters in Tiananmen Square held up a figure resembling the Statue of Liberty as their symbol of political freedom.[5] The mayor of a small village in Africa complained recently to Hollywood executives that American movies encouraged the men of his village to act like "Rambo." Companies throughout Europe are furiously importing the latest American business philosophies, such as "corporate reengineering" and "process redesign." And distinct American brands such as Coca-Cola and McDonald's can be found in almost every corner of the globe. Indeed, America's potential for influence is unmatched in history.

In 1967 Richard Wurmbrand, a great Romanian pastor who suffered fourteen years in prison for his faith, wrote:

> Every freedom-loving man has two fatherlands: his own and America…America is the hope of every enslaved man, because it is the last bastion of freedom in the world.[6]

On the surface, conditions seem positive and prosperous in modern America. As of this writing, our stock market continues to climb higher and higher—breaking one record after another. New

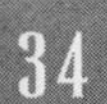

businesses are cropping up everywhere. We have never enjoyed so many personal conveniences. Stores are stocked with amazing goods that our parents' generation could never have imagined. We have several dozen television channels to choose from on our local cable systems—hundreds with direct satellite television. Powerful computers provide new production capabilities to businesses and homes. Information on any topic is a mere keystroke away on the Internet. E-mail messages carry correspondence to the ends of the world in seconds. Jet airplanes can traverse the globe in less than twenty-four hours. Transportation has never been easier or more accessible. We are living longer, healthier lives than ever before. Indeed, as we have progressed through the 20th century, we have created a world of wonder in America which surpasses the greatness of every empire in history.

Blessed for a Purpose

As Scripture tells us, God's blessings come with a purpose. We as a nation seem to have forgotten that life is more than a series of causes and effects. Just as there is a goal, a destination to which God is ultimately leading each individual, God also has a specific and definite goal for each nation. Throughout American history, we see dramatic evidence of God's hand molding and shaping this nation into a vessel He can use. For example:

God gave us a new form of government unlike any the world had ever seen. This government has allowed us to rise above the corruption and inefficiency that grip most of the world's governments and societies. Consider that our form of government has lasted over 200 years. In the same period, France has had seven different forms of government and Italy is on its fifty-first.[7]

Since our nation's founding, *God has sought to weed sin from our midst.* He has rebuked, but never destroyed, us for sins such as slavery and greed. After the materialism of the 1920s, for example, God allowed us to undergo the Great Depression, but He did not abandon us. In fact, within a few years, He restored us to a greater wealth and influence than we had known previously.

God flooded our shores with millions of immigrants and more than half a million international students who possess knowledge and labor skills from every nation on earth. Tens of millions have become American citizens. And while they came to better themselves and their families, God was quietly amassing a multinational spiritual army with the ability to carry the gospel to every culture of the world.

America has been largely spared the blood bath that engulfed so much of the world in the 20th century. In a time of ruthless dictators and the mindless slaughter of tens of millions of people, God has not allowed even one military attack on the mainland of the United States.

Indeed, God has blessed America materially, spiritually, and politically like no other nation in history.

All these blessings speak of a promise of God: "Blessed is the nation whose God is the Lord" (Psalm 33:12). The psalmist David writes these encouraging words: "From the Lord comes deliverance. May your blessing be on your people" (Psalm 3:8).

As we pray for God's continued blessings on America for the 21st century, we are reminded of the promise He made to Abraham and the nation of Israel in Genesis 12:2: "I will make you into a great nation and I will bless you; I will make your name great, and you will be a blessing." Although this promise refers to a spiritual blessing to the descendants of Abraham, this blessing also applies to all nations through the gospel of Christ:

> Consider Abraham: "He believed God, and it was credited to him as righteousness." Understand, then, that those who believe are children of Abraham. The Scripture foresaw that God would justify the Gentiles [non-Jewish people] by faith, and announced the gospel in advance to Abraham: "All nations will be blessed through you." So those who have faith are blessed along with Abraham, the man of faith...The promises were spoken to Abraham and to his seed...meaning one person, who is Christ" (Galatians 3:6–9,16).

In other words, the purpose of the gospel of Jesus Christ was to bless all nations with salvation and goodness.

For 500 years, God has been equipping America with the specific means to accomplish His task of helping to fulfill the Great Commission. Thus, we must regard these blessings as more than mere gifts for our own personal enjoyment.

For example, the Lord had distinct goals in mind when He gave us the strongest economy in the world. While we have been enjoying the material by-products of God's blessings, He has developed specific means by which we can spread His gospel. Modern technology, high-speed communications, and similar innovations spring from God's favor. For the first time in history, America possesses the material resources and technical ability to help share the gospel of Jesus Christ with every person on earth within a very brief period of time.

God fulfilled His end of the covenant with America by providing every tool we need to light the world for Jesus Christ. We dare not miss this God-given opportunity to share the blessings of heaven with others.

Scripture reminds us: "From everyone who has been given much, much will be demanded; and from the one who has been entrusted with much, much more will be asked" (Luke 12:48). God expects each of us—having been blessed with peace, with prosperity, with life—to dedicate ourselves unreservedly to the task at hand, to rebuild our moral and spiritual foundation which was built upon the eternal truth of God. That foundation made America great. It birthed our nation more than two centuries ago. If we pay the price, we will lead our nation to a rebirth and gloriously usher in the "Next American Century"!

What Difference Are We Making?

Our purpose in writing this book is not to celebrate the advances of the last hundred years or to offer false hope that our future will be even better in the 21st century. Instead, we hope to appeal to a certain group of men and women who are uniquely equipped to make a real impact in our world—the true followers of Christ.

As followers of Christ, we are accountable to God for using all the resources He has entrusted to us for His glory. The questions we must answer are:

- How are we as a nation using our influence and affluence for the glory of God?
- Are we exporting positive or negative influences?
- What does God think of what we are sending to the world over our television and radio waves, in our movies and books, and through our Internet connections?

It is increasingly obvious that while America's business stock has peaked internationally, our moral stock is in a free-fall at home. The print and electronic media testify that we have been weighed on the moral scales and found wanting. If we continue on our destructive path, our time for restoring America is very short indeed.

How are we as a nation using our INFLUENCE AND AFFLUENCE for the glory of God?

The words of the late Dr. Charles Malik, brilliant former President of the United Nations General Assembly, go to the heart of our dilemma:

> Having realized that the whole world is as it were dissolving before our very eyes, it is impossible then to ask more far-reaching questions than these three: What is then emerging? Where is Christ in it? And what differences are we making to the whole thing?[8]

The answer is obvious. We are not making the worldwide impact for Christ for which our Founding Fathers dedicated this nation.

Over the last fifty years, the United States of America has reversed its course from a nation where godliness prevailed to a nation that seemingly has no time for God. Our drug/sex/rock culture pervades the whole earth through television and movies, with devastating moral affects, eerily reminding us of the Babylon described in Jeremiah 51:7: "She made the whole earth drunk. The nations drank her wine; therefore they have now gone mad."

This moral decay is why we are so concerned about our country. Most Americans have forsaken the principles and moral standards that come from God through His inspired word, the Bible;

they have traded absolute truth for a humanistic lie. As a result, the nation is reaping the consequences that flow from our unconfessed sin. As in Babylon, America is having a massive party, drinking to the gods of humanism, secularism, materialism, and atheism.

Listen to this biblical warning given to ancient Israel as they stood poised to enter the Promised Land:

> "When you have eaten your fill, bless the Lord your God for the good land he has given you. But that is the time to be careful! Beware that in your plenty you don't forget the Lord your God and begin to disobey him. For when you have become full and prosperous and have built fine homes to live in, and when your flocks and herds have become very large, and your silver and gold have multiplied, that is the time to watch out that you don't become proud, and forget the Lord your God.
>
> "But if you forget about the Lord your God and worship other gods instead, and follow evil ways, you shall certainly perish, just as the Lord has caused other nations in the past to perish. That will be your fate, too, if you don't obey the Lord your God" (Deuteronomy 8:10–14,19,20, TLB).

Friends, this warning to ancient Israel is God's warning to America today. This is our most critical hour! Make no mistake about it. Despite the outward appearance of economic prosperity, we are watching the internal collapse of an empire unless we take immediate corrective action. Daniel Webster warned:

> If we abide by the principles taught in the Bible, our country will go on prospering and to prosper; but if we and our posterity neglect its instructions and authority, no man can tell how sudden a catastrophe may overwhelm us and bury all our glory in profound obscurity.[9]

One Final Chance for America

Nearly 140 years ago, slavery ripped at the seams of the United States. Suffering the cost for that great national sin, America engaged in a bloody Civil War and paid with the lives of more than 600,000 young soldiers. The war today, though not waged with rifles and cannons, poses an even greater threat to the future of our nation. We are losing our moral and spiritual roots, and allowing our national character to be consumed in unprecedented sin. It is as if we are rotting from within, and we are, as Abraham Lincoln warned in 1837, in the process of committing national suicide:

> At what point then is the approach of danger to be expected? I answer, if it ever reach us, it must spring up amongst us; it cannot come from abroad. If destruction be our lot we must ourselves be its author and finisher. As a nation of freemen we must live through all time, or die by suicide.[10]

We need to reconsider who we are as a people and restore God to His rightful place as Lord over our country. If we fail, we will have come so close to achieving that magnificent goal to which our Lord has called us. Yet we will stand in mourning, knowing that God had placed in our hands the ability to reach every individual with the gospel—and we were not found faithful. We will have given up our nation's inheritance, failed our forefathers, and insulted and dishonored our heavenly Father.

By the love and grace of God, the 19th century closed with God's marvelous restoration of "a more perfect union." But tragically, the 20th century has seen the rise of moral decadence, materialism, and atheism, along with many other national sins. The question today is, in light of our continued disobedience, will the 20th century close with judgment and destruction from our just God? As followers of Christ, how will we respond to this present crisis? Will we help to restore the original purpose of this nation and use the tools God has given us to reach the world for Christ? Or will we remain silent and aloof as we have done for at least fifty years, and simply watch as our nation and our God-given mission die?

Our prayer is that this book will play a vital role in reigniting your passion for the gospel and renewing your commitment to restoring America to its original purpose.

Two decades ago, Soviet dissident Alexander Solzhenitsyn warned our Congress, "Very soon, only too soon, your country will require not exceptional men, but great men. Find them in your souls, find them in your hearts. Find them in the depths of your country."[11]

What our ailing nation needs right now is great men and women who will rise to the challenge of the day, who will give us hope based on real truth, not on phony promises, and with godly character, integrity, and principle lead us back into the blessings of God.

Now is the time for heroes, for men and women who will humble themselves before almighty God, who will live according to a higher standard of righteousness, and who will sacrifice themselves to fulfill our nation's calling. Now is the time to live in the spirit of our revolutionary Founders who gave everything they had to the cause of Christ's liberty. Men like Patrick Henry, who said:

> They tell us that we are weak; unable to cope with so formidable an adversary. But when shall we be stronger? Will it be the next week, or the next year?... Shall we gather strength by irresolution and inaction?... Sir, we are not weak, if we make a proper use of the means which the God of nature hath placed in our power... We shall not fight our battle alone. There is a just God who presides over the destinies of nations; and who will raise up friends to fight our battles for us. The battle, Sir, is not to the strong alone; it is to the vigilant, the active, the brave.[12]

The hope lies in the restoration of America's original purpose as "ONE NATION UNDER GOD."

We can be inspired by the great phrase spawned during the civil rights movement: "If not us, who? If not now, when?"

With a revival of righteousness and a renewed commitment from Christ's followers in America, we can still complete our mission. The hope lies not in the restoration of America's former grandeur, but in the restoration of America's original purpose as "one nation under God."

In the next section, we will explore the exciting details of America's godly beginnings, our struggle for moral growth, and the blessings God has given us as a result of living for Him. By reviewing the history of America from the days of Christopher Columbus to the verge of the 20th century, we will see how God moved to create a nation with a specific and holy mission. We will examine the *why* of the American story to discover *where* we should be going in the future.

PART I

A Nation of Purpose

They cherished a great hope and inward zeal of laying good foundations, or at least making some ways towards it, for the propagation and advance of the gospel of the kingdom of Christ in the remote parts of the world, even though they should be but stepping stones to others in the performance of so great a work.

—Governor William Bradford,
referring to the Pilgrims' mission in the New World

CHAPTER 3

Roots of the Republic

At various times throughout history, God has opened the eyes of man to see beyond this world of time and space into the spiritual realm. God revealed to Isaiah the coming of Jesus Christ, the Messiah. From his cell on the Isle of Patmos, the apostle John glimpsed the final battle at the end of time. Occasionally, ordinary men and women have been granted the ability to see current or future events through supernatural eyes.

Such was the case of a Spanish monk named Ramon Lull. While preaching the gospel of Jesus Christ to Muslims on the African continent more than 600 years ago, Lull was severely beaten and lay near death. Two Italian men sympathetic to Lull's gospel message rescued him and put him on a ship to Spain.

Lull did not make it back to Catalonia, his home province. As he lay dying in the bow of the ship crossing the Mediterranean, Lull uttered his last prophetic words. With all of his strength, he pointed westward over the horizon and exclaimed, "Beyond this sea which washes this continent we know lies another continent we've never seen whose natives are ignorant of Christ. Send men there!"[1]

"Send men there!" Those haunting final words lived on in the minds of the two young Italians who cared for Lull in his dying hours. One of them, Stefano Colombo, or Stephen Columbus, was a direct ancestor of the great seafarer, Christopher Columbus.

The words of the Catalonian martyr passed from generation to generation, eventually stirring the heart of the adventurous young Christopher. As he pondered the words of Isaiah, he became convinced that God had chosen him, of all the men in Europe, to travel beyond the seas to spread the good news of Jesus Christ:

> Listen to me, you islands; hear this, you distant nations. Before I was born the Lord called me; from my birth he has made mention of my name...I will also make you a light for the Gentiles, that you may bring my salvation to the ends of the earth (Isaiah 49:1,6).

Had it not been for his firm conviction of God's call on his life, Columbus would have abandoned his mission. In his diary, Columbus later wrote:

> Our Lord Jesus desired to perform a very obvious miracle in the voyage to the Indies...I spent seven years in the royal court discussing the matter with many persons of great reputation and wisdom in all the arts; and in the end, they concluded that it was all foolishness, so they gave it up.[2]

But the voice of God would not let him rest, and Columbus refused to let the vision die. After seven years of hardship and disappointment, the resolute sailor finally won the support of Queen Isabella of Spain and her husband, King Ferdinand. Isabella commissioned Columbus: "It is hoped that by God's assistance some of the continents and islands in the ocean will be discovered...for the glory of God."[3] In a letter to the Pope, Queen Isabella wrote of Columbus' mission "to bear the light of Christ west to the heathen undiscovered lands."[4]

In 1492, Columbus began his world-changing voyage to the Americas. When he landed in the New World on October 12, he christened the first island he encountered "San Salvador," or Holy Savior. In the place where his feet first touched the soil, he knelt and prayed:

> O Lord, Almighty and everlasting God, by Thy holy Word Thou hast created the heaven, and the earth, and the sea; blessed and glorified be Thy name, and praised be Thy majesty, which hath deigned to use us, Thy humble servants, that Thy holy name may be proclaimed in this second part of the earth.[5]

Columbus said that he came to this continent to carry the words of Jesus Christ around the globe. He proclaimed his destiny and ours by planting a large, wooden cross on every island he discovered. With each cross he offered an invocation that the New World would belong, not to any country, but to God. Later recalling his mission, he said:

> It was the Lord who put into my mind the fact that it would be possible to sail from here to the Indies. All who heard of my project rejected it with laughter, ridiculing me. There is no question that the inspiration was from the Holy Spirit, because He comforted me with rays of marvelous inspiration from the Holy Scriptures...No one should fear to undertake any task in the name of our Savior, if it is just and if the intention is purely for His holy service.[6]

Like all of us, Columbus was an imperfect follower of Jesus who admitted that he was a sinner. But his legacy remains. His journey to the New World marked the birth of a covenant between God and the American people which survives to this day.

A Nation of Destiny

From its beginning, America was a nation of vision and destiny. We were created with a mission grounded in an explicit covenant between God and the people of this nation—a sacred contract that would form the core of what we were to become.

The history of America is the story of God's preparation of a people to touch the world with the love of Christ. We are not the stopping point of the gospel, but merely a stepping stone. The visions of Columbus and Lull did not end at our shores, but pointed to lands beyond. In a drama that began more than 500 years ago, we have been carefully molded, disciplined, and guided by God as a nation set apart for a special mission. Although America has changed in many ways, and though we often struggle against great darkness, our mission has not changed. The covenant still stands.

However, additional preparations were necessary before conditions would be right to institute the covenant. After Columbus' historic journey and before the settlers reached North America, events in Europe set the stage for the formation of a democratic government. It began during the Renaissance.

Setting the Stage for America

The Renaissance was a period of tremendous upheaval that dominated Europe beginning in the 14th century. Some changes were good; others were not. The Dark Ages yielded to a flourishing world of art and science, as Michelangelo painted and Da Vinci dreamed. Many of these creations were centered on Christ. At the same time, the Renaissance spawned a culture that paid lip service to Christ while promoting lifestyles that were anything but Christian. In a mixture of Christian and pagan thought, people started thinking of themselves as autonomous and exalting man instead of God. Humanism began to dominate many aspects of life that had previously been the territory of the Church. Humanists taught that man himself, without God, could solve every problem. Russell Kirk, one of the great thinkers of the 20th century, offers this assessment of the Renaissance:

> That intellectual and artistic and social movement called the Renaissance amounted, often, to a denial of the Christian understanding of the human condition. The Renaissance exalted man's egoism, in defiance of Christian teachings of humility, charity, and community. The Renaissance glorified fleshly pleasures... The Renaissance accepted the crafty "power politics" of Machiavelli, as distinguished from the Christian political theories of justice and freedom and order... The Renaissance, a conscious rediscovery of classical civilization, essentially was pagan in its view of human nature.[7]

Then in 1517, a passionate young German monk named Martin Luther nailed his 95 Theses to the door of a church in Wittenberg. That event began the Protestant Reformation, which revolutionized the Christian Church and radically altered man's perception of

God. During the Reformation, the reaffirmation of man's inherent sinfulness led to the creation of concepts such as separation of powers, checks and balances, decentralization, and natural law.

In what Russell Kirk defines as "the wrathful protest of Christians against the rise of an anti-Christian culture,"[8] the Reformation boldly reinstituted biblical Christianity. Followers of Jesus were reminded that God ruled in the affairs of men and nations, not as a distant entity, but as a friend and ally. This realization proved to be a critical factor in shaping the thinking of the American colonists and the government they would create.

During the Reformation, people regained the truth that God ruled every aspect of life. Reformers like Wycliff, Hus, and Luther fearlessly declared that Christ was Lord over government, music, art, literature, and all other disciplines. They taught that man was created in the image of God and that every person had dignity and value through serving God rather than a human ruler. Tremendous freedom ensued as the typical serf realized that he was in God's hands, answerable directly to Jesus Christ—not to the pope or the king. The concept of the "priesthood of all believers" swept society as people were once again taught that every believer has a spiritual ministry and the responsibility to spread the gospel of Jesus Christ.

Religious activities prior to the Reformation were controlled by the elite of the church. During the Reformation, people realized that Jesus Christ was available to all believers on a personal level. For centuries, the Bible had been reserved for the upper echelons of society. Now, due to Bible translators such as Wycliff and innovations like the printing press, ordinary men and women could read the Word of God themselves. A return to biblical teaching gave society a new opportunity for basing their principle of government on God's Word.

The Basis for American Law

Before the Reformation, society was ruled by authoritarian monarchs who instituted arbitrary laws. These laws changed according to the theories and whims of those in charge. Such a system would never have allowed a democratic nation like America to arise. The world needed God's intervention.

In 1644, Scotsman Samuel Rutherford published a book entitled *Lex Rex,* which eventually helped form the foundation of American law. His book popularized a concept first introduced in the Magna Carta a few hundred years earlier. "Lex rex," which translates "law is king," was an earthshaking concept at that time.

Prior to Rutherford's work, the reverse, "rex lex" (the king is law), had been universally accepted. Rutherford maintained that the law itself, and not a person, is preeminent. Therefore the heads of government are subject to the law, not above the law. The law could rightfully be king when it rested upon the Lawgiver, God Almighty, who is both just and infallible. Out of this idea grew the concept of "inalienable rights." In other words, a source above man and above the state—God—grants eternal rights to all mankind. Therefore, these rights cannot be taken away.

When the Jamestown settlers stepped ashore, they immediately planted a cross and CLAIMED THE LAND FOR CHRIST.

Another aspect of laws is that they both form and reflect the values of a society. A society forms laws from its values, but at the same time, laws help form society's values. For example, a law says, "Murder is wrong, and the law demands a high penalty for this crime." This law is created from society's values. The opposite is also true. The absence of a law says something like this, "Abortion cannot be wrong because there is no legal penalty for having one." This law (or lack of one) influences society's values.

The essential point is this: What is behind the law to uphold the values? If a king's decrees are behind the law, then the law is only as good as the king. If he happens to be an immoral, unjust man, the law will reflect that. But if God's holy, inalienable principles form the basis for applying the law, then it will reflect His standards of righteousness and fairness. Thus, we believe divine command is the ultimate source of law.

Some modern activists insist that law derives entirely from the will or need of the people. Law, they say, is ever changing with no absolute truth or principle undergirding it. In America, we consider the democratic process to be extremely important. That is good. However, if the majority view becomes the only standard of the law, then tragedy can result. The following illustration shows what happens when laws are not founded on godly principles, but merely on majority rule.

Several experienced teachers attended a class in humanities as part of a master's degree program. The subject of child pornography laws came up for discussion: Is it right to restrict the free speech of people who produce child pornography?

One woman, who is an excellent teacher and a good student in the class, spoke up. "I have three young children," she said. "Because of them, I believe that child pornography is wrong. But if I lived in a culture where child pornography was considered okay, then I guess I'd have to go along with it too."

How could this concerned mother come to the conclusion that in some circumstances she would accept child pornography—even if it harmed her own children? Because the only standard she had for law was majority opinion or culture.

The only way to build a set of laws that will work in all situations is to base them on an immovable, accurate, loving foundation. The only foundation that can stand this test is God and His Word. By accepting the concept of "lex rex" based on biblical principles, the leaders of the Reformation were setting the stage for a legal system built upon God's standards.

God was clearly working His plan through the Reformation. He once again reminded the Church that He was God and that people were to serve Him alone. For this reason, the new paradigm that came out of the Reformation's upheaval was necessary before the founding of America.

A Covenant With God

In 1607, the Jamestown settlers stepped ashore on pristine soil at Cape Henry, Virginia. They immediately planted a cross and claimed

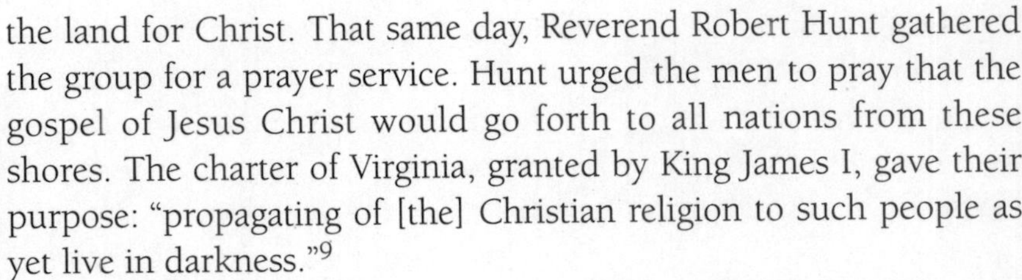

the land for Christ. That same day, Reverend Robert Hunt gathered the group for a prayer service. Hunt urged the men to pray that the gospel of Jesus Christ would go forth to all nations from these shores. The charter of Virginia, granted by King James I, gave their purpose: "propagating of [the] Christian religion to such people as yet live in darkness."[9]

The Pilgrims followed a few years later. They, like the Virginians who preceded them and the Puritans who followed, considered themselves missionaries. They believed they were part of God's plan to raise up a nation from which they and their descendants would not only enjoy the blessings of a new land with religious and political freedom, but also touch the world with the gospel.

William Bradford, governor of the Plymouth Colony, recounts the first moments the Pilgrims spent on American shores:

> Being thus arrived in a good harbor, and brought safe to land, they fell upon their knees and blessed the God of Heaven who had brought them over the vast and furious ocean, and delivered them from all the perils and miseries thereof.[10]

Bradford describes the mission of the Pilgrims:

> They cherished a great hope and inward zeal of laying good foundations, or at least making some ways towards it, for the propagation and advance of the gospel of the kingdom of Christ in the remote parts of the world, even though they should be but stepping stones to others in the performance of so great a work.[11]

The Mayflower Compact of 1620 declares that the Pilgrims came to advance the Christian faith for the glory of God.[12] "Compact" is another word for "covenant." By recording their intent in the Mayflower Compact and similar documents, the Pilgrims were making a covenant, not with each other as men, but with God Almighty.

The Old Testament records many covenants between God and men. One of the most important, spoken through the prophet Jeremiah, is a promise to all believers:

> "This is the covenant I will make with the house of Israel...," declares the Lord. "I will put my law in their minds and write it on their hearts. I will be their God, and they will be my people" (Jeremiah 31:33).

As students of the Bible, the Pilgrims understood the blessings of entering into a covenant with their Creator. They surely also understood the seriousness and the consequences of breaking a covenant with the Lord: "Cursed is the man who does not obey the terms of this covenant" (Jeremiah 11:3). The Mayflower Compact meant serious business to them; they entered into this covenant because they meant serious business with God. This historical compact is one of the founding documents of our government.

The City on a Hill

The Puritans, who arrived on our shores shortly after the Pilgrims, also made a covenant with God. On the deck of the *Arbella* on the voyage between England and America, leader John Winthrop wrote these stirring words:

> We shall be as a city upon a hill. The eyes of all people are upon us; so that if we shall deal falsely with our God in this work we have undertaken and so cause Him to withdraw His present help from us, we shall be made a story and a by-word through the world.[13]

The city on a hill is a powerful image, given by Jesus in Matthew 5:14, which represents the duty each believer has to shine the light of Christ before all men. Winthrop's statement reveals a deep understanding of Scripture, especially God's warning to His people in 2 Chronicles:

> "If you turn away and forsake the decrees and commands I have given you and go off to serve other gods and worship them, then I will uproot Israel from my land, which I have given them, and will reject this temple I have consecrated for my Name. I will make it a byword and an object of ridicule among all peoples. And though this temple is now so imposing, all who pass by will be appalled and say, 'Why has the Lord done such a thing to this land and to this temple?' People will answer, 'Because they have forsaken the Lord, the God of their fathers'" (2 Chronicles 7:19–22).

Winthrop points out that the Puritans understood the powerful significance of making a covenant with God and then disregarding it:

> Thus stands the cause between God and us: we are entered into covenant with Him for this work. We have taken out a commission...But if we neglect to observe those articles, and dissembling with our God shall embrace this present world and prosecute our carnal [worldly] intentions, seeking great things for ourselves and our prosperity, then the Lord will surely break out in wrath against us, and be revenged of a perjured people, and He will make us know the price of the breach of such a covenant.[14]

Clearly Winthrop's band did not risk their lives to settle in a new land only to forsake God and become an object of ridicule. Rather, they intended to let their light "shine before men" so their Father in heaven might be pleased and glorified.

Americans were commissioned to SHINE THE LIGHT OF CHRIST before all men.

The Puritans' proclamation sealed the covenant between America and God. It established the task for future generations: Americans were commissioned to shine the light of Christ before all men. From its inception, the United States of America had a mission.

Given their clear mission, the task before the settlers was to sustain their godly spirit in the midst of wilderness hardship and isolation from the great churches of Europe. Initially their spiritual lives flourished. But after decades of devotion to God, legalism and spiritual lethargy crept in. What would happen to the covenant as future generations arose? Would it be lost? This is one of the most exciting stories in our Christian heritage. In the next chapter, we will see how the colonies kept that flame burning brightly on the hill!

CHAPTER 4

Birth of a Nation

A hush fell over the congregation as the distinguished Christian leader looked across the pulpit into the faces of the crowd. Raising his eyes toward the rafters, he cried out, "Father Abraham, whom have you in heaven? Any Episcopals?" The preacher boldly answered his own question, "No!"

"Any Presbyterians?"

"*No!*"

"Any Independents or Seceders, New Sides or Old Sides, any Methodists?"

"No! No! *No!*"

As the audience sat captivated by the words of the great orator, he roared, "Whom have you there, then, Father Abraham?" With a rush of emotion, the fiery minister echoed once again, "We don't know those names here! All who are here are Christians—believers in Christ, men and women who have overcome by the blood of the Lamb and the word of His testimony!"[1]

George Whitefield, an English evangelist, preached more than 18,000 sermons between 1736 and 1770, the majority on American soil. He was the most prominent voice in a spiritual awakening that swept North America in the mid-18th century. With contemporaries such as Jonathan Edwards and John Wesley, Whitefield helped inspire one of the most powerful revivals in history. During the Great Awakening, tens of thousands of Americans dedicated their lives to Jesus Christ. Men and women across America received Christ and were baptized.

This sovereign move of the Spirit prepared our nation for the struggles that lay ahead. Just six years after Whitefield's death, the colonies plunged into the Revolutionary War. Many who had attended his services sacrificed their lives as the Patriots waged a five-year struggle for independence from England. This spiritual revival had strengthened the colonists for the task.

Benjamin Franklin noted the impact of the Great Awakening: "It seemed as if all the world were growing religious. One could not walk through the town in an evening without hearing psalms sung by different families on every street."[2] Franklin was so impressed that he built an auditorium to accommodate the crowds of more than 30,000 people that his friend, the Reverend Jonathan Edwards, regularly addressed. That auditorium later became the first building on the campus of the University of Pennsylvania.

Edwards himself was astounded by the awakening's impact. In describing one town, he said:

> This work of God, as it was carried on…soon made a glorious alteration in the town, so that in the spring and summer following, Anno 1735, the town seemed to be full of the presence of God. It never was so full of love, nor so full of joy…[T]here were remarkable tokens of God's presence in almost every house. It was a time of joy in the families on the account of salvation being brought unto them, parents rejoicing over their children…, husbands over their wives, and wives over their husbands.[3]

The messages proclaimed from the pulpits during the revival years had a lasting impact on the colonies. The idea that all men are created equal was a radical concept at that time, but the colonists gained new understanding of this principle from the preaching of men like Edwards, Whitefield, and Wesley. They also taught that faith is indispensable to liberty in a society of self-governing citizens.

Through the Great Awakening, the colonists, separated by hundreds of miles in thirteen distinct colonies, began to think of themselves as brothers and sisters in a common cause. As John Wesley preached: "I refuse to be distinguished from other men by any but the common principles of Christianity...Dost thou love and fear God? It is enough! I give thee the right hand of fellowship."[4]

The idea of a free and independent community began to grow in the hearts of the people. To be sure, Christians even then adhered to strict denominational lines; but, for the most part, they agreed on their greater goals. Nurtured by a shared vision of faith and freedom, the once-fragmented colonies were becoming one.

By the time of the American Revolution, 99.8 percent of the colonists claimed to be believers in Christ.[5] Christian principles therefore pervaded every aspect of their society. As Daniel Webster later stated in a speech commemorating the arrival of the Pilgrims:

> Let us not forget the religious character of our origin. Our fathers were brought hither by their high veneration for the Christian religion...They sought to incorporate its principles with the elements of their society, and to diffuse its influence through all their institutions, civil, political, or literary.[6]

Education in the Colonies

Learning in those days had a purpose with a moral context. When an illiterate people cannot read God's Word for themselves, they are unable to judge the practices of government against biblical teachings. To avoid the civil abuses that occurred in Europe, the early settlers enacted the first law establishing grammar schools in 1642. Titled the "Old Deluder Satan Law," it stated that since "one chief objective of that old deluder, Satan, [is] to keep men from the knowledge of the Scriptures, as in former time," children must be taught to read and write to ensure that everyone could learn the Scriptures.[7]

For nearly two hundred years, all schools were Christian schools in which Christian values were paramount. Since 1691, school children learned the alphabet by studying the *New England Primer*, which used Bible stories to teach reading and writing. Generations of children learned from verses that taught them: "A—In Adam's Fall, we sinned all; C—Christ crucify'd, for sinners dy'd; and N—Noah did view, the old world and new."[8]

Another book widely used in America's schools was the *New Guide to the English Tongue*, written in 1740 by Englishman Thomas Dilworth. From its pages, school children learned spelling and grammar with such phrases as: "No man may put off the law of God. The way of God is no ill way. My joy is in God all the day. A bad man is a foe to God."[9]

The Northwest Ordinance, which would later be signed into law by our U.S. Congress, required that schools be instituted for the purpose of teaching religion:

> Religion, morality, and knowledge, being necessary to good government and the happiness of mankind, schools and the means of education shall forever be encouraged.[10]

In the colonies, a Christian education did not end with grammar school. Almost all of the first institutions of higher learning were established as Christian schools.

Harvard, the first college in America, was founded in 1636. Its *Rules and Precepts* stated: "Let every student be plainly instructed, and earnestly pressed to consider well, the main end of his life and studies is to know God and Jesus Christ which is eternal life, John 17:3, and therefore to lay Christ in the bottom as the only foundation of all sound knowledge and learning."[11]

The charter for the College of William & Mary, founded in 1692, states its purpose: "that the Christian faith may be propagated . . . to the glory of God."[12]

In 1701, Yale College was founded to "propagate in this wilderness the blessed Reformed, Protestant religion,"[13] with the goal that "every student shall consider the main end of his study to wit to know God in Jesus Christ and answerably to lead a Godly, sober life."[14] Like Harvard, its founders required that "all scholars shall live religious, godly, and blameless lives according to the rules of God's Word, diligently reading the Holy Scriptures, the fountain of light and truth; and constantly attend upon all the duties of religion, both in public and secret."[15]

Princeton University, founded in 1746, had as its second president Reverend John Witherspoon, a signer of the Declaration. Witherspoon's emphasis on incorporating biblical principles in government had an impact on our Founding Fathers, 87 of whom attended Princeton. The university's first president declared: "Cursed be all learning that is contrary to the cross of Christ."[16]

Education's Christian foundation would last for over two centuries. In all, 106 of the first 108 colleges in America were founded on the Christian faith. By the time of the Civil War, non-religious universities could be counted on one hand. College presidents were almost always clergymen until around 1900.[17]

The Laws of the Colonists

Colonial law also reflected Christian values. A man who greatly influenced the shaping of American law was renowned English jurist Sir William Blackstone (1723–1780). At the time of the American Revolution, there were more copies of Blackstone's *Commentaries on the Laws of England* in this country than there were in England. In a study of the nearly 15,000 documents written by the Founding Fathers between 1760 and 1805, researchers discovered that Blackstone was the second most frequently quoted person.[18]

Blackstone proposed that there were only two foundations for law: nature and revelation in the Holy Scriptures. He wrote, "These laws laid down by God are the eternal immutable laws of good and evil...This law of nature, dictated by God Himself, is of course superior in obligation to any other. It is binding over all the globe, in all countries, and at all times: no human laws are of any validity if contrary to this."[19]

Another man who had a profound impact on American law was Baron Charles Montesquieu, a French philosopher. Next to the Bible, Montesquieu was the individual most quoted by our Founding Fathers.[20] In 1748 he wrote a highly influential book called *The Spirit of the Laws,* in which he proposed separating the powers of government due to man's inherent sinfulness and desire for control. Montesquieu devised an ingenious plan of government dividing the powers into three branches, based on Isaiah 33:22: "The Lord is our judge [the judicial branch]; the Lord is our lawgiver [the legislative branch]; the Lord is our king [the executive branch]."[21]

Montesquieu's work was studied intently by our Founding Fathers, who would later use his plan of government for our own. The structure of American government is therefore derived directly from Scripture.

The governments of the individual colonies were also greatly influenced by Christian principles. In all but one of the colonies, the people were even taxed to support the preaching of the gospel and the building of churches.

A Christian consensus dominated colonial society with few dissenters. With so many people listening for the "still small voice of God," it is undeniable that God was the author of what was about to happen.

A Spirit of Independence

During the early settlement of America, rebellion against the British Crown was unthinkable. At the same time, Christians considered tyranny a violation of God's law. This idea pointed back to the concept of "lex rex," where law is king and God is the foundation for the law. The Declaration of Independence reflects this when it states that if the laws of nature and of nature's God are violated, a God-fearing people would be justified in severing ties of kinship with the British Empire.

On the other side of the Atlantic, events were occurring that caused the colonists to accuse the King of "absolute tyranny over the states." By 1760, many British leaders began to fear the Americans. The colonists would soon outnumber Englishmen, and the growing strength of the American economy meant that one day the Americans would expect representation in the British government. As long as the Americans posed no threat to the authority of the Crown, the King encouraged their self-government. But as perceptions about the colonists began to change in England, some began advocating that the colonies be "put in their place."

Soon England passed oppressive ordinances against the colonies. The Stamp Act of 1765 imposed direct taxes on a wide range of products. The Quartering Act required the colonists to provide room and board in their homes for British soldiers—who in most cases acted as spies. The Declaratory Act, the Townshend Acts, and other authoritarian measures contributed to the tension between the colonies and their mother country.

The colonists began to revolt against the tyranny. After all, John Knox and Samuel Rutherford had taught that all tyranny comes from the devil—not from God, who wants people to be free. Therefore, the English king had violated, not just man's law, but God's law, and the colonists felt justified in seeking independence.

Under this oppressive taxation, the colonists identified with the Israelites suffering oppression in Egypt and appealed to God. The men of Marlborough, Massachusetts unanimously declared: "A free-born people are not required by the religion of Jesus Christ to submit to tyranny...[We] implore the Ruler above the skies, that He would make bare His arm in defense of His Church and people, and let Israel go."[22] The Provincial Congress of Massachusetts, which organized the famous Minutemen, issued a statement to the inhabitants of Massachusetts Bay: "Resistance to tyranny becomes the Christian and social duty of each individual...Continue steadfast, and with a proper sense of your dependence on God, nobly defend those rights which heaven gave, and no man ought to take from us."[23]

The structure of American government is derived DIRECTLY FROM SCRIPTURE.

In 1765, the Reverend Jonathan Mayhew of Boston's renowned West Church made a powerful plea for independence that helped incite the colonists against England. He said:

> The king is as much bound by his oath not to infringe the legal rights of the people, as the people are bound to yield subjection to him...As soon as the prince sets himself above the law, he loses the king in the tyrant. He does, to all intents and purposes, un-king himself by acting out of and beyond that sphere which the constitution allows him to move in...The subject's obligation to allegiance then ceases, of course, and to resist him is no more rebellion than to resist a foreign invader.[24]

When circulated in flyers and newspapers of the day, such words inflamed the people, inspiring the 1770 Boston Massacre and the 1773 Boston Tea Party. (It is a little known fact that the participants in the Boston Tea Party actually paid for the tea they dumped into the harbor. While they were determined to make a powerful statement by their act of defiance, they also believed that it would be stealing to not pay for the tea themselves.[25])

The colonies soon resounded with the cry, "No King but King Jesus!"[26] In short order, the groundwork for revolution was in place. War was inevitable.

A Declaration of Faith

The first order of business was declaring independence. The Declaration of Independence, the single most important document in the establishment of the United States of America as a free and independent nation, was both a political and a religious document. In studying its message, it is apparent that the document is as much a Declaration of Dependence upon the Lord as it is a Declaration of Independence from civil tyranny.[27] The Declaration states that all men are created, that their Creator has given them rights, and that these God-given rights are inalienable. It also states their firm reliance on God's protection and appeals to the Supreme Judge of the world.

From the wording in this historic document, it is clear that the Founding Fathers believed they were building their nation with the authority of the Supreme Being, who alone should be King. As the Declaration of Independence was being signed, Samuel Adams, often called the "Father of the Revolution," declared:

> We have this day restored the Sovereign to Whom all men ought to be obedient. He reigns in heaven and from the rising to the setting of the sun, let His kingdom come.[28]

As the Declaration reached the hands of the King of England, the Americans braced for war. Yet, having just stated their reliance on God's protection, they were willing to undergo whatever God had planned for them. John Adams wrote:

> It is the will of Heaven that these two countries should be sundered [separated] forever. It may be the will of Heaven that America shall suffer calamities still more wasting and distresses yet more dreadful. If this is to be the case, it will have this good effect, at least: it will inspire us with many virtues which we have not, and correct many errors, follies and vices which threaten to disturb, dishonor and destroy us...The furnace of affliction produces refinements in states, as well as individuals.[29]

The colonies had no human chance of winning a war with England. The British Empire at that time possessed the most formidable fighting forces on the face of the earth. The ragtag assembly of volunteers, farmers, and tradesmen who composed the ranks of the American military were out-manned, out-gunned, out-financed, and out-generaled. Only a miracle could bring success in a war with Great Britain. That is exactly what happened.

Miraculous Intervention

Time and again throughout the war, God preserved the American cause. Both American and British observers recorded strong impressions that God had sided with the colonies and against the English. From Brooklyn Heights to Yorktown, God's hand brought mysterious fogs, unexpected floods, and other phenomena that aided the side of the colonies.

One example was the night the Continental Army was evacuated under the noses of the British near Brooklyn. On August 27, 1776, 20,000 British soldiers nearly surrounded the 8,000 poorly trained American troops. General George Washington was waiting for the final assault that would finish off the Continental Army and cause the colonists to lose the war.

But for some unknown reason, General Howe did not press the attack. All throughout the next day, the Americans still waited, but there was no action from the British. Rain came and a northeast wind arose, preventing the British fleet from sailing up the East River.

Knowing that time was running out, Washington outlined a daring and possibly foolhardy plan to his officers. Using small boats, he would evacuate his entire army to safety across the mile-wide river.

How could he expect such a plan to succeed? How many trips would it take across the open water in sight of the British? Providentially, a company of expert oarsmen were among the American troops. After nightfall they began laboring across the choppy water, trip after trip, carrying a few soldiers at a time. Hour after hour passed. Washington set a screen of men in front positions to fool the British. The enemy did not notice a thing!

At midnight the wind died down so the boats could be loaded with even more men. As the sky lightened, the oarsmen knew the boats would become easy targets. The men remaining on shore waited nervously in the trenches. Would their turn to escape come or was it too late?

Just as the sun peered over the horizon, a dense fog arose from the ground. Visibility dropped to a mere six yards. The fog remained until the last boat, carrying General Washington, set off across the river. Then the fog lifted, and the British were stunned to see the shore empty of the 8,000 American troops. Guns were fired at the last departing boat, but it was out of range!

Many American soldiers kept diaries of this miraculous event, and almost all attributed the "coincidental happenings" to the intervention of God.[30]

During the battles, the fighting was fierce, and many Americans died without seeing victory. But after five long years, England finally gave up. On October 19, 1781, General Charles Cornwallis surrendered his army to General Washington at Yorktown, Virginia. After receiving word of Britain's surrender, Washington ordered his men to set up prayer tents to thank God for protecting the army and preserving the colonies throughout the war.

The Faith of the Founding Fathers

Who were these leaders who stood fast during the war and formed our nation? Almost to a man, our Founding Fathers sought to serve and glorify Jesus Christ with their lives. One study found that of 15,000 writings by the Founding Fathers included in newspaper articles, pamphlets, books, monographs, and other documents, 94 percent of all quotes either directly or indirectly cited the Bible.[31]

Fifty-two of the 55 framers of the Constitution were avowed Christians. From their hearts flowed the documents and structures to form the foundations for this modern nation.

In September 1774, the First Continental Congress opened its initial session with prayer. Psalm 35 was read aloud: "My soul shall be joyful in the Lord; it shall rejoice in his salvation...Awake and rise to my defense! Contend for me my God and Lord" (vv. 9,23).[32]

Those in attendance later recalled the atmosphere as they prayed fervently for America and for the Congress: "[W]ho can realize the emotions with which they turned imploringly to heaven for divine interposition and aid. It was enough...to melt a heart of stone."[33] John Adams remarked that he had never seen a greater effect on an audience. "It seemed as if Heaven had ordained that Psalm to be read on that day."[34]

Of all the Founders' writings, 94 PERCENT either directly or indirectly CITED THE BIBLE.

George Washington often spent hours in prayer without interruption. In his prayer book, he wrote: "Direct my thoughts, words, and work. Wash away my sins in the immaculate Blood of the Lamb, and purge my heart by Thy Holy Spirit...Daily frame me more and more into the likeness of Thy Son Jesus Christ."[35]

The famous portrait of Washington pausing in battle to pray for the safety of his men depicts an actual scene witnessed by a British reporter. He later confessed that the sight of Washington on his knees convinced him that God must be on the side of the rebels. No wonder God used Washington to father a nation dedicated to spreading the gospel of Jesus Christ!

In his dying words, Alexander Hamilton, signer of the Constitution, spoke of his faith in Christ: "I have a tender reliance on the mercy of the Almighty, through the merits of the Lord Jesus Christ. I am a sinner. I look to Him for mercy."[36]

Patrick Henry, whose "give me liberty or give me death" speech helped spark the war, declared in his will, "This is all the inheritance I give to my dear family. The religion of Christ will give them one which will make them rich indeed."[37]

To discover the faith of some of the other Founders, consider the following words from their wills:

Samuel Adams, signer of the Declaration: "First of all, I resign my soul to the Almighty Being who gave it,... relying on the merits of Jesus Christ for the pardon of my sins."[38]

Gabriel Duvall, delegate to the Constitutional Convention and U.S. Supreme Court Justice: "I resign my soul into the hands of the Almighty who gave it in humble hopes of His mercy through our Savior Jesus Christ."[39]

Charles Carroll, signer of the Declaration: "On the mercy of my Redeemer I rely for salvation and on His merits; not on the works I have done in obedience to His precepts."[40]

Other signers of the Declaration include John Witherspoon, a Presbyterian pastor; William Treat Payne, a military chaplain; and Benjamin Rush, who founded the Pennsylvania Bible Society.[41]

Of those who signed the Constitution, Charles Pinckney and John Langdon founded the American Bible Society, James McHenry founded the Baltimore Bible Society, and Rufus King helped found a Bible Society for Anglicans. Abraham Baldwin was a chaplain in the Revolution, and four others were theological writers.[42] The list could go on and on.

Even those who were known as nominal Christians deeply respected God and the Bible. Thomas Jefferson and Benjamin Franklin, considered heroes by the anti-Christian secular movement of our day, clearly acknowledged divine authority in the affairs of men and never questioned God's role in the founding of this nation.

Franklin wrote to the president of Yale College, "Here is my creed. I believe in one God, the Creator of the universe. That He governs it by His providence. That He ought to be worshiped. That the most acceptable service we render to Him is in doing good to His other children...As to Jesus of Nazareth,...I think the system of morals and his religion, as he left them to us, is the best the world ever saw, or is likely to see."[43]

Franklin's most stirring speech was delivered at the Constitutional Convention of 1787. Representatives from the various colonies had spent days of bitter dispute over the terms of agreement and were on the verge of disbanding and going home. Then they received an angry rebuke from the 81-year-old diplomat:

> I have lived long, Sir, and the longer I live the more convincing proofs I see of this truth—that God governs in the affairs of men. And if a sparrow cannot fall to the ground without His notice, is it probable that an empire can rise without His aid? We have been assured, Sir, in the Sacred Writings, that "except the Lord build the house, they labor in vain that build it." I firmly believe this; and I also believe that without his concurring aid we shall succeed in this political building no better than the builders of Babel.[44]

Then Franklin called for prayer and urged that every session of the government in the future begin with prayer. Following their corporate prayer, the assembly adopted the Constitution and framed the outlines of the American government.

While Thomas Jefferson was not what many would consider a biblical believer and follower of Jesus, he claimed, "I am a real Christian; that is to say, a disciple of the doctrines of Jesus."[45] He wrote to Dr. Benjamin Rush (also a signer of the Declaration of Independence):

> My views...are the result of a life of inquiry and reflection, and very different from the anti-Christian system imputed to me by those who know nothing of my opinions. To the corruptions of Christianity I am, indeed, opposed; but not to the genuine precepts of Jesus himself. I am a Christian in the only sense in which he wished anyone to be; sincerely attached to his doctrines in preference to all others.[46]

Built on Christian Principles

With the Revolutionary War over and our nation's independence won, our Founding Fathers sought God's guidance in establishing a righteous government built on Christian principles.

These men knew that the freedoms that had been won can only exist within a nation guided by biblical principles. Our laws are rooted in a moral and religious tradition dating from the time that Moses received the Ten Commandments. James Madison, known as the "Chief Architect of the Constitution," declared:

> We have staked the whole future of American civilization, not upon the power of government, far from it. We have staked the future of all of our political institutions upon the capacity of mankind for self-government; upon the capacity of each and all of us to govern ourselves, to control ourselves, to sustain ourselves according to the Ten Commandments of God.[47]

John Adams, who with Benjamin Franklin and John Jay negotiated the treaty with Great Britain ending the war, wrote in his diary:

> Suppose a nation in some distant region should take the Bible for their only law book, and every member should regulate his conduct by the precepts there exhibited!...What a Eutopia, what a Paradise would this region be.[48]

What he envisioned was becoming reality. His son, John Quincy Adams, stated, "The highest glory of the American Revolution was this; it connected in one indissoluble bond the principles of civil government with the principles of Christianity."[49]

The Declaration of Independence affirms that our nation was built on God-given principles: "We hold these truths to be self-evident, that all men are created equal. That they are endowed by their Creator with certain inalienable rights, that among these are life, liberty, and the pursuit of happiness."

The United States Constitution established a nation that was Christian from the ground up. Between the lessons taught by God through the Reformation and the moral character reinforced by the Great Awakening, the Founding Fathers laid the framework for what has become the most successful form of government in history.

Now the stage was set. The first settlers established the covenant with God; the Founding Fathers set up a government based on godly principles. How would the mandate and purpose established by our ancestors affect our history? As usual, God's work in history takes His chosen course. In the next chapter, we will look deeper into our national purpose and how America was shaped to fulfill it.

CHAPTER 5

God's Purpose for America

How much would you give up to spread the gospel of Jesus Christ? That is a hard question for many of us to answer because few of us have experienced hardship or persecution because of our walk with Christ. But after the Revolutionary War, many Christians looked at the frontier, at the thousands of people clearing farmland in the wilderness, and at the lack of a witness for Christ. Through necessity and innovation, a new method of evangelism made its rounds—the circuit-riding preacher.

Just what was it like to ride a circuit? Francis Asbury, the great Methodist preacher, gave up everything for Christ. He never married and never bought a home. He rode his faithful horse carrying two saddlebags that held everything he owned. When he was older and no longer able to handle the jostle of horseback, he still made his rounds bumping over trails in a carriage. Traveling more than 270,000 miles, he preached over 16,000 sermons during his years and saw many thousands come to Christ.

Many circuit-riding preachers were not highly educated or well-respected intellectuals. Often converted at a camp-meeting, they became so filled with the fire of God's Spirit that they opted to live their lives on horseback, just to help fulfill the Great Commission and teach scriptural values to families isolated from other religious influences.

Imagine the scene. The preacher gallops into town, dusty and tired, his horse sweating. He tacks up a notice to announce his meeting. It might be held in a home, schoolhouse, barn, or even a tavern. This was more excitement than that little town had seen for weeks! Everyone read the sign and ran to get dressed in their Sunday-go-to-meeting clothes and wash the dirt from their faces.

If this town was his last stop for the day, the preacher stayed with a Christian family or even spread his blanket under the summer sky. How exciting if the preacher came to your house, helped you read the Bible, prayed with you, and gave you news of the surrounding communities! Through rain, sleet, snow, and searing sunshine, the circuit rider kept going. Many traveled a circuit of 200 to 500 miles every two to six weeks.

Circuit-riding preachers helped change the frontier. Their methods of spreading the gospel were innovative and uniquely served the needs of the people. Thus the powerful spirit of the gospel adapted to conditions not found in Europe or even on the East Coast of America where towns and villages were more accessible. These pioneering evangelists and teachers inspired the formation of churches and helped frontier families build a tradition of serving God.

Created to Be an Influence

This innovation was just one way God worked in our midst. From the days of Columbus on, He used great care in forming the United States of America, creating us to be a worldwide influence. Although we had won our independence, God was still shaping us to become a sovereign nation.

Shortly after we miraculously survived the Revolutionary War, which could have crippled our infant nation, we were once again embroiled in war with Great Britain. Sometimes referred to as the "Second War of Independence," the War of 1812 was the first major test of our national spirit. Responding to British blockades of American ports, the United States government tried several diplomatic channels to avoid conflict. But on June 18, 1812, President James Madison signed a Declaration of War against Great Britain.

A series of major victories on the high seas led to triumph in 1815. American confidence soared as we successfully defended our honor once again. With this important victory, it became clear that we were no longer just an experiment in democracy. America was here to stay!

Other victories for American sovereignty came with the Monroe Doctrine of 1823 and the Mexican War of 1846–48. With these successes, God was equipping us to one day be a world leader. America was becoming powerful and greatly revered among nations. The American government grew more stable through effective leadership and a growing economy. We had solid diplomatic relationships abroad, and we were universally recognized as a free and independent state.

America was, indeed, a new experiment in history. Never before had a nation been created under such circumstances, and then succeeded so conspicuously. The nations of the world were beginning to listen to what we had to say. With our enhanced visibility, God was positioning us to impact the world with the gospel.

Fulfilling His Purpose

Throughout every stage of our growth, the Creator was careful to mold and guide our nation to accomplish His purposes for us: to propagate the Christian faith and help fulfill the Great Commission.

In a speech on July 4, 1837, the 61st anniversary of the Declaration of Independence, John Quincy Adams proclaimed:

> Why is it that, next to the birthday of the Savior of the world, your most joyous and most venerated festival returns on this day?
>
> Is it not that, in the chain of human events, the birthday of the nation is indissolubly linked with the birthday of the Savior? That it forms a leading event in the progress of the gospel dispensation?
>
> Is it not that the Declaration of Independence first organized the social compact on the foundation of the Redeemer's mission upon earth?[1]

Former Librarian of Congress and renowned historian Daniel

Boorstin writes that early Americans believed the victories and miraculous growth of our nation were for a greater purpose:

> From the beginning, Americans had been unwilling to believe that their emigration, their expansion, their diplomacy, and their wars had no high purpose, and they commonly defined that purpose as a "mission."[2]

Even Herman Melville, the American novelist who was no great friend of Christians, compared the American experience with that of the Israelites in Scripture. In 1850, Melville wrote: "We Americans are the peculiar, chosen people—the Israel of our time; we bear the ark of the liberties of the world."[3]

This is our high purpose—to bring liberty, hope, and renewal to those lost in sin. In her infancy, America entered into a covenant with God to extend the light of Christ's love to the world, to become, as John Winthrop said, "a shining city on a hill."

As the New England Confederation proclaimed in 1643:

> We all came to these parts of America with the same end and aim, namely, to advance the Kingdom of our Lord Jesus Christ.[4]

This great covenant was not restricted to those early settlers, but extended to an entire nation for all posterity. The Scriptures make it clear that God is never concerned with a single generation; His perspective spans many generations at once. We see this in the instructions Moses gave to his people:

> Hear now, O Israel, the decrees and laws I am about to teach you. Follow them so that you may live and may go in and take possession of the land that the Lord, the God of your fathers, is giving you. Do not add to what I command you and do not subtract from it, but keep the commands of the Lord your God that I give you...Only be careful, and watch yourselves closely so that you do not forget the things your eyes have seen or let them slip from your heart as long as you live. Teach them to your children and to their children after them (Deuteronomy 4:1,2,9).

Having experienced God's guidance and protection, our forefathers were entrusted with the responsibility to tell what God had done and share His great blessings with others.

Sharing God's Message

When we consider the type of nation we have become over the last 500 years, the plan and purpose of God for America becomes apparent. Nineteenth-century historian Charles Bancroft recognized that America was destined to exert great influence:

> America, then, will colonize ideas extensively when her institutions are thoroughly matured. The process indeed commenced with her birth, and her spirit sails with her ships in every sea and visits all lands.[5]

Bancroft was not saying that America would one day hold colonies as Britain did, but that our ideas would be carried by our people to every nation on earth. Political leaders in America may desire to influence other nations to change from dictatorial to democratic forms of government. While this is a worthy goal, it is not our main objective. Our most important influence has been in exporting, not just material wealth and political wisdom, but the gospel of Jesus Christ. Of all the good we have done, this is the greatest. In this way, our blessings do not just benefit us, but also those who receive the gospel message.

A goal of world evangelization, however, does not mean that we attempt to force our beliefs on others through colonization or empire building. Instead, out of deep gratitude to God, we share His love and compassion, which helped us build our own country. Every culture and people group in the world is valuable, and our responsibility is to share God's Word with them and encourage them to serve God according to the guidelines of His holy Word—within their own culture. Because of our love for Christ and our concern for others, we share the message of God's free gift of salvation with all people, regardless of who they are or where they live.

But I want to make this point clear. No one has the power to convert another person, nor should anyone try to do so. Only God can change the heart of a person. In the past, many well-meaning Christians believed that the American way of life was somehow the "godly life." They wrongly tried to make people accept scriptural beliefs by forcing them to give up their ways of life.

America today is a pluralistic society, a melting pot of people from many nations representing many religions and cultures. As Christians, we need to be sensitive to the beliefs of recent immigrants, international students, and foreign visitors who hold religious views different from ours. We should be quick to inform them of our Christian heritage and emphasize why God has made America the greatest nation in history. However, we should not pressure them or their families to follow our Lord. Only the Holy Spirit can reveal truth to someone and transform him or her into a new person.

Our role is to tell everyone who will listen about Jesus and that, according to the Bible, there is no other person who can reconcile us to God. We do this from hearts filled with joy and excitement about our Lord Jesus Christ, and with compassion for the lost. Christ commanded us to love our neighbors—and even our enemies—as ourselves. We simply share the good news that God loves them and offers a wonderful plan for their life, and ask the Holy Spirit to do His work in their heart. (To learn more about God's plan for your life, read *Have You Heard of the Four Spiritual Laws?* in Appendix B.)

Spreading the Gospel Near and Far

As the United States became a beacon of liberty to other nations, attracting a continuing influx of immigrants, new generations of Americans were growing up who needed to hear the gospel message. The Second and Third Great Awakenings at this time were probably the most influential events of the post-Revolutionary years. This was the era of the circuit riders and camp meetings. Great prayer revivals helped bring the focus of our people back to God. These spiritual renewals spawned the abolition movement, the growth of Sunday schools and Bible societies, and many social reforms. New Christians flooded the existing churches and the newly formed Methodist and Baptist denominations, expanding their memberships.

Through a seemingly minor event, another American spiritual tradition began that has gained momentum to this day. Samuel Mills, Jr., had been converted in a revival meeting in 1801. While studying at Williams College in western Massachusetts, he became impassioned with foreign missions.

One hot August day in 1806, he and four friends decided to meet for prayer in a field near the college campus. While they were praying, a huge thunderstorm rolled in and began to pelt them with rain. They ran to take shelter in a nearby haystack. As they continued praying, despite the roaring thunder, God laid on their hearts a passion to reach people around the world for Christ.

This "Haystack Prayer Meeting" was the beginning of the foreign mission movement in America. From this initial gathering began a missionary group called the Society of the Brethren, which was joined by pioneer missionary Adoniram Judson and others. After their appeal to the Congregational Ministers in Massachusetts for assistance, the first American foreign missions society was formed in 1810. By 1821, the society had already sent out 81 missionaries. That tiny effort, multiplied over the years, has helped America become the primary missionary-sending country in the world today.

By now, the pattern was unmistakable. God was raising up a nation to impact the world—a special nation with a special destiny. As we would soon learn, however, that destiny would not be accomplished easily. To complete our mission, we would need to be purified; but purity comes at a price. By mid-century, the Refiner's fire was burning brightly throughout America as we braced ourselves for America's toughest hour.

CHAPTER 6

Purification and Preparation

How does God view continual sin? What does He do about a lack of repentance? An illustration of His dealings with sin among His people is found in the book of Exodus. Moses had just met with God at the burning bush in the middle of the desert. It was an awesome experience, one that Moses would never forget. The holiness of God was so overpowering that Moses had to take off his shoes to approach the bush.

At that holy spot, God commissioned Moses to go back to where he had grown up in the palace of Pharaoh and lead the Israelites to freedom. After hearing God's plan to set His people free after four hundred years of bondage, Moses returned to Egypt. But the Bible says, "At a lodging place on the way, the Lord met Moses and was about to kill him" (Exodus 4:24).

Think about it! From the beginning of time, God had chosen Moses as a vessel through whom He would free His chosen people. Every moment of Moses' life had been orchestrated for that precise purpose. Why was God so angry? Because Moses had not done what God demanded: he had not circumcised his own son. This was an act of disobedience and dishonoring to God.

God demands obedience, and He will not use an unclean vessel to do His will. The Lord was willing to forego using Moses in His divine plan because Moses had disobeyed God's clear rules. But in that moment of terror, Moses' wife, Zipporah, circumcised her son and, by her act, saved Moses' life.

In a similar way, God could not use the United States to liberate men and women from the bondage of sin while we denied freedom to one segment of our own people—slaves. No matter how great our mission to the world, our most important duty is obedience to God. No matter how things looked on the surface at that time, judgment was imminent.

One Flagrant Sin

By 1830, America was widely considered a beacon of moral integrity. The French philosopher Alexis de Tocqueville visited the United States and chronicled the depth of faith that made the American republic the most remarkable experiment in the history of human government. "In the United States the sovereign authority is religious," he said in one memorable passage. "There is no country in the world where the Christian religion retains a greater influence over the souls of men than in America, and there can be no greater proof of its utility and of its conformity to human nature than that its influence is powerfully felt over the most enlightened and free nation of the earth."[1]

Yet we still allowed that one great moral outrage—slavery—against the principles that had formed our way of life. Paul had strong words that addressed the relationship among believers:

> You are all sons of God through faith in Christ Jesus, for all of you who were baptized into Christ have clothed yourself with Christ. There is neither Jew nor Greek, slave nor free, male nor female, for you are all one in Christ Jesus (Galatians 3:26–28).

Unfortunately, America had not lived by that principle of equality given in Scripture. For hundreds of years, farmers and manufacturers celebrated their own freedom while condemning an entire group of their brothers and sisters to forced servitude.

Why was this such a serious breach of obedience? Our Founding Fathers stated in the Declaration of Independence that all men are created equal, and that all have God-given rights that are inalienable, including life, liberty, and the pursuit of happiness. Yet a short time later Americans neither respected the life of, nor granted liberty to, those among them who were slaves. The United States, which had fought for its independence from tyrannists, was now denying independence to and tyrannizing others.

The hypocrisy resulted from a compromise of basic principles in the earliest stages of American history. They knew that denying a slave his freedom was not only hypocritical but morally wrong. Many of the Founding Fathers, including George Washington and Thomas Jefferson, personally detested the institution of slavery. Russell Kirk writes:

> It has been remarked that this bold affirmation of the right to liberty ignored a considerable part of America's population, the Negro slaves, which had no voice in the Congress. Was it liberty simply for those already free? Jefferson, in his original draft [of the Declaration of Independence,] included a denunciation of slavery and the slave trade though [he was] a considerable slaveholder himself.[2]

They feared division among themselves and problems with the economy more than they feared A RIGHTEOUS GOD.

Out of deference to the delegates from South Carolina and Georgia who argued that slavery was essential to their labor-intensive economy, the issue of slavery was deleted from the Declaration of Independence. At the same time, our Founding Fathers admitted that they did not know how to change the situation. Jefferson left instructions that his slaves should be freed upon his death; Washington, however, was never at peace about how to deal with the issue.

The Founding Fathers demonstrated a lack of faith when they compromised on the slavery issue. They feared division among themselves and problems with the economy more than they feared a righteous God.

Historian Paul Johnson questions how a Christian people could have justified the existence of such a sinful practice:

> Christianity was the one great religion which had always declared the diminution, if not the final elimination, of slavery to be meritorious; and that no real case for slavery could be constructed, in good faith, from Christian scripture. The fact that Southerners from a variety of Christian churches were prepared to do so, in the second half of the nineteenth century, was a shocking and flagrant stain on the faith.[3]

General Robert E. Lee, Confederate general and a devout Christian, observed: "Slavery as an institution is a moral and political evil in any country...The doctrines and miracles of our Saviour have required nearly two thousand years to convert but a small part of the human race, and even among the Christian nations what gross errors still exist!"[4] Yet Lee himself fought to protect the practice!

The North and the South were equally guilty of the scourge that tainted the land. Some tried to justify slavery; others tried to ignore it or to claim that it was someone else's moral choice. They pretended not to notice the hypocrisy of stating that all men are created equal, while at the same time allowing slavery.

Yet God's Word warns us that we cannot hide our head in the sand when we see sin in our midst: "Don't try to disclaim responsibility by saying you didn't know about it. For God, who knows all hearts, knows yours, and he knows you knew! And he will reward everyone according to his deeds" (Proverbs 24:12, TLB).

The Second Great Awakening

Only God Himself could prepare our nation for what was to come: judgment for our hideous sin. Just as the Great Awakening preceding the American Revolution filled the colonists with the heart, faith, and will to create a new Christian nation, in the 1820s and 1830s God again poured out His Spirit in the Second Great Awakening. Men like Charles Finney saw hundreds of thousands of Americans give their lives to Jesus Christ.

During this Second Awakening, many people became aware

that slavery displeased God. In his Pulitzer Prize-winning chronicles of the Civil War, *Battle Cry of Freedom*, author and historian James McPherson considers the social legacy of the Second Great Awakening as it affected slavery:

> This evangelical enthusiasm generated a host of moral and cultural reforms. The most dynamic and divisive of them was abolitionism. Heirs of the Puritan notion of collective accountability that made every man his brother's keeper, these Yankee reformers repudiated Calvinist predestination, preached the availability of redemption to anyone who truly sought it, urged converts to abjure sin, and worked for the elimination of sins from society. The most heinous social sin was slavery. All people were equal in God's sight; the souls of black folks were as valuable as those of whites; for one of God's children to enslave another was a violation of the Higher Law, even if it was sanctioned by the Constitution.[5]

Thus challenged by the voice of God, our nation headed into the greatest trial it has ever endured.

Unimaginable Horror

The Civil War, begun on April 4, 1861, was the bloodiest war our country has fought. More American soldiers were killed in that four-year period than in all other wars combined. Over 600,000 men paid for the sin of slavery and financial greed with their lives. Well over half of the casualties were Northerners, indicating that in God's eyes both sides were equally guilty for condoning slavery.

At times that war must have seemed like hell on earth. Unlike modern wars where missiles are launched and artillery shells fired from miles away, the Civil War was personal, intimate, and bloody. Men stood across from one another, looking their adversary in the eye as they fired their weapons. James McPherson recounts one bloody day during the war:

> Night fell on a scene of horror beyond imagining. Nearly 6,000 men lay dead or dying, and another 17,000 wounded groaned in agony or endured in silence. The casualties at Antietam numbered four times the total suffered by American soldiers at the Normandy beaches on June 6, 1944. More than twice as many

Americans lost their lives in one day at Sharpsburg as fell in combat in the War of 1812, the Mexican War, and the Spanish-American War combined.[6]

Suddenly, what was perceived as a minor compromise with sin turned into a crisis that almost destroyed the union. We were on the brink of collapse.

This war was a painful lesson in holiness. Though God had a glorious plan to use the United States, He held us accountable for our sins—possibly because of that plan. The emotional and physical toll on the nation was immeasurable, but the nation arose from the great disaster purged, stronger, and perhaps a more perfect union. We were far from solving the problems of race and forming a more equitable society, but we had at last begun the process of granting full equality to all people.

God's Man of the Hour

Do you recall the Bible story of Queen Esther, the beautiful wife of King Xerxes? She risked her life to tell the king of Haman's wicked plot to destroy her people, the Jews. These powerful words, spoken by her uncle Mordecai, had persuaded Esther to take her brave course of action: "Who knows but that you have come to royal position for such a time as this?" (Esther 4:14).

If ever a man was prepared by God "for such a time as this," that man was Abraham Lincoln. Just as God raised up George Washington to give birth to our country, He used Lincoln to save the nation from internal destruction.

Born in obscurity, a self-educated lawyer from Illinois, Lincoln spent his early life drifting in and out of politics and in and out of church. Known as "Honest Abe," Lincoln had a passion for righteousness and a sincere love for the Bible.

In 1856, Abraham Lincoln left the Whig Party to join the new anti-slavery Republican Party. He surprised the nation by winning the presidency in 1860. When the South responded by immediately seceding, Lincoln entered the White House determined to preserve the Union.

Perhaps more than anyone else, Abraham Lincoln recognized

that the Civil War was God's judgment on both the North and the South for allowing the sin of slavery to continue. He stated, "American slavery is one of those offenses which, in the providence of God...He now wills to remove, and that He gives to both North and South this terrible war as the woe due to those by whom the offense came."[7]

Lincoln observed that the North and South read the same Bible and prayed to the same God, and concluded that God was using the war to change the nation:

> Insomuch as we know that, by His divine law, nations like individuals are subjected to punishments and chastisement in this world, may we not justly fear that the awful calamity of civil war, which now desolates the land may be but a punishment inflicted upon us for our presumptuous sins to the needful end of our national reformation as a whole people?[8]

In his hour of testing, Lincoln stood firm, winning freedom for millions of enslaved men, women, and children. With God's guidance, Lincoln preserved the Union he believed God meant to use as the "last, best hope of earth."[9]

The Civil War was GOD'S JUDGMENT for allowing the SIN OF SLAVERY to continue.

However, Lincoln did not live to see a reunited America. His wife, Mary Todd Lincoln, reported the final words of the President as they sat in Ford's Theater just five days after the Civil War ended. "He said he wanted to visit the Holy Land and see those places hallowed by the Savior. He was saying there was no city he so much desired to see as Jerusalem. And with the words half spoken on his tongue, the bullet of the assassin entered his brain, and the soul of the great and good president was carried by the angels to the New Jerusalem above."[10]

In his own assessment of our national tragedy and the task before us at the end of the Civil War, Lincoln said: "With malice toward none, with charity for all, with firmness in the right, as God gives us to see the right, let us strive on to finish the work we are in, to bind up the nation's wounds."[11] His vision did not include the bitterness and rancor that followed the war during the Reconstruction era. Some historians suggest that, had he lived, the period of adjustment might have been less painful. But Lincoln's mission passed to other hands.

Years later, Theodore Roosevelt recalled the achievements of the Civil War:

> Thank God for the iron in the blood of our fathers, the men who upheld the wisdom of Lincoln and bore the sword or rifle in the armies of Grant! Let us, the children of the men who carried the great Civil War to a triumphant conclusion, praise the God of our fathers that the ignoble counsels of peace were rejected; that the suffering and the loss, the blackness of sorrow and despair, were unflinchingly faced, and the years of strife endured; for in the end, the slave was freed, the Union restored, and the mighty American Republic placed once more as a helmeted queen among nations![12]

The Veil Is Lifted

With the nation free at last from the bondage of slavery, God once again began preparing our country for its great task. Immediately following the postwar recession of the 1870s, an explosion of new ideas and inventions changed our country and the world.

Thomas Edison's lightbulb and Alexander Graham Bell's telephone were tools unlike any ever seen. Edison's phonograph made it possible to record a message for later playback. Samuel Morse perfected the telegraph. On the very first telegram, sent from Baltimore to the U.S. Supreme Court in Washington, D.C., Morse wrote the words: "What hath God wrought!"[13] Railroad lines that carried industry and ideas across plains and mountains were dramatically improved. Daniel Boorstin describes this vigorous American spirit:

> The years after the Civil War when the continent was only partly explored were the halcyon days of the Go-Getters. They went in search of what others had never imagined was there to get. The Go-Getters made something out of nothing, they brought meat out of the desert, found oil in the rocks, and brought light to millions. They discovered new resources, and where there seemed

> none to be discovered, they invented new ways of profiting from others who were trying to invent and to discover…All over the continent—on the desert, under the soil, in the rocks, in the hearts of the cities—appeared surprising new opportunities.[14]

Motion pictures were invented. The automobile was created. Steamships were improved. America was on the move. Massive corporations like General Electric, AT&T, and Standard Oil became industrial giants securing America's economic might. Within a few years, the United States scarcely resembled the agrarian nation it once was. A cascade of new developments in manufacturing and technology made the United States the premier industrial and military power in the world.

These were such vital years in America's history. For ages past, technology had developed slowly, but suddenly the world was being transformed. At the very moment we were cleansed from the sin of slavery, the scales began to fall from our eyes. In God's perfect timing, America was acquiring the tools that would allow her to grow into a dominant world power. We were gaining the communication and information resources to evangelize the world. Wealth, power, and political acumen combined to assure us the capability to spread God's message to the farthest reaches of the globe.

Evangelism and Immigration

Another great force shaped America after the Civil War—immigration. Millions of people came to our shores during this time. The inscription at the base of the Statue of Liberty, penned by 19th-century poet Emma Lazarus, declares the greater vision of the American experiment:

> Give me your tired, your poor, your huddled masses yearning to breathe free, the wretched refuse of your teeming shore. Send these, the homeless, the tempest-tossed to me, I lift my lamp beside the golden door![15]

The most important resource in America is not her vast natural resources, her democratic institutions, or even her great spirit of independence, but the soul and vision of her people. In business, entertainment, religion, science, and every other field in which this nation excels, our greatest resource has always been the broad and complex interaction of those who compose the "melting pot." We are not defined by color, race, ethnicity, or our common language. We are men and women of every nation, brought together by providence and history to become "one nation under God."

From 1820 to 1975, 47 million people flooded the shores of America to begin a new life. Men, women, and children of every nation and tribe made the journey in hopes of discovering and living out the American Dream. There is no question that immigration is one of the greatest legacies of our heritage.

Few things stir our sense of awe and patriotism as much as the photographs, films, and personal memoirs of the thousands of immigrants who entered this nation through Ellis Island in New York Harbor during the immigration years. New citizens, striving to support their families, took up residence in New York, Detroit, Boston, Chicago, and many other urban centers. They enriched our lives in every area. Among them are such well-known names as Irving Berlin, Levi Straus, Oscar Hammerstein, Henry Steinway, Werner von Braun, and Henry Kissinger.

> **We have the way; we have the resources. If only we had the will, we could CHANGE THE WORLD for Jesus Christ.**

God never intended America to be an elitist or arrogant nation. After all, in our history, it was not the kings or princes or clerics who built our institutions and way of life. It was the meek, the humble, and the poor. The homeless Puritans seeking religious freedom. The slave brought in the stinking hold of a ship. The peasant farmer who wanted to own land for the first time in his life.

Have you ever stopped to think how truly unique our immigration policies are? Anyone can become an American citizen. All those who come to the United States and take citizenship can join the great melting pot of American people, regardless of their ethnic background. This is as true today as it was a century ago. Unlike the chosen people of Israel, it is not our birthright that sets us apart as God's chosen instrument—it is our great national purpose.

G. K. Chesterton once observed that America is the only nation ever founded upon a creed.[16] Not on geographical borders, not on culture, and certainly not on ethnicity. In his assessment of the impact of American immigration, British historian Paul Johnson says:

> America will never be an ordinary country; it is always going to be extraordinary. Every time I visit—and I must have been in the U.S. 100 times or more—I am continually astonished by its diversity. When people in England attack America, which they often do, I say: If you are anti-American, you're anti-human race, because that is what America is about. You don't need the United Nations, you've already got it.[17]

On these shores, God amassed a populace comprising almost all the people groups on earth. All of them are Americans, yet all of them retain some unique understanding of the cultures from which they came. Each was meant to thrive, prosper, and learn from a Christian nation.

From its beginning to today, American immigration has been the cornerstone of God's plan to use America to help redeem the modern world with the love of Jesus Christ. Today, we have an army of potential servants of Jesus Christ who have knowledge of every culture and language on the planet. When properly grounded in faith and bearing the message of Christ's love, armed with the resources of America, these "ambassadors" have the ability to spread the gospel to the farthest reaches of the earth. We have the way; we have the resources. If only we had the will, we could change the world for Jesus Christ.

As Joseph Stowell, president of Moody Bible Institute, said, "Christians are not here on earth to change culture, but to change lives which will have an affect on the culture in which they live. Lives changed for the better!"[18]

Were we ready, willing, and able to complete the task for which He had prepared us? Would we combine our resources and carry out our historical mandate?

Even now the answer to those questions are not clear. In the next section, we will see that this nation prepared by God to complete the Great Commission would turn from its lofty vision and begin to reject the truths and values we once held sacred. In the 20th century, our nation has rejected God in every way imaginable. Will this be our end? Or could there be another way? Will someone take the initiative to rescue us from our disobedience as Zipporah rescued Moses? Will America be given another chance?

PART II

A Nation Unravels

Progress has brought us both unbounded opportunities and unbridled difficulties. Thus, the measure of our civilization will not be that we have done much, but what we have done with that much. I believe that the next half century will determine if we will advance the cause of Christian civilization or revert to the horrors of brutal paganism. The thought of modern industry in the hands of Christian charity is a dream worth dreaming. The thought of industry in the hands of paganism is a nightmare beyond imagining. The choice between the two is upon us.

—President Theodore Roosevelt, 1909

CHAPTER 7

The Battle for America's Soul

During the first few decades of the 20th century, exciting things were happening in our country. American optimism was high, and we were having a positive influence on the world. It seemed as if technology could solve almost any problem. One example of the energy and enthusiasm of American enterprise was the building of the Panama Canal. The French had tried in the 1880s, but disease and poor planning had foiled their efforts. Some estimates place the French death toll at nearly 20,000.

When the United States received the rights to build the canal, American engineers and workers flooded the Isthmus of Panama. They found the project extremely difficult. Mosquitoes carrying malaria took their toll; whole sides of mountains collapsed into newly dug ditches; high humidity caused unbearable working conditions; and mold grew on almost everything. But the Americans kept digging.

After spending $352 million and ten years, the United States completed the project. More than 5,500 people had died during the construction, including 350 Americans. But the project was a success. The elaborate system of locks opened on August 15, 1914, saving ships thousands of miles of travel around the tip of South America. It seemed as if America could accomplish anything.

The Passion for Souls Continues

Exciting things were also occurring in the world of Christianity. If the 18th century was America's foundation and the 19th the era of spiritual testing and growth, then surely the 20th century would be God's final preparation for America to attain her purposes in His divine plan of redemption. At the turn of the century, that seemed possible.

At that time, America took the lead in sending out missionaries. Hundreds of Americans set off for places they had only seen on maps to spend the rest of their lives serving God. Many died of disease or martyrdom, but their passion for winning the world for Christ inspired others to follow in their footsteps. These missionaries began to use their specialized skills on the field and a new cross-cultural dialog began replacing the old colonialism of the 19th century.

For the first time, single women like Lottie Moon and Johanna Veenstra took a more active role in the Christian community. The Student Volunteer Movement inspired daring young students from colleges and universities to forego prestigious careers and follow Christ. It is estimated that half of the Protestant missionary force came from this movement alone. John R. Mott, a great missionary statesman, was its foremost speaker. Sherwood Eddy wrote of his experiences as a student volunteer:

> In retrospect, I find I have spent half a century along the far-flung battle line of missions. I was one of the first of sixteen thousand student volunteers who were swept into what seemed to us nothing less than a missionary crusade. We were considered fanatical by some, and we made numerous mistakes which we ourselves came to realize later in bitter experience. Many sacrificed early plans and ambitions for wealth, power, prestige, or pleasure to go to some distant country about which they knew little save its abysmal need. Not wholly unlike the unity of Christendom achieved during the Middle Ages was the feeling of these student volunteer

missionaries that they were one team, working for one world, under one Captain.[1]

Also getting their start during this time were faith missions, where missionaries are primarily responsible for raising their own support. A. B. Simpson founded the Christian and Missionary Alliance, Peter Cameron Scott the African Inland Mission, and C. I. Scofield the Central American Mission. God raised up Christians who had a burden for such varied parts of the world that it seemed as if the whole earth would soon be covered. These men and women had a deep passion for Christ's work. Jim Elliot, who was martyred for his faith, echoed their heart for the lost: "May we who know Christ hear the cry of the damned as they hurtle head-long into the Christless night without ever a chance...May we shed tears of repentance for those we have failed to bring out of darkness."[2]

Faith mission societies became some of the most vibrant and innovative segments of the Christian world. J. Herbert Kane, a missions historian, writes:

> Most of the innovations in the twentieth-century mission have been introduced by the faith missions, including radio, aviation, Bible correspondence courses, gospel recordings, tapes, cassettes, saturation evangelism, and theological education by extension.[3]

Although times were hard during the Great Depression, the missionary spirit never died in evangelical circles. Clarence Jones began the first missionary radio effort; William Cameron Townsend trained missionary linguists and founded Wycliffe translators; Joy Ridderhof birthed and expanded gospel recordings. This period also saw the beginning of medical missions.

On the home front, evangelist Billy Sunday, a former professional baseball player, made waves across America during the first half of the century. It all began when Sunday and his friends went to a bar to have a few drinks. They walked outside to listen to the rescue mission musicians. There on the street next to the bar, Billy Sunday was struck in the heart by the old hymns and the testimonies. He sobbed and sobbed, and though his friends mocked him, he accompanied a young man to the Pacific Garden Mission. There he fell on his knees in repentance.

From that day on, Sunday gave up drinking and betting. Although he continued his baseball career, he never played on Sundays. A few years later, he felt called to tell others about Jesus Christ. He prayed for a release from his contract with the Philadelphia team, and when it came, he went into full-time Christian work. For almost twenty years, he packed auditoriums as he preached the message of Jesus Christ.

The Battle Begins

Unfortunately, this exciting time for Christ's kingdom was also the hour of Satan's frantic attempt to thwart God's purposes. Despite the many challenges to our national purpose over the centuries, the battle for America's soul did not begin in earnest until the 1920s. Then we began using God's blessings for our personal gain. Millions of dollars were traded in stocks, bonds, and commodities. Prohibition against alcohol was flaunted in speakeasies. Money, fashions, and entertainment consumed the American mind, while traditional morals and values were discarded.

> One idea is flung against another with the heavy ring of contact. WHOSE IDEAS will win the battle?

C. S. Lewis once taught, "One of the dangers of having a lot of money is that you may be quite satisfied with the kinds of happiness money can give and so fail to realize your need for God. If everything seems to come simply by signing checks, you may forget that you are at every moment totally dependent on God."[4] That is also true for nations. America's wealth and material prosperity in the 1920s blinded us to our greater need for God. By mid-decade, this rebellion reached into mainstream America and tempted hundreds of thousands away from traditional beliefs.

Two distinct forces were lining up to do battle for the soul of America. Paul outlines the heart of the battle:

> Our struggle is not against flesh and blood, but against the rulers, against the authorities, against the powers of this dark

> world and against the spiritual forces of evil in the heavenly realms (Ephesians 6:12).

In *The Great Evangelical Disaster*, the late Dr. Francis Schaeffer describes the conflict in human terms:

> The primary battle is a spiritual battle in the heavenlies. But, this does not mean, therefore, that the battle we are in is otherworldly or outside of human history. It is a real spiritual battle, but it is equally a battle here on earth in our own country, our own communities, our places of work and our schools, and even our own homes. The spiritual battle has its counterpart in the visible world, in the minds of men and women, and in every area of human culture. In the realm of space and time, the heavenly battle is fought on the stage of human history.[5]

Potent forces were threatening to unravel our society. In 1830, Alexis de Tocqueville captured the essence of who we were as a nation, our successes, and the dangers to our future:

> I sought for the key to the greatness and genius of America in her harbors...in her fertile fields and boundless forests, in her rich mines and vast world commerce, in her public school system and institutions of learning. I sought for it in her democratic Congress and in her matchless Constitution. Not until I went into the churches of America and heard her pulpits flame with righteousness did I understand the secret of her genius and power. America is great because America is good; and if America ever ceases to be good, America will cease to be great.[6]

In the 1920s, America traded her relationship with God for worldly pursuits. We subscribed to ideals that put us at enmity with God without acknowledging that it was God who had made America great in the first place. What went wrong was that America was no longer "good." The battle had begun.

The Battle of Ideas

What kind of foe were we facing? Imagine a great army of spiritual beings battling in the heavenlies with sharply honed swords. These swords are not made of tempered steel, but of strong ideas. One idea is flung against another with the heavy ring of contact. Whose ideas will win the battle? How we use the ideas we wield will determine who wins the battle for America's soul. Will we keep our swords sheathed or come out fighting with the ideas we know will win—the principles of God's Word?

Indeed, the 20th century could be labeled the battle of ideas. The Scopes Trial of 1925, which took place in tiny Dayton, Tennessee, is a good example. It revolved around the question of whether evolution should be taught in public schools. While the ruling upheld the Christian belief in creationism, Clarence Darrow and the ACLU leveled great public scorn upon God, the Bible, and Christianity. The true goal of Darrow's efforts in the Scopes Trial was revealed several years later when he returned to Dayton and saw a new church under construction. He scoffed, "I guess I didn't do much good here after all."[7]

Journalists like H. L. Mencken denounced Christianity as "a childish theology founded upon hate" and called Christians "morons." His angry diatribes, combined with those of other intellectuals, penetrated mainstream thinking as many Americans began to believe they could actually live without God.[8]

In the 1920s, Margaret Sanger, founder of Planned Parenthood and a believer in the science of racial purity known as eugenics, began her work to popularize birth control. She stated, "Birth control appeals to the advanced radical because it is calculated to undermine the authority of the Christian churches. I look forward to seeing humanity free someday from the tyranny of Christianity."[9] Sanger's work formed the foundation for the radical feminist movement, and her birth-control crusade led to promiscuity and a collapse of sexual purity. Sanger's Planned Parenthood became the world's leading provider of abortions. Men and women such as Darrow, Mencken, and Sanger knew well that they were engaged in a war of ideas—and a war against God.

Another idea that challenged the Christian faith was existentialism, a humanistic philosophy based on disillusionment and the emptiness and despair of secular life. Philosophers such as John-Paul Sartre, Albert Camus, Martin Heidegger, and Karl Jaspers disseminated this idea. In one outburst, French writer and social critic Sartre said, "There is no human nature because there is no God to have a conception of it. Man simply is ...Man is nothing else but that which he makes of himself. That is the first principle of existentialism."[10] These beliefs provided the foundation for the radical hippie movement of the 1960s. And from these roots arose some of the most threatening anti-Christian ideologies and social policies.

In the wake of World War I, philosophers and scientists began putting forth an entirely new way of thinking. Ideas from intellectuals such as Karl Marx, Charles Darwin, Friedrich Nietzsche, and Sigmund Freud conveyed much the same message to the generation of the '20s—that the world was not what it seemed to be. People began to question almost everything.

Sigmund Freud, founder of modern psychology, believed that the world revolves around sexual dysfunction. Some of his supposed "findings" are graphically sexual. In one of his most famous works, *The Future of an Illusion*, Freud compared religion to a "childhood neurosis." He argued, "Religious ideas have sprung from the same need as all the other achievements of culture: from the necessity for defending itself from the crushing supremacy of nature." Freud concluded that "the more the fruits of knowledge become accessible to men, the more widespread is the decline of religious belief."[11]

These men and women were well aware that they were engaged in a war of ideas—and a WAR AGAINST GOD.

Before long, Marxism and the new field of study spearheaded by Freud, called psychoanalysis, filled people with doubt and anxiety. Paul Johnson explains:

> Marxist and Freudian analysis combined to undermine, in their different ways, the highly developed sense of personal responsibility, and of duty towards a settled and objectively true moral code...The impression people derived from Einstein, of a universe in which all measurements of value were relative, served to confirm this vision of moral anarchy.[12]

Seduced by the "logic" of the age, many people turned their

backs on the God of their fathers. They developed a thirst for anything spiritual that could add significance to their empty lives. Eventually, some experimented with drugs, hoping that the release from pain and the hallucinatory experiences might provide a mystical vision that was missing in their de-Christianized lives. Others drowned themselves in alcohol and sex.

When Aldous Huxley published his astonishing novel *Brave New World* in 1932, he predicted that future societies would advocate the use of drugs to help alleviate the emptiness of life. As other experimental works helped introduce Eastern metaphysical concepts drawn from the Hindu religion, thousands more were enticed by such exotic ideas and tempted away from belief in God. In *Time Must Have a Stop*, Huxley lamented, "If we must play the theological game, let us never forget it is a game. Religion, it seems to me, can survive only as a consciously accepted system of make-believe."[13]

Huxley wrote of man's dilemma: "If God were there and the world had meaning, then he had to accept God's meaning and God's rules. But, if he said there were no God there, and everything was meaningless, then he could make his own rules."[14] Suddenly, we come to the heart of the matter.

As we sped toward World War II, we willingly turned our eyes away from the truth of God to pursue our own passions and pleasures. We hardly took note of Mussolini's rise to power in Italy or the virulent propaganda and dangerous threats of Adolf Hitler in Germany. Nor did we recognize the threat of communism, which had by then overtaken Russia.

Thanks to their promotion by intellectuals and educators, America dabbled in dangerous and potentially destructive new ideas. While some of these developments seemed harmless at the time, these chilling influences soon threatened our sense of national purpose and our very survival as a nation.

Our Moment of History

In the continuing escalation of ideological hostilities, the outcome will determine whether this nation will be able to fulfill the role for which God gave us birth. What we do with our moment of history, as Theodore Roosevelt observed, will make all the difference in our destiny. Will we leave a legacy of destruction and death, or one of blessing and eternal life? Will we come back to God and receive His blessings, or will we reap the whirlwind of the evils we have sown? Author Paul Johnson describes how these choices affect our future:

> By the last decade of the twentieth century, some lessons had plainly been learned. But it was not yet clear whether the underlying evils which made possible its catastrophic failures and tragedies—the rise of moral relativism, the decline of personal responsibility, the repudiation of Judeo-Christian values, not least the arrogant belief that men and women could solve all the mysteries of the universe by their own unaided intellects—were in the process of being eradicated.
>
> On that fact depends the chances of the twenty-first century becoming, by contrast, an age of hope for mankind.[15]

In the closing years of the 20th century and the beginning of a new millennium, the legacy that we leave our children and grandchildren is yet to be decided. Our possibilities are limitless through the power of God. Imagine what we could do for the cause of Christ with computer technology, satellite communications, new methods of language translation, and advances in transportation and medical science. We have the ability: all we need is the dedication, personnel, and the finances.

Our Measure of Devotion

Our Founding Fathers signed the Declaration of Independence with full knowledge that if they lost the war with England they would be executed as traitors. They willingly risked their lives for their beliefs. The Declaration, in fact, ends with the powerful statement, "We mutually pledge to each other our lives, our fortunes and our sacred honor." They sacrificed everything to guarantee our freedom to worship and tell others about our Lord Jesus Christ. Our duty is to protect these freedoms. Should we not demonstrate the same measure of devotion in our willingness to sacrifice to help bring about a rebirth of faith for our future generations? Former President Ronald Reagan highlights the importance of diligence:

> Freedom is never more than one generation away from extinction. Madison knew, and we should always remember, that no government is perfect—not even a democracy. Our test today must be to reaffirm the ideals of those days. Let it be said of this generation of Americans that when we pass the torch of freedom to the new generation, it will be burning as brightly as when it was passed to us. Then we will know that we have kept faith with Madison and those other remarkable men we call the Founding Fathers, and we will have kept faith with God.[16]

Sadly, as we stand at the threshold of a new millennium, our torch of freedom is burning dimly. Looking back over the 20th century, we can chart the downfall of our nation and her great mission. At each critical step, we have shifted our focus further from God and onto ourselves. The church has fallen into widespread decay and missed many opportunities to fulfill its commission. The United States of America, far from being a shining city on a hill, is in great danger of losing her sense of purpose and her blessings. How do we stop this process of decay? How important is it to regain what we have given away? If this generation cannot rise up and reverse the disastrous trend of rejecting God, who can say where this downfall will end?

"[W]hen we pass the torch of freedom to the new generation, ...we will have kept FAITH WITH GOD."

In this section of *Red Sky in the Morning*, we will take a look at the consequences of integrating ungodly ideals into the heart and soul of America. We will also discover the tragedies we have inflicted on our families, schools, and society by abandoning our biblical foundations.

CHAPTER 8

The Darker Side of Life

Perhaps you have seen the award-winning photographs taken by Dorothea Lange in the 1930s during the Great Depression. She captured the haunting eyes of children who had nothing; the tragedy of families who left their farms in the Midwest to travel in a dusty old car to California; and the poverty of migrant workers who survived from day to day. These were the true-life stories of Americans who suffered immensely during the lean years of the 1930s.

Why did God allow the Great Depression to afflict our nation? The Bible is clear about the results of ignoring our faith: "We must pay more careful attention, therefore, to what we have heard, so that we do not drift away. For if the message spoken by angels was binding, and every violation and disobedience received its just punishment, how shall we escape if we ignore such a great salvation?" (Hebrews 2:1–3). God would allow the nation He had so carefully created to stray only so far without discipline. As He did throughout the history of the Jewish people, He chose to capture America's attention by allowing us to face serious trials. Therefore, in 1929 America was plunged into a deep economic depression.

In three short years, American wages dropped more than 50 percent; combined personal income fell from $87.4 billion to only $41.7 billion. Nearly 70,000 businesses and family farms collapsed in bankruptcy. For a time, suicide was the leading cause of death in America. Unemployment soared to 4 million by 1930, doubled in 1931, then topped 12 million in 1932.[1]

At times, more than 25 percent of the American work force was jobless.[2] Many of the more fortunate workers brought home barely enough to live on. When it seemed as if the crisis could get no worse, the Dust Bowl of the mid-1930s blasted the heartland with the worst drought our nation has ever experienced.

The capitalist dream seemed to collapse before our eyes. I believe that God was trying to show us that the American dream was not about money, but about human souls. Tragically, instead of returning to God, we looked to our own resourcefulness to rebuild America's dreams, acting as if we no longer needed God. In so doing, we augmented the downward spiral begun in the previous decade.

The New Deal

Franklin Roosevelt rose to power during our national humiliation and led the nation for the next twelve years. Roosevelt's economic program, the New Deal, though well intentioned, was our attempt to solve our own problems without God's help. The federal government began its journey into debt—from the $16 billion federal debt of the early '30s to the over $5.3 trillion in 1997.[3]

Federal expenditures during the New Deal were astronomical. More than $10.5 billion was spent on public works, and more than $2.7 billion on other government-sponsored projects—an enormous amount of money for that day. More than eight million people joined the government payroll as 122,000 public buildings, 77,000 bridges, 285 airports, 664,000 miles of roads, and 24,000 miles of storm and water sewers were constructed.[4]

While these projects benefited America greatly, they set a precedent of government intervention that redefined vital roles in American society. Through programs such as Social Security, public housing projects, and welfare, the federal government expanded its control over nearly every aspect of American life. For the first time, the American people looked to big government as their source of supply, as Roosevelt promised to get them out of the Great Depression.

Roosevelt sincerely tried to help a hurting nation, and it is unlikely that he intended to escalate the federal bureaucracy to the size it has grown. But his policies served to turn our nation further away from our historic dependence on God. Financial expert Larry Burkett explains the impact of Roosevelt's New Deal on America:

> Once the federal government assumed the role of protector and provider for the general public, the role of the church diminished proportionately until, today, few people see the church and God as their financial resource in times of need.[5]

The New Deal helped alleviate some of the pain temporarily, but big government supplanted the function that community and church had fulfilled in the past. Policies such as Social Security, intended to be a temporary means of assistance for those incapacitated by economic hardship, quickly became a permanent fixture of government. And as churches relinquished to the government their responsibility to help the poor, along with it went their opportunity to share the gospel with those needy families. In 1993, Burkett wrote:

> Whether we like to admit it, our parents and grandparents traded our freedoms for the government's handouts during the thirties. From that point forward, the government has intruded further and further into our daily lives until the average American now considers the massive federal bureaucracy to be normal. Most of the controls we see now are economic in nature. The next wave likely will be aimed at the family structure.[6]

This decision to rely on ourselves changed the nature of our country in a manner that proved devastating in coming years. From the destruction of the Protestant work ethic to the breakup of the nuclear family, we are reaping the consequences of those decisions.

The Valley of the Shadow

In the end, it took a war to bring us out of the Depression. World War II did help us reestablish a national sense of purpose, but it also destroyed our innocence and changed our way of living. The horror of concentration camps and genocide in Europe shattered America's idealism. By the end of the war, family structures had changed dramatically. Many husbands and fathers were either dead or missing; wives and mothers had entered the workplace as breadwinners. Although many women originally went to work out of financial necessity, this break from the status quo planted seeds for the later women's movement, in which radical feminists would claim that women could find fulfillment only outside of the home.

On September 30, 1938, British Prime Minister Neville Chamberlain agreed to allow Germany to conquer part of Europe without England's interference. When Chamberlain and Adolf Hitler met to sign the Munich Pact, Winston Churchill uttered this prophetic warning:

> The people should know that we have sustained a defeat without a war…they should know that we have passed an awful milestone in our history…and that the terrible words have for the time being been pronounced against the Western democracies: "Thou art weighed in the balance and found wanting." And, do not suppose this is the end. This is only the beginning of the reckoning. This is only the first sip, the first foretaste of a bitter cup which will be proffered to us year by year unless, by a supreme recovery of moral health and martial vigor, we arise again and take our stand for freedom as in the olden times.[7]

With an insight and moral courage that made him a legendary figure, Churchill saw the hand of God in our diplomatic crises.

We had been given historical warnings about the consequences of forsaking our Christian heritage. Nazi Germany is one of the most obvious examples of what happens to a nation that rejects God. Adolf Hitler's rise to power was aided by two main factors. First, the church in Germany endured a sustained period of secularization and decline. Second, Germany's economic structure collapsed and left widespread depression and chaos. Having forsaken God, the German people fell prey to this charismatic leader. Hitler promised a new era of material success and world domination, for a thousand-year reign, through the military power of the Third Reich.

Although Germany was one of the most highly educated, technologically sophisticated, and scientific cultures in the world, its people were unable to withstand the allure of Nazism. Despite the highest literacy rate, the best universities, the most distinguished scientists, the Germans could not fend off barbarism once they turned their back on God.

While it is unlikely that a leader like Adolf Hitler could come to power in America today, the similarities between prewar Germany and present-day America are unsettling. Our churches have steadily declined in godly influence. Compromise has tainted the purity of the gospel message and lessened its impact. Believers regularly fail to obey Jesus' command to be "salt and light" to their culture. A large proportion of those who claim to be Christians live in a shallow, superficial manner.

In the prewar days, arguments favoring abortion and euthanasia pervaded the daily discourse of the German people. Few spoke against Hitler's regime for conducting social engineering and medical experiments on helpless victims. New Age religions fueled the demonic rage of Hitler and many of his followers. These influences are present in our culture today.

THE SIMILARITIES between prewar Germany and present day America ARE UNSETTLING.

From the Holocaust to the atomic bomb, from fascist dictatorships to brutal communist regimes, Americans saw the darker side of life. As a result, Americans spent decades building and improving bomb shelters, investing wealth and energy into avoiding the destruction of the "final war." C. S. Lewis describes the paranoia:

> As a Christian I take it for granted that human history will someday end; and I am offering Omniscience no advice as to the best date for that consummation. I am more concerned by what the Bomb is doing already. One meets young people who make the threat of it a reason for…evading every duty in the present.[8]

Despite the incredible loss of innocence, through the grace and provision of God we arose from the war as leaders of the free world. In August 1945, Churchill told the British House of Commons, "America stands at this moment at the summit of the world."[9] Just imagine what impact we might have made for the cause of Jesus Christ had we used our influence for God by sending thousands of missionaries to those countries devastated by the war.

But once again America ignored her purpose. Despite God's protection and guidance through the firestorms of two world wars, our fighting forces returned to America to focus on themselves. As our prosperity, pride, and privileges increased, the ideological demons introduced during the '20s reappeared even stronger in the '40s.

Decline Reaches Main Street

Have you ever watched the professional demolition of a multistory building? Dynamite is placed in strategic spots inside the structure. Seconds after the detonator is pressed, the building implodes, falling into a surprisingly small pile of rubble.

Historian Will Durant once said that a great civilization cannot be destroyed from the outside until it falls first from the inside. No matter how well we might arm ourselves against enemies outside our borders, the greatest enemies are those who place destructive devices inside our strategic institutions—causing us to morally implode. British broadcaster Malcolm Muggeridge observed, "Since the beginning of the Second World War, Western Society has experienced a complete abandonment of its sense of good and evil. The true crisis of our time has nothing to do with monetary troubles, unemployment, or nuclear weapons. The true crisis has to do with the fact that Western man has lost his way."[10]

Muggeridge described the danger of subtle changes to culture in his famous "pot of frogs" illustration. If you drop a frog into a pot of boiling water, the frog will immediately jump out. But if you place the frog in a pot of lukewarm water and slowly turn up the heat, the relaxed frog will just swim around, growing accustomed to the increasing warmth until it eventually boils to death. This is what happens with cultural decay. It is a gradual process that slowly dulls our senses until what was once seen as unacceptable somehow becomes acceptable.

Since the 1940s, America has allowed sin to creep into our nation as never before. As a result, we have become desensitized to sin and our moral judgment is impaired. Even worse, at each step along the way, we eliminated Jesus Christ from our lives and culture. The gospel was no longer politically correct, and many Americans embarked on a new "crisis of faith" that would be the catalyst for national despair. Dr. Charles Malik, former President of the United Nations General Assembly, addressed this crisis of faith:

> I really do not know what will remain of civilization and history if the accumulated influence of Jesus Christ, both direct and indirect, is eradicated from literature, art, practical dealings, moral standards, and creativeness in the different activities of mind and spirit... The heart of the whole matter is faith in Jesus Christ.[11]

In the years following World War II, General Omar Bradley warned America, "We have grasped the mystery of the atom and rejected the Sermon on the Mount...The world has achieved brilliance without conscience."[12] Though we had helped to win a great military and moral victory in Europe, we were becoming a world of "nuclear giants and ethical infants."[13] Success and power blinded most Americans to their need for God. One by one, all across America, the great institutions that had been fountains of righteousness began to fall away from God. Like the frog, we had begun to swim in a pan of lukewarm moral water and never noticed the temperature rising.

A Court Without God

One tremendous influence in turning our nation away from God has been the alarming number of anti-God court decisions arising from the Supreme Court. In a very real sense, the United States Supreme Court has been the official judge standing between God and the American people. For most of our nation's history, the Justices recognized that they were subject to a higher law found in God's Word. The Court viewed law as President Calvin Coolidge did when he declared, "Men do not make laws, they do but discover them. Laws must be justified by something more than the will of the majority. They must rest upon the eternal foundations of righteousness."[14] Let us look at a few of the historic cases that reaffirmed biblical principles:

- *Vidal v. Girard's Executors* (1844): The Court produced a ruling which said, "Christianity is not to be maliciously and openly reviled and blasphemed against, to the annoyance of believers or the injury of the public." The Court's decision asked the question, "Where can the purest principles of morality be learned so clearly or so perfectly as from the New Testament?"[15]
- *Holy Trinity v. United States* (1892): The Supreme Court cited document after document from American history and concluded, "There is no dissonance in these declarations. There is a universal language pervading them all, having one meaning; they affirm and reaffirm that this is a religious nation." The ruling states bluntly, "This is a Christian nation."[16]
- *United States v. Macintosh* (1931): The Supreme Court declared, "We are a Christian people... according to one another the equal right of religious freedom, and acknowledging with the reverence the duty of obedience to God."[17]

But in early 1947, an entirely new agenda gripped the Court. In *Everson v. Board of Education*, the Supreme Court ruled that the First Amendment erected a "wall of separation" between church and state which must be kept "high and impregnable." Supreme Court Justice Hugo Black, author of the decision, stated, "We could not approve the slightest breach" of that separation.[18] The Court cited no precedent from previous rulings. The case was an official betrayal of America's Christian heritage.

The *Everson* case put forth a radically new idea: "separation between church and state"—a removal of religious principles from government. Our Founding Fathers placed the First Amendment in the Constitution specifically to prevent such erroneous rulings. The fact that we are a nation based on the Word of God has been restated throughout our history.

From the time of *Everson* until today, decisions by the U.S.

Supreme Court have helped to bring about the greatest decline in American civilization. It was as if the Supreme Court had declared a bloodless revolution in America—a revolution more subtle than, yet just as destructive as the Russian revolution under Lenin. Over the next three decades, we witnessed a stream of liberal court rulings that gradually reshaped who we are as a nation.

- *Engel v. Vitale*, *Murray v. Curlett*, and *Abington v. Schempp* (1962–1963): Within two years, three separate cases effectively removed prayer, religious instruction, and Bible reading from America's public schools.
- *Florey v. Sioux Falls School District* (1979): The Court ruled it unconstitutional for a student to ask at a school assembly, "Whose birthday is celebrated on Christmas?"[19]
- *Grove v. Mead School District* (1985): The Supreme Court refused to remove from the required curriculum of a class a book that referred to Jesus as "a poor white trash God."[20]

Other Supreme Court rulings in the past thirty years have stated:

- It is unconstitutional for a war memorial or any public monument to be designed in the shape of a cross.
- It is unconstitutional for public schools to teach biblical doctrine or principles; however, the Bible may be used in a course on history or comparative religions.
- It is unconstitutional to post the Ten Commandments in public schools. The Supreme Court gave this reasoning: "If the posted copies of the Ten Commandments are to have any effect at all, it will be to induce the schoolchildren to read, meditate upon, perhaps to venerate and obey the Commandments. This...is not a permissible...objective."[21]

Founding Father Benjamin Rush foresaw the danger of these court decisions. Two hundred years ago, he warned:

> The great enemy of the salvation of man, in my opinion, never invented a more effectual means of extirpating [removing] Christianity from the world than by persuading mankind that it was improper to read the Bible at schools.[22]

Since 1947, our tradition of faith and our rich history of allegiance to Almighty God have been systematically stripped away, while most of the church has been slumbering. By officially declaring that America has turned its back on God, the Supreme Court and the majority of our public institutions invited evil into our midst. Thus the battle for America's soul, which began in the 1920s and has continued to this day, has changed our fortunes forever.

I am sure you have noticed that when fabric unravels it follows a pattern. First a stitch becomes loose. At that point, it is easy to repair the fabric to make it as strong as ever. But if left untended, the loose stitch affects the one next to it. Now the hole is twice as large. From there, many loose threads cause the fabric to completely unravel and fall apart.

Our tradition of faith and our rich history of ALLEGIANCE TO ALMIGHTY GOD have been systematically stripped away.

We have seen how essential moral stitches in our national fabric were pulled loose during the 1920s. We did not attend properly to those holes in our moral character. Suddenly, today it seems as if our entire society is unraveling—from the government to the family.

What would unravel next? In our next chapter, we will see how the problems left untended early in the century caused multiple problems in the second half of the century. How would these problems affect our nation? Furthermore, what does God's Word say about our moral predicament? Surely, the gathering storm on our national horizon is gaining strength!

CHAPTER 9

Torn Apart at the Seams

Years ago, while I was speaking on a large university campus, a radical young man confronted me. He stood in the assembly and railed against me because I was encouraging students to follow Christ as their Savior. As the head of the Communist Party on this prestigious campus, he had other plans for these students.

Rather than argue, I invited him to come to our home for dinner, which he did. He was a brilliant young man, articulate and winsome. As we chatted through dinner, we talked about many things. I found him to be an interesting guest. As we finished our dessert, I reached over and picked up my Bible and said, "I want to read something to you from the Bible."

He reacted with obvious irritation. "I have read the Bible from cover to cover," he exclaimed. "It's a ridiculous book. It's filled with contradictions, lies, and myths. I don't want to hear anything from the Bible."

"If you don't mind, I will read it anyway," I replied gently. I began reading to him from the Gospel of John. Chapter one begins, "Before anything else existed, there was Christ, with God. He has always been alive and is himself God. He created everything there is—nothing exists that he didn't make. Eternal life is in him, and this life gives light to all mankind... To all who received him, he gave the right to become children of God. All they needed to do was to trust him to save them. All those who believe this are reborn!" (vv. 1–4,12,13, TLB).

Remember—he had told me that he did not believe the Bible and that he had read it from cover to cover. When I concluded reading this passage from John, he said, "Let me see that. I don't remember reading that." He read it thoughtfully, then handed the Bible back to me without comment.

Then I turned to Colossians, chapter 1: "Christ is the exact likeness of the unseen God. He existed before God made anything at all, and, in fact, Christ himself is the Creator who made everything in heaven and earth, the things we can see and the things we can't; the spirit world with its kings and kingdoms, its rulers and authorities; all were made by Christ for his own use and glory. He was before all else began, and it is his power that holds everything together" (vv. 15–17, TLB).

These young people had high ideals, but their HEARTS WERE STILL EMPTY and confused.

Again he said, "I've never seen that before. May I read it?"

I handed the Bible to him. Again he was very sober. He handed it back to me. As I read Hebrews 1:1–5 and 1 John 2:1,2, the words deeply moved this young man. His entire countenance changed. We chatted briefly, and after a time he stood to leave. I asked him if he would write in our guest book. He penned his name and address, after which he wrote these words: "The night of decision." He left facing a major decision about receiving and following Christ.

When Campus Crusade for Christ first began on the UCLA and Berkeley campuses during the '50s and '60s, my staff and I encountered many hostile students like him who were caught up in the protests and riots of those days. These young people had high ideals, but their hearts were still empty and confused. Because of

God's mercy, we were able to touch the lives of many and see the miracle of the new birth change their attitudes. But many, many more across the country were deeply affected by the climate of unrest.

Asleep in the Pew

Years before the student unrest shook up our society, Alexis de Tocqueville wrote:

> If the lights that guide us ever go out, they will fade little by little, as if of their own accord...We therefore should not console ourselves by thinking that the barbarians are still a long way off. Some people may let the torch be snatched from their hands, but others stamp it out themselves.[1]

That is an accurate description of what we have allowed to happen in our country. As the 20th century progressed, we stamped out morality. Though the decades of the '20s and '30s brought negative social and cultural changes, they were nothing compared to the nation's full-scale rejection of traditional values during the '60s and '70s. The intervening decades were crucial. The late '40s and '50s were pleasant and uneventful, often called the "happy days." Yet despite the peacefulness and calm on the surface, important changes took place during that transitional period. The departure from God and biblical Christianity that occurred then was more subtle than the insurrection that was to come in the following decades.

Throughout the '50s, Christians were doing the right things, but often for the wrong reasons, or for no reason at all. Many churches were viewed as stuffy, uninspiring, and out of touch. Pastors and their flocks often lacked a sense of passion or vision for ministry, missing the cultural mandate that lies at the heart of Christianity.

Then suddenly, a tidal wave of rage and revisionism swept across the landscape during the '60s and '70s, almost demolishing the values and moral standards that had guided our nation for centuries. These eruptions caught Christians off-guard. Had the church been properly mobilized at the time, perhaps the chaos that erupted in places such as Haight-Ashbury, New Haven, and Chicago might have been averted.

The '60s became the pivotal decade in the breakdown of the

American culture. Subtle disorders that had lain dormant for years finally erupted onto the scene. When the upheaval came, the Church could not respond coherently; Christians had been lulled to sleep in the pews.

Stitch by stitch, our nation unraveled. First came rebellion against the status quo. Soon we embraced humanism, followed by moral relativism. The hunger for spiritual meaning quickly spawned New Age religions. One by one, the moral standards that formed the fiber of our nation frayed and fell apart.

Radical Ideals

Os Guinness believes that the crisis was set in motion by the sheer mass of unresolved issues that converged on America in the '60s. We had not dealt with the apathy and neglect that caused the nation to turn its back on God. "So many things happened at one time almost by spontaneous combustion," he says, "but there were certain common features."[2] The '60s were a time of idealism. Young people were seeking justice, freedom, and community, but not by conventional methods.

Christians did not disagree with many of the goals of the young radicals; believers also wanted justice, freedom, and community. In the beginning, the revolutionaries rejected everything that was hollow or hypocritical, and that was good; but they also revolted against the values of the '50s, and that meant rejecting Christianity as well. Guinness says of the rebels, "They were like the Greek figure Icarus who flew too close to the sun; his wings melted, and he crashed to the ground and died. Their ideals were right, but without a basis, they soared up and collapsed."[3]

Judge Robert Bork, a professor at Yale University during those turbulent years, witnessed the chaos firsthand:

> To understand our current plight, we must look back to the tumults of [the '60s], which brought to a crescendo developments in the '50s and before, that most of us had overlooked or misunderstood. We noticed Elvis Presley, rock music, James Dean, the radical sociologist C. Wright Mills, Jack Kerouac, and the Beatles. We did not understand, however, that far from being isolated

> curiosities, these were harbingers of a new culture that would shortly burst upon us and sweep us into a different country.[4]

Student activism started in earnest with a group called Students for a Democratic Society (SDS). They met in 1962 in Port Huron, Michigan, and produced a document they called the "Port Huron Statement." This manifesto stated that man is perfectible, and if we can keep changing the culture long enough, we can make man into what he should be. It was the dream of a manmade utopia—a heaven on earth. Judge Bork explains how those improbable and idealistic dreams made their way into modern-day liberalism:

> SDS became the center of the student revolution, the center of what they called the "New Left." The New Left disintegrated politically because their program was too amorphous for anyone to know what it was exactly, except destruction. It persists today in individual groups; that is, some of them focus on environmentalism, racial problems, or on radical feminism, and so on. Altogether, they add up to what the New Left used to be.[5]

Many social issues that plague us today—such as radical feminism, abortion on demand, and homosexuality—came out of the radicals' programs in the '60s. This is not surprising when you consider how many of these revolutionaries held the cherished traditional values of this nation in utter contempt.

Today, our major universities are staffed by many of these former radical activists who embraced ANTI-GOD VIEWS AND PHILOSOPHIES.

What happened to these students? Today, our major universities are staffed by many of these former radical activists who embraced anti-God views and philosophies. They are now tenured professors and administrators working to propel the next generation of revisionists into completing the revolution they started more than thirty years ago. Under the leadership of the radical New Left, many of the most famous, prestigious universities have become hotbeds of anti-Judeo-Christian values. Consider the words of one professor from Vermont's Middlebury College:

> After the war, a lot of us [anti-war graduate students] didn't just crawl back into our library cubicles, we stepped into academic positions. With the war over, our visibility was lost, and it seemed for a while—to the unobservant—that we had disappeared. Now we have tenure, and the work of reshaping the universities has begun in earnest.[6]

The values that were considered radical, immoral, and unprincipled during the decade of the '60s became the established norms of the '90s. Policies we once found outrageous are now the status quo. One can easily see how public virtues and social mores that Tocqueville once called "habits of the heart" were turned upside down.

The Poverty of Self-Fulfillment

In his classic book, *How Should We Then Live?*, Francis Schaeffer uncovered two factors that helped bring about the carnage following the '60s revolution:

> As the Christian-dominated consensus weakened, the majority of the people adopted two impoverished values: personal peace and affluence... Personal peace means just to be let alone, not to be troubled by the troubles of other people, whether across the world or across the city—to live one's life with minimal possibilities of being personally disturbed. Personal peace means wanting to have my personal life pattern undisturbed in my lifetime, regardless of what the result will be in the lifetimes of my children and grandchildren. Affluence means an overwhelming and ever-increasing prosperity—a life made up of things, things, and more things—a success judged by an ever-higher level of material abundance.[7]

Parents, brought up in a disciplined, structured environment, told their rebellious children, "Keep your mouth shut and don't rock the boat." Disarmed by a culture that had provided them with unprecedented peace and affluence, they could not handle the fury of the revolution instigated by their children. Robert Bork observes:

> Every generation is composed of barbarians that have to be civilized by their families, by churches, by schools, and so forth.

> [The Baby Boomer] generation was so big that they swamped the institutional capacity to civilize them.[8]

As member of the "hippie" generation, pastor Greg Laurie of Harvest Christian Fellowship in Riverside, California, witnessed the '60s from the other side. He says, "A lot of people look back at the '60s through rose-colored granny glasses. It is this idyllic era that is celebrated today. But in reality what we did in the '60s was open a Pandora's box. What our society sowed in the '60s, we are reaping in the '90s. As the Bible says, 'You sow the wind, you reap the whirlwind.'"[9]

For centuries, the moral and spiritual fabric of American society rested upon what Schaeffer called the "Christian-dominated consensus." Both Schaeffer's and Laurie's generations rebelled against the biblical precepts on which this nation was founded. Schaeffer's generation rebelled against the poverty and hopelessness of the Great Depression. Determined never to suffer such loss and disappointment again, they resolved never to allow their children to suffer either. As their search for prosperity overshadowed their religion, they neglected to pass on their Christian foundation to their children. Laurie's Baby Boomer generation rebelled against the spiritual poverty of making self-fulfillment and ease the main goal. They rejected their parents' materialism and morals, and sought other means to satisfy their spiritual hunger. Each revolt led its generation further away from God.

The Humanist Credos

Beneath the intellectual veneer of the '60s' revolution was a dramatic shift in values that helped usher in a new set of beliefs. These ideals, which exalted humankind and dishonored God, had their root in humanism.

Earlier, Darwin, Freud, and others proposed radical theories that claimed to solve the riddle of humanity. Each contributed to a belief that man could live without God. Educators, philosophers, scientists, and social theorists would later proclaim these theories as fact.

Darwin's friend and advocate, Thomas Huxley, made the statement that "skepticism is the highest of duties, blind faith the one unpardonable sin."[10] Even some Christians claimed that human discovery is superior to divine revelation, challenging the basic tenets of the Christian religion. This new "theology" had no room for faith.

Published in 1933, the *Humanist Manifesto* articulated the fundamental precepts of modern secular humanism:

> Religious humanists regard the universe as self-existing and not created. Humanism asserts that the nature of the universe depicted by modern science makes unacceptable any supernatural or cosmic guarantees of human values.[11]

Secular humanists believe that God does not exist. Man is therefore solely responsible for his own destiny; he is captain of his own fate and master of his own soul. Therefore, man need not subject himself to any law higher than himself. Humanism places mankind at the center of all things and makes him the measure of all things. The original Humanist Society included such influential members as John Dewey and B. F. Skinner. They propagated views that appeared scientific on the surface but were based on the presupposition that man is in charge of his own destiny.

Humanism places mankind at the CENTER OF ALL THINGS and makes him the MEASURE OF ALL THINGS.

The *Humanist Manifesto II*, published in 1973, restated the humanists' hostility toward Christianity:

> As in 1933, humanists still believe that traditional theism, especially faith in the prayer-hearing God, assumed to love and care for persons, to hear and understand their prayers, and to be able to do something about them, is an unproved and outmoded faith. Salvationism, based on mere affirmation, still appears as harmful, diverting people with false hopes of Heaven hereafter. Reasonable minds look to other means for survival.[12]

Prominent Americans such as Ed Doerr from Americans United for Separation of Church and State, Alan Guttmacher of Planned Parenthood, and Betty Friedan of the National Organization of Women signed the *Humanist Manifesto II*.[13] Excerpts from the *Humanist Manifesto II* show the firm stand humanists take against traditional standards, ideals, and morality:

> We believe, however, that traditional dogmatic or authoritarian religions that place revelation, God, ritual, or creed above human needs and experience do a disservice to the human species...We reject those features of traditional religious morality that deny humans a full appreciation of their own potentialities and responsibilities...Often traditional faiths encourage dependence rather than independence, obedience rather than affirmation, fear rather than courage...Promises of immortal salvation or fear of eternal damnation are both illusory and harmful...Ethics [are] autonomous and situational, needing no theological or ideological sanction. Ethics stem from human needs and interest...We believe that intolerant attitudes, often cultivated by orthodox religions and puritanical cultures, unduly repress sexual conduct. The right to birth control, abortion, and divorce should be recognized...It also includes a recognition of an individual's right to die with dignity, euthanasia, and the right to suicide.[14]

Could there be a more thoroughly anti-Christian document?

In *A Christian Manifesto*, his famed response to the *Humanist Manifesto*, Dr. Francis Schaeffer argued, "[The humanists] have reduced Man to even less than his natural finiteness by seeing him only as a complex arrangement of molecules, made complex by blind chance."[15]

The ideals of humanism produced a revolution in science that viewed man as little more than a cosmic accident. Eventually, this theory pervaded every segment of society.

Scientific Revolution

Did you know that modern science has its roots in the Christian faith? Men like Galileo, Copernicus, Johannes Kepler, and Sir Isaac Newton all believed that they were studying God's majestic creation. They worshipped a God of order who made an orderly creation. Because the personality of this knowable God was displayed through His creation, scientists could discover the secrets of this loving, intelligent Creator.

None of these early scientists would have guessed that their fields of inquiry would one day be used to "disprove" the existence of God. Yet, in this century many in the scientific community have tried to rid mankind of its belief in God and its relationship with Jesus Christ.

What kind of effect have these anti-God beliefs had? Author Paul Johnson explains that the work of scientists often impacts broader reaches of society:

> The scientific genius impinges on humanity, for good or ill, far more than any statesman or warlord. Galileo's empiricism created the ferment of natural philosophy in the seventeenth century which [foreshadowed] the scientific and industrial revolutions. Newtonian physics formed the framework of the eighteenth century Enlightenment, and so helped to bring modern nationalism and revolutionary politics to birth. Darwin's notion of survival of the fittest was a key element both in the Marxist concept of class warfare and of the racial philosophies which shaped Hitlerism ...So, too, the public response to relativity was one of the principle formative influences on the course of 20th century history. It formed a knife, inadvertently wielded by its author, to help cut society adrift from its traditional moorings in the faith and morals of Judeo-Christian culture.[16]

In the early years of American history, many who propagated anti-Christian goals were discreet and covert about their agendas. However, during the '60s, the scientific community began to attack Christianity and biblical principles more boldly than ever.

One theory that anti-Christian forces have been pursuing vigorously is evolution. If science can "prove" that evolution is true—that man has not been created by a loving God as stated in the Genesis account—then the Bible is immediately "proven" false and unreliable. This single attack on Christianity has done the greatest damage to evangelism. With the credibility of the Bible destroyed, there is no reason for the lost to trust God's Word—and to place their faith in Jesus Christ as revealed in that Word. And with God's standards removed, every man can do what seems right in his own eyes.

In 1985, Michael Denton, molecular biologist and evolutionist, wrote in *Evolution: A Theory in Crisis*:

> It was because Darwinian theory broke man's link with God and set him adrift in a cosmos without purpose or end that its impact was so fundamental. No other intellectual revolution in modern times...so profoundly affected the way men viewed themselves and their place in the universe.[17]

Today in America there is a concerted effort to promote evolution as absolute truth, despite the fact that it is based on little scientific data. In his 1859 work introducing the concept of evolution, *On the Origin of Species by Means of Natural Selection*, Charles Darwin admitted that blind chance could not produce a seeing eye:

> To suppose that the eye with all its inimitable contrivances for adjusting the focus to different distances, for admitting different amounts of light, and for the correction of spherical and chromatic aberration, could have been formed by natural selection, seems, I freely confess, absurd in the highest degree.[18]

Darwin also acknowledged in his watershed study that the geological record seriously lacked the data to support his proposition:

> Why then is not every geological formation and every stratum full of such intermediate links? Geology assuredly does not reveal any such finely graduated organic chain; and this, perhaps, is the most obvious and serious objection which can be urged against the theory. The explanation lies, as I believe, in the extreme imperfection of the geological record.[19]

Yet 140 years and a quarter of a million fossils later, humanistic scientists are still searching for a shred of proof in support of his theory. They are clinging with religious fervor to the theory of our Godless origin, because the alternative is unthinkable to them. In 1980, H. S. Lipson, physics professor at the University of Manchester in England, stated, "Evolution became in a sense a scientific religion;...many are prepared to 'bend' their observations to fit in with it."[20] Darwin himself admitted in a letter to a colleague, "But, alas, how frequent, how almost universal it is in an author to persuade himself of the truth of his own dogmas."[21]

Despite Darwin's doubts and all the scientific evidence in recent years that supports the biblical account of creation, the teaching of creationism is openly scorned. Meanwhile, Darwinian evolution is being taught as established fact in public schools and colleges.

In *School Science Review*, G. W. Harper stated, "The teacher of Darwin's theory...undoubtedly is concerned to put across the conclusion that natural selection causes evolution while he cannot be concerned to any great extent with real evidence because there isn't any." He concludes that "our current methods of teaching Darwinism are suspiciously similar to indoctrination."[22] That is exactly what humanists had in mind. W. R. Bird wrote in *The Origin of Species Revisited*, "Even John Scopes...said that 'if you limit a teacher to only one side of anything, the whole country will eventually have only one thought.'"[23]

The reason the humanists insist on teaching evolution is clear. According to Dr. Michael Walker, senior lecturer on anthropology at Sydney University: "Many scientists and technologists pay lip-service to Darwinian theory only because it supposedly excludes a Creator."[24] Author T. Rosazak agrees: "The main purpose of Darwinism was to drive every last trace of an incredible God from biology. But the theory replaces God with an even more incredible deity—omnipotent chance."[25] The doctrine of random chance that underlies Darwin's theory lies at the core of the humanistic belief system. Many humanists perpetuate a belief that they suspect is a lie rather than be forced to acknowledge the reality of God.

The Results of Humanism

Humanism and Christianity are polar extremes, two entirely separate and incompatible ways of viewing the world. They directly conflict each other and always work toward opposite ends. Humanistic teachings, rooted in materialism and a finite view of human life, naturally oppose supernatural Christianity. Since humanists view themselves as competitors to the church, they wage war against all who follow Jesus Christ.

Christians believe in God as the Creator and sustainer of all life;

humanism places man at the center of all things. God-centered Christianity gave birth to the great institutions of American society; humanism is at the root of the collapse of modern culture.

Francis Schaeffer articulated the root problem of the humanist philosophy: "The humanist is really a materialist. The humanist holds that energy and material have existed forever in some form and that its present configuration is purely by chance."[26] If the universe came into being merely by chance, we would have no basis for laws. Values would be constantly evolving in response to the latest vogue or the whims of the elite minority. The belief that all material substances are shaped purely by chance, asserts Schaeffer, leads to a belief in "a silent universe that has nothing to say about the meaning of life, the values of life, or a basis for law."[27]

Such logic is contrary to the Christian perspective, which recognizes an infinite, personal, loving Creator who has a definite and discernible personality. To dismiss Christian values and to believe in the humanist world view, says Schaeffer, "brings forth the very things which are tearing our society to pieces today."[28]

> **"The main purpose of Darwinism was to DRIVE EVERY LAST TRACE of an incredible God from biology."**

A Case of Cultural AIDS

A fervent devotion to humanism has led to the deterioration of the family, the home, the church, the community, political parties, and every other social institution. Kay Coles James, former member of the Reagan and Bush administrations, describes humanism's affect on America as a case of "cultural AIDS":

> AIDS is a virus that is not usually the cause of one being terminally ill. It breaks down the immune system, and, as a result of that, leaves the body vulnerable to all sorts of aggressive viruses. Our immune system as a culture has broken down. The things that made us strong were strong families, firm morals, and institutions like churches. When those have become weak, and in some

> cases destroyed, it leaves us open to things that have existed in society since the beginning of time. Violence, drug abuse, teen pregnancy, pornography—when you look at all the concerns of society, most of us will agree that they have been present in society from the beginning, but we've been immune to them.[29]

How could this "cultural AIDS" occur? The answer may be found in a deeper look at our body's immune system. We live in a sea of microbes, and our bodies provide an ideal growing place for many harmful substances that constantly try to invade us. In a healthy body, the complex immune system resists foreign substances such as viruses, bacteria, and toxins. Whenever one of these substances invades the body, the immune system goes to work fighting off the invader.

Poor nutrition, stress, smoking, drugs, lack of exercise, and insufficient rest weaken our immune system. This increases the body's susceptibility to all types of diseases, from the common cold to serious conditions like cancer or chronic bronchitis. Once an infection takes hold in a body with a suppressed immune system, disease multiplies dramatically until it takes over the body. If not stopped, the disease eventually causes death.

Like harmful invaders, radical elements infiltrated our country. As godless philosophies such as humanism spread throughout our society, our nation's weakened immune system did not withstand the invasion. As one social disease took hold, it further weakened society so that a second social disease could invade. Soon the social body was so weak that almost any kind of social ill could gain a foothold. The once-healthy American society began to disintegrate.

Today, we can see many results of the weakened state of our country. Crime, suicide, sexual permissiveness, broken homes, drug addiction, and so many more social ills are all symptoms of underlying philosophical diseases like humanism.

In our next chapter, we will consider a second philosophical disease which took hold on the heels of humanism. Called moral relativism, it accelerated the shift away from biblical morality. And it sprang from a surprising source.

CHAPTER 10

A Relative Disaster

Once a nation begins to unravel, no area is left untouched. Destruction finds its way into unusual places.

In the early years of the 20th century, Albert Einstein published his famous studies on the properties of light and matter called the "theory of relativity." A popularized version of Einstein's theory, applying the ideas beyond scientific arenas, was circulated publicly. Humanists jumped to adopt a broad application of relativity—that everything is relative in all spheres—including the moral, ethical, and spiritual spheres. Suddenly the idea of flexible, relative time and space gave rise to the notion that ethics and morality were likewise flexible and relative. Through this idea of "moral relativism," humanists proposed that there is no absolute or universal truth.

Having his work applied to morality shocked Einstein because his theory dealt strictly with mathematics and physics, not ethics. He repeatedly declared in public addresses, "The real problem is in the hearts and minds of men. It is not a problem of physics but of ethics. It is easier to denature plutonium than to denature the evil spirit of man."[1]

Historian Paul Johnson reports that Einstein "lived to see moral relativism, to him a disease, become a social pandemic, just as he lived to see his fatal equation bring into existence nuclear warfare. There were times, he said at the end of his life, when he wished he had been a simple watchmaker."[2]

By the 1960s, the theory of moral relativism bore fruit in public education: situational ethics. Under its influence, public education discarded the teaching of absolute truth and biblical virtues, teaching instead that morality changes with each situation. Today moral relativism is taught without question in America's public schools. When asked if they believe in absolute truth, most high school students answer with a resounding *no!*

This moral relativism is a result of humanistic beliefs. Although humanism places mankind at the center of all things, it inevitably devalues life by removing the belief in man's eternal state. Man lives, dies, and that is the end. Without a belief in the sanctity of life that comes through faith in God, the right to life for all human beings is put at risk, leading to consequences society can scarcely survive. From cloning and genetic manipulation to abortion and euthanasia, human life is merely a plaything to be created and destroyed at will. With moral relativism, every choice becomes relative to the specific situation.

The Winds of Revolution

In this new era, the American people either resisted moral relativity or redefined their values to allow them to act as they pleased. As philosopher Bertrand Russell told a British television audience, when God and His purpose for the universe are removed, man is "freed up to pursue his own erotic desires."[3] Russell and his colleagues preferred relativism to the truths of Scripture. Without a God to give us standards of behavior, man is free to do what is right in his own eyes.

Os Guinness reminds us that "relativism is not a fact, it is a philosophical conclusion—it is the idea that there is no absolute, independent, objective truth. In the Christian view, truth is true even if we do not like it; falsehood is false, even if everyone believes it. But, now there is no truth, truth is dead... Obviously, that [viewpoint] is very deadly, not just to the Christian faith but to much of the tradition out of which America comes."[4]

Alan Keyes, radio host, former UN ambassador, and 1996 presidential candidate, explains that in the absence of immutable moral truths, our culture cannot sustain stability:

> There have been people trying to set up this experiment where they would not have God and would somehow be free to do whatever they wanted to do. That sounds attractive. The truth of the matter is that it leads to an understanding of freedom that becomes self-destructive. It is not based on respect for any type of law, not even the law from which we get our freedom in the first place.[5]

Do Your Own Thing

Moral relativism, which grew from the sterile roots of secular humanism, led to another new value—moral permissiveness. "Do your own thing!" became the theme of the '60s as Americans pursued lifestyles that would have horrified our Founding Fathers.

"In the Christian view, TRUTH IS TRUE even if we do not like it; FALSEHOOD IS FALSE, even if everyone believes it."

In 1961 the birth control pill arrived on the scene. Millions of people were led to believe that sexual experimentation, infidelity, and all forms of sensual gratification were safe. Author and researcher Eric Johnson believes that the introduction of the birth control pill was one of the watershed events of American history. "Popular culture increasingly saw sex as just one of life's pleasures, one that now could be easily separated not only from procreation, but also from marriage, and emotional and spiritual commitment, thanks to the Pill."[6] Sexual immorality exploded.

Several unconnected events served to fuel the fires of moral defiance. The first of these was the tragic slaying of John F. Kennedy, witnessed worldwide on television. Kennedy was a man admired by many; even those who disagreed with his politics acknowledged his charisma. As the nation was dealing with its grief, other national heroes vanished: Bobby Kennedy and Martin Luther King, Jr.

The entire nation was in turmoil throughout these years. Assassinations. Racial confrontations. The Black Panther movement. The Vietnam War protests as our nation sent its young men to fight and die in a seemingly senseless war. Flag burning. Riots at the 1968 Democratic Convention in Chicago. The Cold War and the threat of a nuclear confrontation with the Soviet Union. The Watergate scandal of the early '70s and the collapse of the Nixon presidency. In the span of just ten short years, the United States appeared to be in danger of collapse.

For example, in his study *A Generation of Seekers*, Wade Clark Roof chronicles the deep impact the Vietnam War had on the Baby Boom generation of the '60s:

> Americans lost faith in their country's moral superiority and in a technology that tried to make the nation's military might increasingly invisible and remote. Seeing the napalm-scarred faces of children on television and hearing day after day about "body counts" and "loss ratios" eroded what confidence was left in the nation's war machine.[7]

Roof reports that those most affected by the war were older Boomers, who had grown up with confidence in their government only to be disappointed by the atrocities and senselessness of the war. According to Roof, the impact of those years continues to shape Boomers' perceptions to this day: "Boomers (born from 1945 through 1975) still feel some distance from almost every institution, whether the military, banks, public schools, Congress, or organized religion. Alienation and estrangement born out of the period continue to express themselves as generalized distrust of government, of major institutions, and of leaders."[8]

In a generation that came of age during their own rebellion, then suffered through a series of national tragedies, many lost all hope of finding God and abandoned the faith of their families. Add to that the passivity of their parents, along with the ideas spread through television, radio, film, and popular culture, and the search for spirituality apart from the Christian church proliferated. Instead of finding freedom and salvation in Jesus, most of this generation fell for paganism.

That New Age Religion

Since the '60s, Americans have exhibited a deep spiritual hunger. But by rejecting the Scriptures, they left themselves open to spiritual counterfeits. Chuck Colson explains:

> People will always worship something, because people are naturally religious. The problem is that when we don't have good teaching, when Christianity is mocked and ridiculed, when people aren't forced to recognize that there is truth that they are to seek in life, then they seek alternatives. The enemy of true religion is not nothing—it is false religion. People begin to worship themselves or what is common today—worship of the earth, worship of nature, naturalism, putting nature on the same level as God. What you end up with is a new age, occultic earth worship.[9]

C. S. Lewis said that when people cease to believe in God, it is not that they believe in nothing. It is that they believe in anything. This approach leads to the blind acceptance of any new "religion." Such worship might consist of sitting alone in a closed room, listening to the sounds of trees and rushing waters, or meditating while chanting random syllables. Buddhism has become a major influence, along with the art of "visualization." The first thing many Americans do each day is check their horoscope in the local newspaper. Some organize their day around what "the stars" predict. Psychic television networks and telephone hotlines proliferate.

Traveling "psychic fairs" are springing up all across the country, at which New Age practitioners set up in shopping malls or parks to hawk their wares for a couple of days in each city. For a few dollars you could seek your fortune from numerologists, psychics, channelers, and astrologers; others claim to tell your future by reading your horoscope, your palms, tarot cards, or tea leaves. You could even have your "aura" photographed.

While such occult practices may seem ridiculous, they actually involve dangerous attitudes and behaviors. First, they blatantly ignore the teachings of the Bible forbidding such practices. Second, these philosophies deny the existence of Jesus Christ as the Son of God, the Savior, and the Judge of all mankind. They therefore reject the inevitability of judgment. Third, many New Age practices have been adapted from the occult and from pantheistic religions, which teach that everything in nature is divine.

The early Israelites practiced pantheism. After they conquered the Promised Land, they began to intermarry with the local inhabitants—a practice forbidden by God because it would lead to the acceptance of alien gods. That is precisely what happened.

Hosea records: "There is no faithfulness, no love, no acknowledgment of God in the land. There is only cursing, lying and murder, stealing and adultery; they break all bounds...A spirit of prostitution leads them astray; they are unfaithful to their God" (Hosea 4:1,2,12).

In their unfaithfulness to God, the Israelites became SPIRITUAL PROSTITUTES... Are we in the same position today?

In their unfaithfulness to God, the Israelites became spiritual prostitutes. Their spiritual infidelity drove a wedge between themselves and God and compromised their prospects for peace, security, and happiness.

Are we in the same position today? How does the God who created this nation view us? He must look upon the mass of Americans who worship many gods as harlots who have sold themselves cheaply to the lowest bidder. Surely we must see the risks we embraced as a direct result of the rise of relativism and humanism. No man or woman can live securely without faith in God. And no nation formed by His hand can hope to survive if it turns its back on its Maker. Oh, that America will come back to Him while there is still time!

Rays of Hope

I, too, was affected by these forces. Since my high school years, I had been a "happy pagan"—a humanist and a self-sufficient, independent materialist. Gold was my god. As a businessman and a member of the extension faculty of Oklahoma State University, I worked day and night to make my fortune to fulfill the American dream. Then through my mother's prayers and the influences of the First Presbyterian Church of Hollywood, California, I became a follower of Jesus.

In the spring of 1951, I was touched by the Lord in an unusual way. The Lord revealed to me that He wanted me to help fulfill the Great Commission, beginning on the college campuses where the leaders of tomorrow are trained. I believed then and even more so now that if we can capture the student generation, we can change our country within a few years. As Abraham Lincoln observed, "The philosophy of the school room in one generation will be the philosophy of government in the next."[10]

At the time that Vonette and I received the mandate to begin Campus Crusade for Christ, we had no idea what God had in mind. But He changed the way we thought and the values we held, and gave us a firm foundation in His holy principles. Over the past fifty years, His powerful Spirit has enabled us to present the gospel to almost three billion people around the world, using tools such as the *Four Spiritual Laws* and the *JESUS* film. I am so grateful for what He has done!

Although at times it may seem as if God has completely abandoned us in the latter half of our century, exciting things are happening in our country and around the world. God is still shaping and guiding His people. I believe that He is getting us ready for a great spiritual revolution, which will result in the greatest spiritual harvest of all time. For example, the Navigators, which was founded just before World War II by my good friend the late Dawson Trotman, is now reaching people around the world. Billy Graham, one of the greatest evangelists of all time and a beloved friend and encouragement for over fifty years, has reached millions with the gospel. Thousands of other godly organizations are making a powerful impact for our Lord. And most importantly, countless faithful believers are witnessing to their neighbors or teaching a Sunday school class, serving God where they live.

It is true that our country is unraveling, yet we can all influence our culture—one person at a time. God is just waiting to send His Spirit in all His fullness to knit together our torn and bleeding people. Let me give you an example from my own experience.

In the early 1970s, Vonette and I started the Christian Embassy in Washington, D.C. We spent about one week each month helping to reach and disciple our nation's leaders for Christ.

During this time, I visited the office of a senator whom I had never met. After we had talked for a few minutes, a natural opportunity arose for me to ask if he was a Christian. I was able to share the good news of the gospel with him through the *Four Spiritual Laws*. Before I left his office, the senator said he would like to receive Christ.

Another time I was invited to a congressman's home to speak to other congressmen and their spouses. After the meeting, several individuals requested personal appointments. The following day as I met with each one, I asked, "Did what I said last night make sense to you?"

The first congressman I met with replied, "It surely did!"

"Would you like to receive Christ?" I asked. He said he would and we knelt beside his couch to pray.

Down the hall, I shared my faith with another congressman. He too received Christ. Both of these men and many others like them continue to walk with God, seeking His wisdom to help them lead our nation wisely. Scores of godly congressmen, senators, and other leaders meet regularly to study the Bible and pray together. Today, our organization has a large staff who minister full-time to reach leaders not only in the nation's capital, but in various capitals of the world.

I mention these stories to encourage you. I am confident that believers can win the battle, that we can repair the fabric of our society through the leadership of God's Holy Spirit. Much of the success in this spiritual battle has to do with the power of prayer.

You may never have a chance to witness to a senator or congressman, but you can pray. Prayer changes things. Later, we will learn about ways we can remember government leaders in prayer.

In addition, we can all reach out to coworkers, neighbors, relatives, friends, and even strangers.

But despite these exciting examples of God's work in our midst, our country is still marching down the broad road to destruction. Think of it as a ghoulish parade winding down the center of Main Street America, a specter of "isms" that captures our applause. Humanism, represented by a towering image of humankind with godlike features, leads the parade. The crowd roars its approval at the deified man. Then comes relativism, a float containing figures dancing to every kind of aberrant behavior. The roar intensifies as people clap and shout for the thrills they want to experience for themselves. Some even hold up their children so they can get a better glimpse of the whirling figures.

> **A ghoulish parade is winding down the center of Main Street America, a SPECTER OF "ISMS" that captures our applause.**

What is next in the gaudy lineup? Just down the street comes a huge golden statue, arms raised, tall, proud, but without a heart. What does it represent? In the next chapter, we will learn more about this massive golden idol.

CHAPTER 11

The Golden Touch

When a goal is lost, something takes its place. For example, a child who loses a toy will turn his attention to another toy. An employee who loses his job will look for a new one. If a person loses at a game, he will either play again or find another pursuit to entertain himself.

Do you remember the story of Midas? He was a good king who lost his goal of being a good ruler. Instead, he wished for incredible wealth. He was granted his wish and received the "golden touch"—everything he touched turned to gold. He ran around his kingdom touching here, touching there—becoming more wealthy than he ever dreamed. Unfortunately, the more he touched, the more he wanted. Tragically, he touched his daughter, and she turned into a golden statue. She was beautiful to look at, but she had lost all of her life, her warmth, her vitality. Midas had his little daughter forever, but she was no longer the vibrant person he knew and loved.

Somewhere during the 20th century America lost its goal to be a godly nation and spread the gospel to people who have never heard the name of Jesus. Instead, Americans embraced a trio of "isms." We saw how humanism dethroned God and exalted man,

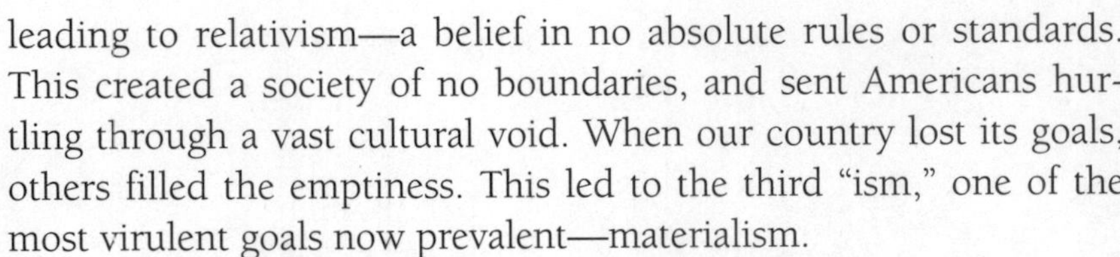

leading to relativism—a belief in no absolute rules or standards. This created a society of no boundaries, and sent Americans hurtling through a vast cultural void. When our country lost its goals, others filled the emptiness. This led to the third "ism," one of the most virulent goals now prevalent—materialism.

God has given our country "the golden touch." He blessed us with unimaginable wealth out of His love and as a reward for obeying His Word. But what have we done with it? We have desired more and more. We run around like Midas, trying to acquire everything we can touch. In our greed, we destroy the very things we love—including our children.

Never Satisfied

Marty Pay and Hal Donaldson agree that the lust for money has affected America's relationship with God:

> Materialism. Greed. Consumption. These words have become synonymous with the American version of capitalism. Economic concerns and the sweeping lust for money have unquestionably had their effect on this nation's commitment to the Almighty. "No man can serve two masters."[1]

In an ironic twist, as the pursuit of wealth became our primary passion, it made us forget the God who gave it to us. As the great Pilgrim leader, Cotton Mather, described it, "Religion begat prosperity and the daughter devoured the mother."[2]

Throughout the 20th century, America's insatiable desire for worldly riches has infiltrated every aspect of our culture. From the church house to the White House, from rural communities and farms to inner cities and slums, from college campuses to halls of science and medicine, the love of money consumes nearly all Americans. In *When Choice Becomes God,* Professor F. LaGard Smith writes:

> Gone are the days when children bought savings stamps at school and took their nickels, dimes, and quarters to the bank in plastic Hopalong Cassidy piggybanks. Now, the quarters feed hungry computer games in the video arcade. Just as the good guys in Hollywood westerns have been replaced by the Teenage Mutant

Ninja Turtles, so too savings stamps and piggybanks belong to a bygone era.[3]

Ours is no longer a nation of savers, but spenders. Smith points out that this is true even when we do not have the money, claiming that is where we have taken the quantum leap: "The pro-choice generation is also the credit card generation."[4] Certainly two of the most popular words in America today are "charge it."

The pursuit of more—more wealth, more material goods, more choices in everything—is nothing more than greed. No matter how much we possess, we feel it is not enough. We cannot seem to obtain "more" fast enough. Messages of rampant consumerism drive our purchases and debts: "Why wait when you can have it all today?" "You deserve it." "Buy now, pay later!"

Catch phrases urge consumers to exercise "rightful choices" beyond their reach. "Why wait for that second car when you can buy it today on credit?" "You can have those $100 athletic shoes. Just charge them." This greed spreads beyond the material realm. "Why wait for sex in marriage when you can enjoy it all tonight?" And of course the ultimate compromise, "Why not abort the baby since a child will dampen your lifestyle?"

> **America's insatiable DESIRE FOR WORLDLY RICHES has infiltrated every aspect of our culture.**

We have a terminal addiction to spending money. America is in debt and the federal government is the biggest debtor of all. But rather than deal with our addiction honestly, we prefer to define the problem away. Therefore, the question is no longer, "Can I afford it?" or "What will I accrue in interest over the life of the debt?" but rather, "What will my monthly payment be?" The writer of Ecclesiastes understood the root of the problem:

> Whoever loves money never has money enough; whoever loves wealth is never satisfied with his income. This too is meaningless. As goods increase, so do those who consume them. And

what benefit are they to the owner except to feast his eyes on them? (Ecclesiastes 5:10,11).

Jesus warned about greed: "Watch out! Be on your guard against all kinds of greed; a man's life does not consist in the abundance of his possessions" (Luke 12:15). In fact, in the New Testament, greed is identified as idolatry! That makes so much sense. What if you could buy that one special car that you have wanted for years? Would you treat it like a treasured idol? What do you have in your home that you cannot bear to give up? How much time do you spend caring for your possessions? How much time and money are left for God? No wonder Jesus warned us to be on our guard, because when we become greedy, we are worshipping another god!

How much time do you spend caring for YOUR POSSESSIONS? How much time and money are LEFT FOR GOD?

It comes down to choice. F. LaGard Smith writes,

> Choice is the god of instant gratification, and the credit card and easy credit have become its guardian angels, promising on-demand money at the 24-hour automatic teller machine and on-demand purchases in the shopping malls where we regularly go to worship the god of choice. "On-demand" has been the creed of a pro-choice generation ever since.[5]

Our materialistic values are reflected in how we reward others. Top athletes sign contracts for millions of dollars while school teachers earn barely enough to cover daily essentials. Corporate executives cash in on multi-million-dollar stock options and demand "golden parachutes" to protect them for life while the average married couple shells out a large portion of their income for taxes and pays dearly for basic household needs. Movie stars pocket millions of dollars per film then parade as compassionate protectors of the poor and needy.

The greatest danger in astronomical incomes is not that the few wealthiest Americans control much of our country, but that their salaries inspire unhealthy dreams in the hearts of Americans. Greed is as addictive as gambling. Everyone wants their fair share, but they often do not want to work for it. Some people commit crimes such as stealing, armed robbery, even embezzlement from their employer to enjoy "the good life." They justify themselves by saying, "They owe it to me." Such rationalizations are not uncommon anymore. When greed takes root in the popular culture, it leads to increasing envy and irresponsible behavior until the combination of greed and the love of money rips society apart.

Get Rich Schemes

Millions of Americans who are captivated by super-wealth spend vast sums of money on legalized gambling. The tentacles of this sophisticated form of "robbery" reach into every area of life. Forbidden by law for more than 300 years, that vice is now openly sanctioned by state and local governments to help educate our children or provide programs for the needy. Every day, men and women buy lottery tickets at local convenience stores, gas stations, and now on the Internet hoping that theirs will be the one ticket in a million to win the big one. Some cash-strapped workers shell out their entire paycheck. Casinos and gambling riverboats are opening all over the country. The result? Americans are losing the value of honest labor and hard work. Work, they say, is for losers. After all, gambling, selling drugs, or stealing is the fast way to make big bucks. Sooner or later, we will strike it rich!

Instead of investing time, effort, and education to build a business or career, some Americans buy into "get rich quick" schemes. A promotional video for one new multilevel marketing company actually states, "Money can buy happiness." The video includes "testimonies" of people who made fortunes with minimal effort. Each success story features photographs of those who made it big, standing next to exotic cars, extravagant homes, or luxurious RVs. They had reached their goals: more money, more things, more leisure, and less responsibility—the good life!

The Forgetfulness of Self-Reliance

In *Whatever Happened to the American Dream*, Larry Burkett tells a hypothetical story about a man who travels through time from the 1950s to present-day America:

> [The man from the '50s] would be awed by the array of material advancements. The cars are faster, smoother, and more reliable. Virtually all middle-income American homes have air-conditioning, color televisions, microwave ovens, and a plethora of other marvels of ingenuity and engineering; and the homes are nearly twice the size of those in the fifties.[6]

Everything from hospital technology to computers, satellites, cellular telephones, faxes, and mass transportation amazed the time traveler. But his excitement gave way to distress as he began surfing through the endless array of programming on cable television. Burkett continues:

> He would have to wonder how anyone ever decides what to watch. Then, if he happened upon one of the cable movie channels, likely he would stop and blink in disbelief as the television displayed, in living color, sex scenes that would have made a sailor blush in the fifties. He would soon realize that we are a sex-dominated society.[7]

The visitor flips to a news program discussing the crime problems in New York, Miami, and other large cities. The violence displayed on the screen is so shocking, it takes several minutes before the time traveler figures out that this is not another movie scene.

> He stares at the scenes from the Los Angeles riots as waves of people from mobs bent on looting and destroying everything in their paths, without regard for the rights of anyone around them ...Now our visitor ponders: It has only been forty years or so since I left my own time. How could things have changed so drastically and so quickly?...The gadgets and gizmos of the nineties are marvelous, but society has lost something fundamental.[8]

The traveler was horrified at the homosexuality openly celebrated and promoted in public school classrooms. He was bewildered by our $4 trillion national debt. He felt devastated by legalized abortions and frightened by America's flirtation with euthanasia. All these derive from the same mindset being promoted by the materialism and greed of this culture: "I want what I want, and I want it now!"

God has given America tremendous natural resources and an abundance of opportunity. But Scripture says that to whom much has been given much, much will be required. Instead of using our wealth to glorify God and His Son Jesus Christ, we have squandered those same resources. God warns us about what happens to nations consumed by materialism—they forget the Lord (Deuteronomy 8:10–14).

This forgetfulness happens so easily. When a person becomes wealthy, he begins to think he has accumulated everything through his own strength. Inevitably, he forgets that at every moment, he is held back from utter ruin, and even death, by the hand of God. Self-reliance takes over as he begins taking credit for what he did not accomplish. Ultimately, he forgets all about the God he thinks he no longer needs.

Repeating the Pattern

The writer of Deuteronomy explains, "You may say to yourself, 'My power and the strength of my hands have produced this wealth for me.' But remember the Lord your God, for it is he who gives you the ability to produce wealth, and so confirms his covenant, which he swore to your forefathers" (Deuteronomy 8:17,18).

> Sadly, the first ones affected by OUR NATIONAL SIN are the most vulnerable—OUR FAMILIES.

Does this not describe the same pattern we have experienced in our history? Our forefathers covenanted with God; and He blessed us and gave us the ability to produce wealth. Now we have claimed the credit for ourselves. We say, "Who is God? We cannot see Him. Our success has been made by our own hands."

Reading on, Deuteronomy offers this warning about impending judgment:

> If you ever forget the Lord your God and follow other gods and worship and bow down to them, I testify against you today that you will surely be destroyed. Like the nations the Lord destroyed before you, so you will be destroyed for not obeying the Lord your God (vv. 19,20).

Is this not true? Are the storms amassed on our horizon more ominous than ever before? The evidence that destruction is already coming upon America is becoming painfully obvious.

The storms are beginning to crash around us. What are we destroying? Sadly, the first ones affected by our national sin are the most vulnerable—our families.

CHAPTER 12

Broken Hearts, Broken Homes

People love to watch weddings. Whenever a network television program includes a marriage ceremony, ratings go up. A young couple saying their vows with radiant faces makes us think of a happily-ever-after life. People also love babies. Today, one of the most popular television advertisements shows a young couple holding their newborn. The picture is so warm, it makes us think of bright, rosy futures for this baby and his family.

Throughout history, the family has been the most essential building block of society, the foremost institution of culture. More than government, schools, or any other center of influence, the family is the principal source of stability. Just think what would happen without families. How tragic if parents dropped their babies off at a facility just after they were born and did not take any part in raising their sons and daughters. What a cold, impersonal world that would be! Now compare the joy of young couples as they take home their new infant for the first time.

Families are essential to social life. The home is the best place to teach values. It is the place where we first learn to interact and build positive relationships. The family setting should also be where children learn to respect others and to be accountable to God.

Families give us our first sense of community. A child learns how to say "I love you" and hug his parents and to experience how important grandma and grandpa are. Families introduce us to the rules of daily life and personal interaction outside the home walls. By being held accountable to family do's and don'ts, children learn that bad actions have bad consequences. Families give a first critical glimpse of the way the kingdom of God works. How precious when a little child first hears the story of God's love from the lips of his mother or father. Fragmented families, however, result in little lives riddled with emotional and relationship problems.

Paul believed that healthy families are essential to the household of faith. "Give the people these instructions, too," he writes, "so that no one may be open to blame. If anyone does not provide for his relatives, and especially for his immediate family, he has denied the faith and is worse than an unbeliever" (1 Timothy 5:7,8).

Family Values

Pastor T. D. Jakes recently observed that the family has become an "endangered species."[1] Christians should be among the first to stand up for traditional family values, for rebuilding parent-child relationships, and for religious education in the home. This is the real source of strength, virtue, and integrity for future generations.

Yet today millions of Americans have accepted the lie that family values are outdated. This lie is defended by those who want us to accept the immoral values of modern humanism. The idea that "it takes a village" to raise a child, for example, is a misleading assault on traditional child-rearing. A village of faith and virtue may provide a protective buffer for America's kids, but there is no substitute for a united, caring, supportive, affirming, God-fearing family for raising healthy, well-adjusted children. No village on earth can do the job of a mom and dad together. You just cannot improve on God's formula for the family: one man, one woman, for one lifetime. Any other formula leads to broken hearts and broken homes.

The corrosion of family values first became visible in the mid-1940s when traditional family structures began breaking down as a result of World War II. When fathers went to war, mothers were forced into the workplace—in the plants, factories, and marketplaces—to carry on the critical work. For the first time in our history, large numbers of children were alone, in the care of strangers, or at best with elderly grandparents. This trend continues today.

An even greater threat to the family is the exploding divorce rate. In the 1970s, California passed the nation's first no-fault divorce laws. Since then, divorce has skyrocketed more than 250 percent. In fact, since 1960, the divorce rate has shot up over 400 percent; out-of-wedlock childbirths are up 500 percent; and the number of single-parent homes is up more than 300 percent. Today, half of all first marriages end in divorce, and the figure for second marriages is much higher.[2]

The Gallup Organization reports that 4 in 10 American children go to bed without a father in the home; 26 percent of teens have been physically abused in the home; one-fourth of all Americans say that drinking is a problem in their home; and 6 out of 10 marriages this year will end in divorce.[3] When we fail to provide stable home lives, we propagate despair throughout society. For example, multiple studies have shown that children raised in dysfunctional families continue the patterns as adults in their own homes.

Unsupervised Children

Due to pressures such as re-socialization, the feminist agenda, and a rising standard of living, tens of thousands of American mothers who would prefer to stay at home and nurture the next generation have been pushed into the workforce. Against their wishes and maternal instincts, these women leave the majority of the training and modeling for their children to others. Radical feminists tell women they have been cheated out of equality in the workplace by a history of male exploitation. As part of this massive plan of indoctrination, many stay-at-home mothers feel like second-class citizens and believe they are "unfulfilled."

More and more children are left alone. Because of high taxes and increased cost of living, most mothers and fathers feel pressured to have two incomes. In addition, most single moms have no choice but to leave their kids and seek employment outside the home. Consequently, more than 57 percent of American children do not have full-time parental supervision. Is it any coincidence that 45 percent of all violent juvenile crimes occur between 3:00 p.m. and dinnertime, the period when children are most likely to be unsupervised because both parents work?[4] On the other hand, are there any more reassuring words to a young child coming home from school than to hear a positive response to "Mom, I'm home."

Tens of thousands of unsupervised children across America spend their after-school hours soaking up destructive values. More than 63 percent of young people say that movies, television, and music lyrics encourage teenage sex "a great deal" or "quite a lot."[5] If this is the influence that occupies our kids, why are we shocked to discover that the United States has the highest teen pregnancy rate in the industrialized world?

Even Christian families are tempted to forsake what is really important. Under perceived pressures of not enough time and money, many parents fail to make their children's spiritual well-being a priority. Some Christian parents abdicate their roles as moral guardians by allowing their kids to feed on a steady diet of rock and alternative music, MTV, daytime television, and weird shock-jocks. Then these parents wonder why they have lost control of their kids—and why the kids lose interest in Sunday school, Bible study, and family devotions.

Redefining the Family

Former presidential candidate Alan Keyes believes that the greatest threat to America is the collapse of the traditional, two-parent, marriage-based family. "Every study I look at," he says, "when they talk about what correlates with crime, with poverty, with gang involvement, with poor performance in school, it is always the same. When kids come from broken families, those kids have the deck stacked against them."[6]

Keyes argues that while we are busily throwing money at our problems, we fail to confront the root cause: the collapse of the family. "We can spend all the money we want, but if we don't work to put that institution back together—including the moral values of commitment, sacrifice, and respect for obligation that are really the foundation for family life—then we're never going to get anywhere."[7]

This battle is waged on several fronts: by homosexuals who seek legitimacy through legal marriage; by heterosexuals who see no need for marriage to maintain a family; by social theorists who advocate "open marriage" or other kinds of "committed relationships"; and by married men and women who see no reason to abide by their marriage vows.

Those who want to redesign God's model for healthy families claim that traditional values are repressive and dangerous, while their immoral values are their "right." Is this not just what the Bible describes as calling evil good and making a lie the truth?

The family is God's original design, and no amount of re-socialization will allow us to reengineer the family. No matter how hard anyone tries to mimic the traditional family structure, only biblically based families will thrive in the real world.

> **The GREATEST THREAT to America is the COLLAPSE of the traditional, two-parent, marriage-based FAMILY.**

Can homosexuals living together become a family? From Hawaii to the East Coast, state legislatures are considering legalizing and, thus, legitimizing homosexual marriages. Many of America's largest companies, including Disney, Levi-Strauss, AT&T, American Express, and EDS, offer health care and family benefits to the live-in lovers of homosexual employees. The implications for medical insurers, not to mention the obvious moral consequences, may prove disastrous.

Keith Fournier of the Catholic Alliance recounts a recent article by a radical homosexual activist who said that the real danger was from those who would discriminate by requiring "opposite sex restrictions on marital choice."[8] How is that for reframing the issue?

Keith Fournier debated this issue with a homosexual activist.

"[The activist] took exception to my saying that homosexual sex was not creative. What he actually said was, 'In this technological age, of course it is, we will just use test tubes.' I thought to myself, *How far have we come?* I asked him, 'Is this the brave new world that you are proposing? Where the womb is replaced by a test tube?'" The activist obviously saw no problem with that model. But Fournier quickly adds, "It won't work. It simply won't work."[9]

As Christians, we must speak out against sexual license and destructive social policies. However, we should not lash out at homosexuals. Our duty as followers of Jesus Christ is to proclaim His love to those caught in the grip of sin. Like Christ, we are to love the sinner, but hate the sin, to show compassion as Christ was compassionate. When we come face-to-face with sin, we need to remember Jesus' words, "It is not the healthy who need a doctor, but the sick. I have not come to call the righteous, but sinners to repentance" (Luke 5:31,32).

Every sinner is someone who needs Jesus; someone God loved enough to send His Son to sacrifice His life. Like any other sin, homosexuality needs to be recognized as sin, confessed, and rejected. Only God has the power to forgive and make it possible to conquer temptation. As believers who have access to the love and grace of God, we can support and encourage those who turn from the bondage of sin to live as new creations in Christ.

This does not mean, however, that we condone or encourage homosexuality. We risk incurring God's judgment by legitimizing homosexuality, permitting gay marriage, and misusing science for procreation. If we legalize homosexual marriage in America, we will once again go "on the record" as disregarding God's laws and offending the laws of nature. We would do well to count the cost of such disobedience before we reap divine displeasure.

Single Parent Households

Another redefinition of the family to sweep the land in recent decades is the acceptance of single-parent families as healthy and desirable. The unprecedented increase in the number of single-parent households ranks as one of the greatest moral failures of our time. I do not mean this as an indictment of those who have been deserted by spouses and left to raise their children alone. Single parents need our understanding and support. But there are some who, as a result of their own sins of promiscuity and infidelity and because of the availability of easy divorce and government subsidy, have brought disgrace and dysfunction upon themselves and their family.

Paul Johnson attributes the rise in single-parent homes to misleading information about contraception and other reproductive choices. The spread of contraceptives and the growing availability of abortion-on-demand have made fortunes for pharmaceutical firms and abortion clinics, but have been catastrophic for society. Johnson writes, "In a hedonistic and heedless society, [these practices] did not appreciably diminish the number of unwanted children. One striking and unwelcome phenomenon of the 1970s and still more of the 1980s was the growth of what were euphemistically termed 'one-parent families,' in most cases mothers, usually dependent on welfare payments, looking after children on their own."[10]

Like Christ, we are to LOVE THE SINNER, but HATE THE SIN, to show compassion as Christ was compassionate.

Some sociologists argue that family fragmentation is actually good for us. But Johnson says there is no point in pretending that one-parent families and illegitimacy are anything other than "grave social evils, devastating the individuals concerned and harmful for society."[11]

We need to recognize the valiant efforts of the single men and women who are struggling, through no fault of their own, to raise their children. Parents who do their best to lead godly lives as single moms and dads need to be commended and supported. The same is true for those who have come to know Christ as Savior and are now struggling to make the best of past bad decisions. Jesus cares about each one of these families, and the Word of God provides answers that really work. Christians need to be quick to support those who have come to Christ in their time of need.

Damage Report on America's Children

The turmoil in America's families has damaged our children almost beyond repair. According to research by the Barna Group, the children of divorced parents receive less parental attention and discipline than their peers in two-parent homes. These children have more frequent and more serious health and emotional problems, and they are more pessimistic about the future. They lack good role models and are more likely to suffer depression than children from intact families. They are more likely to commit crimes or to struggle with low self-esteem, anger, guilt, and lower levels of achievement in school. Similarly, a government study discovered that children from broken homes are more likely to be expelled or suspended from schools than those from two-parent homes.[12] Even the American Medical Association recognizes that the condition of America's young people is a "national emergency" and that we are facing an "unprecedented adolescent crisis."[13]

If we lose the BATTLE for the minds of our young people, the Judeo-Christian ethic can be LOST IN ONE GENERATION.

Dr. James Dobson, president of Focus on the Family, points out the problem: "There is a battle for the hearts and minds of teenagers today. I am more convinced of it than ever before that if we lose the battle for the minds of our young people, the entire understanding of the Judeo-Christian ethic, which was so predominant from the foundation of this country to the present day, can be lost in one generation."[14]

Even the attitudes and behaviors of teenagers who have accepted Christ as their personal Savior have been impacted by our popular culture. Consider the following 1995 study by the Barna Group:

> When we look at how the born-again kids think and live in comparison to their non-Christian peers, there are some encouraging signs and some not-so-encouraging signs. Among the not-so-encouraging signs is the fact that the behaviors we tested are

virtually identical among Christian and non-Christian teenagers. Both segments were equally likely to volunteer their time to help the needy, to cheat on an exam, to steal possessions, to look through a pornographic magazine, to have had sexual intercourse, to have attempted suicide and to spend time watching MTV during the week.

Born-again teenagers were slightly less likely to have watched an X-rated or pornographic movie or to have used an illegal, non-prescription drug within the last three months. They were also more likely to have discussed their religious beliefs with other kids their age and to have felt God's presence at some time in their lives. Overall, however, apart from their engagement in religious activity, most teenagers' lives do not seem to have been substantially altered by their faith views.

Among the encouraging signs, however, is that born-again kids hold views on marriage and family that are more in line with biblical mores than do non-Christian youth. They are more likely to perceive that God intended marriage to last a lifetime; more likely to uphold the importance of the traditional family to the health of our society; and less likely to believe that divorce is inevitable for people who get married.

Teenage believers are also more likely to assert that having just one marriage partner for life is a very desirable circumstance. Overall, the differences between the views of Christian and non-Christian teenagers on family issues are not huge, but at least the nature of the existing differences are as we might hope for: the Christian teens are more likely to have a biblical position.[15]

The Impact of a Culture

When moral chaos and confusion reign, certain segments of our society are affected more deeply than others. Our children are the most susceptible. The pattern follows a well-worn course. First nonscriptural ideas and loose morals leave upcoming generations with no truth. Inevitably, families begin to fall apart. This damages young lives. Reflecting society's values, schools become part of the problem rather than part of the solution. In the end, our youth reap a crisis because they have no sense of belonging or moral foundation to shape their behavior.

The outbreaks of juvenile crime and gang violence show that

the young feel no sense of community or shared values. According to an Associated Press report, American children are five times more likely to die violently than children in twenty-five other industrialized countries; they are twice as likely to commit suicide. Both the homicide and suicide rates have tripled among teens since 1950.[16]

The Problem With Education

Other areas also show the impact of a culture that has abandoned God. The educational deficit is one prime example. In the early 1960s, the Supreme Court declared that students could not learn about God in the classroom. Since then, spending on education has tripled, but standardized test scores have plummeted. Some humanists have proscribed that public schools were to be the state church of the unbeliever. Many students in public schools today are taught that evolution is fact, that America was founded by deists, and that God is irrelevant.

D. James Kennedy observes that what has been taking place over the last three decades is like something out of George Orwell's ominous novel, *1984*. In that story, the Department of Truth was dedicated to turning truth into lies. Kennedy says, "That is what we have in revisionist historians. It starts with their own atheism, their own unbelief, and then they go back and attempt to revise and rewrite history in their own image."[17] Already, the agenda has taken a tragic toll on America's schools and our students. One can only imagine what will happen as those young people begin to assume positions of leadership throughout the nation.

Consequently, our schools have become battlefields. In a now-famous study from 1940, teachers reported the seven most serious problems in the public schools: talking out of turn, chewing gum, making noise, running in the halls, cutting in line, dress-code violations, and littering. In 1990, public school teachers again listed the top problems in schools: drug abuse, alcohol abuse, pregnancy, suicide, rape, robbery, and assault. This shows how far we have fallen.

Research conducted by Eric Johnson reveals a deep sense of sadness and a yearning for innocence among many of today's hardened youth. Johnson reports on a recent program on CBS television which focused on the teenagers of the '90s:

> They showed educational films from the '50s about family life, teen dating, peer pressure, manners, etc , to a group of high school students on a Miami, Florida, campus composed of Hispanic, black, and white teens. As I watched, I laughed. I grew up during the '50s and these films were so hokie and corny, I could not believe it. But, what was more shocking was the unexpected response of these 1990s students. They did not laugh or make fun of these incredibly corny films, instead they were totally mesmerized by them. The students were asked later what they thought about the films. One after another said, "I wish it could be like that today." The innocence, simplicity, security, and safety of the 1950s (except of course without the prejudice and racism) is something today's youth know nothing about but would give anything to experience. Students today say, "I'm afraid of getting shot, raped, or getting AIDS."[18]

The violent and explosive climate faced by today's children comes in a large part from the teaching they receive in public schools. The U.S. Supreme Court, based on an appeal from the state of Kentucky, ruled that "the Ten Commandments may not be posted in public schools, for fear that the mere presence of God's laws may induce children to read, meditate upon, perhaps to venerate and to obey the commandments."[19] Who would imagine that the words of God handed down at Mt. Sinai are dangerous to the young? Yet, the public schools are free to distribute condoms, teach homosexuality as an acceptable lifestyle, and provide abortion counseling without the consent of parents. Public schools today have abandoned the proven components of a classical education—the Three R's of reading, writing, and arithmetic—to focus on the Three S's—sensitivity, self-esteem, and safe sex. In the modern classroom, *feelings* are presented as more important than facts. As one example, problem-solving exercises in some social science and mathematics programs give "pretty good guesses" as much credit as correct answers.

In a report from the American Enterprise Institute, one of the new radical mathematics concepts called MathLand or Interactive Mathematics reveals the bizarre thinking of educators. These math standards, author Lynn Cheney says, recommend that students get together with peers in cooperative learning groups to "construct" strategies for solving math problems. Rather than learning math concepts from their teachers, students invent their own ways of adding, subtracting, multiplying, and dividing. There is no penalty for wrong answers, since program designers consider socialization skills more important than mere numerical accuracy.[20]

No More Rules

Not only do many educators deny students real learning, but they also believe it is dangerous to teach students moral principles that could save their lives. Years ago, people knew the most common Bible stories, the Ten Commandments, the Golden Rule, and the Sermon on the Mount. They had probably learned some of the books of the Bible and could quote Scriptures from memory. They seemed to know more about God, who He is, and how He works.

> More than 86 percent of teens claim to be Christians, yet only 42 percent say FAITH IS VERY IMPORTANT in their lives.

Today, however, I find that fewer young adults have a knowledge of the basic facts or principles of the Bible. They are unaware of the standards God expects of us, or the principles He gave us in His Word. Some see Him as a dictatorial despot, not realizing that He loves us and knows what is best for us. One's view of God affects the way he thinks and acts, the books he reads, the music he enjoys, and the friends he attracts. Our view of God determines every detail of our lifestyle.

In our society, the worldviews and moral philosophies of contemporary culture have been boiled down to the level of soundbites and infomercials. We have bought into a theology of consumerism and the philosophy that we only go around once, therefore nothing really matters, so anything goes. Many people feel that rules and laws don't apply to them, or that they can be bent to suit their needs. In this environment of selective morality, we think we can pick and choose which of God's laws we want to follow.

Read the findings in a 1993 survey conducted by the Josephson Institute of Ethics:

- 91 percent of Americans admit to lying regularly to the people closest to them.
- 77 percent see no point in observing the Sabbath.
- 74 percent admit they would steal items from those who would not really miss them.
- 56 percent say they will drink and drive if they feel they can handle it.
- 55 percent say they would consider cheating on their spouse.
- 50 percent say they regularly procrastinate at work and admit that they do nothing for one full work day each week.
- 40 percent confess they would use illegal drugs.
- 30 percent claim they would cheat on their taxes.
- 93 percent of adults and teens say that "they and nobody else determine what is and what isn't moral in their lives."[21]

How would you come out if you took this survey? Would you fail the moral test on one or two items? Perhaps even three or four? All of us are susceptible to conforming to our society's values or lack of values.

Overcoming Ignorance

Without absolute standards of right, law has no meaning and civilized behavior has no foundation. Chuck Colson sums up the result: "There is no longer any moral authority, because the leading nations of the world have rejected the basis for that authority—ultimately, the law of God. Without a basis in divine law, human law is only a matter of opinion, imposed by force."[22]

Administrators who do not teach that violence is morally wrong should not be surprised when their teachers are threatened with bodily harm by students or when they are assaulted and raped in the classroom. Should it surprise us that 160,000 students skip school every day in fear of their lives? If we do not teach our children that violence is wrong, why are we surprised to learn that 20 percent of high school students carry guns, knives, razors, clubs, and other lethal weapons to school?[23]

If our culture can offer young people no reason why drug use is wrong, then we must expect that many will turn to drugs. According to the Partnership for a Drug-Free America, the average age for the first use of marijuana in America is 13. Marijuana use by eighth graders has doubled since 1991, and 20 percent of fourteen-year-olds say they have used marijuana at least once.[24]

When we offer no reason why teenagers should abstain from sex outside marriage, they will have sex. Despite parental objections, Planned Parenthood of Syracuse, New York, distributed pamphlets to teens that say, "Many people believe that sex relations are right only when they are married. Others decide to have sex outside of marriage. This is a personal choice."[25] How can we win the battle against teen pregnancy, sexually transmitted diseases, or abortion-on-demand when ideas like these are promoted among the young?

And how about these disturbing statistics? More than 86 percent of American teens claim to be Christians, yet only 42 percent say that faith is very important in their lives. More than 55 percent say they believe all prayers are heard by God, regardless of one's religion, or lack of it.[26]

The Lost Generation

Left to fend for themselves in almost every area of life, America's children are becoming a lost generation. Adults have neglected their responsibility of teaching them the Word of God. In the public schools, they have been inoculated against the Christian faith. Consequently, we have raised a generation of outlaws who, unless God should mercifully change the situation, may contribute to the annihilation of civilization as we know it.

Solomon said, "Train a child in the way he should go, and when he is old he will not turn from it" (Proverbs 22:6). We have chosen the opposite—to turn the children loose on the streets without moral guidance—and they have gone astray.

James Dobson and Gary Bauer, president of Family Research

Council, made an urgent appeal in *USA Today* titled "Stop and Listen, America." They urged:

> The American people know we are in a crisis. According to a poll conducted by Pew research, eighty percent believe immorality is our greatest problem as a nation. It's time we all pulled together—Americans of every political party and religious faith—and began working together to recover a sense of what it is that God wants us to do for our nation.
>
> Let's do everything in our power to reverse the blight of violence and lust that has become so pervasive across this land. Radical individualism is destroying us! The creed that says, "If it feels good, do it!" has filled too many hospitals with drug-overdosed teenagers, too many prison cells with fatherless youth, too many caskets with slain young people, and too many eyes with tears.[27]

In an environment of arrogant secularism, humanism, and moral chaos, it will be difficult for many of these young men and women to find their way to God. But God has not given them up. He has given us powerful resources, including truth. With such weapons, combined with fasting and prayer, we can win many battles against evil for our children—even the entire war. Jesus said, "You will know the truth, and the truth will set you free" (John 8:32). This is still our best hope of reversing the confusion in our land and restoring strong families.

> **In the public schools, America's children have been INOCULATED against the Christian faith.**

The demise of moral education results in upcoming generations who do not have the moral fiber to become great leaders, to raise strong sons and daughters, and to influence culture. Because of this and other factors we have examined, deterioration has affected every part of our culture. Some of these areas are technology, art, and the law. As we will see next, these areas are also under siege in our country.

CHAPTER 13

Backward Advances

Despite all her critics, America is still a great nation. It seems, however, that for each step we take forward, we take two steps backward. So far, we have examined several areas of deterioration that have hurt our nation's progress:

- The battle over ideas that began in the 1920s and 1930s
- The materialism and greed that grew out of the Depression and World War II
- The overt revolution of the 1960s and 1970s
- The chaos and confusion now rampant in our families, schools, and streets

Right now you are probably thinking, *This is enough! There could not be more!* But we have not looked at several areas that have made catastrophic contributions to our freefall: the technological revolution, new artistic expressions, the rise of cults, and the breakdown of law. All of these are the result of our national embrace of humanism, relativism, and materialism.

Incredible Advances in Technology

Today, thanks to incredible advances in technology, we can broadcast messages around the globe by television, films, radio, and the Internet. Innovations in technology are marvelous tools intended to broadcast the glory of God. One example is the use of the *JESUS* film. Initiated in 1978–1980 and based entirely on the book of Luke, by 1998 this film of the life of Jesus had been translated into more than 450 languages and viewed by more than 1.2 billion people. The film has been shown in 222 countries by thousands of Christian groups and denominations with tens of millions being introduced to our Lord Jesus Christ. It thrills me to think of how the body of Christ has the ability to spread the gospel and build up believers in their faith in the most remote areas of the world by using all kinds of technological advances.

Indeed, the power of invention is a gift from God. As the Creator, His nature is the essence of invention and discovery. Throughout history, He has revealed secrets of His infinite wisdom and power to His chosen servants. As Psalm 25:14 records, "Friendship with God is reserved for those who reverence him. With them alone he shares the secrets of his promises" (TLB). Almost without exception, early American inventors gave credit to God for what they discovered. For example, Samuel Morse, inventor of the telegraph and Morse code, once told reporters that he never felt he deserved the honors he received for his invention because it was all through God's help.

It is not surprising that the first message he telegraphed was taken from Scripture: "What hath God wrought!" (Numbers 23:23).

The Technology Revolution

But somehow we have been deluded into believing that we are the creators and discoverers—that we are like gods who hold the keys to all knowledge and science. What a sad misunderstanding of who we really are. Consequently, we have taken the technology that God provided for reaching the world for Christ and used it for our own benefit. In so doing, what God meant as a blessing has become a curse. Judge Robert Bork explains:

> A culture obsessed with technology will come to value personal convenience above almost all else, and ours does. That has consequences...Among those consequences is impatience with anything that interferes with personal convenience. Religion, morality, and law do that which accounts for the tendency of modern religion to eschew proscriptions and commandments and turn to counseling and therapeutic sermons; of morality to be relativized; and of law, particularly criminal law, to become soft and uncertain. Religion tends to be strongest when life is hard, the same may be said of morality and law. A person whose main difficulty is not crop failure but video breakdown has less need of the consolations and promises of religion.[1]

Paradoxically, although we have instant access to information on every conceivable topic, we continue to be relatively uninformed. With an incredible overload of information at our fingertips, we find ourselves gravely undernourished in wisdom. Daniel Boorstin, former head of the Library of Congress, remarks that science once boasted of our species as *homo sapiens*, the being who is wise; but today we might merely be classified as *homo optidatum*, the being who possesses the best and latest facts. Sadly, he concludes, *homo optidatum* is a "dunce"![2]

Technology has brought about the "easy life." The harder facts of God like holiness, repentance, and evangelism lose their appeal when a nation becomes fat and rich, sated with convenience and affluence. Instead of employing these new resources to evangelize the nations, we use them to create a life that costs us nothing.

Judge Bork believes the new technology, along with our affluence, has helped usher in a state of complacency that will prove dangerous, if not disastrous.

> Affluence brings with it boredom. Of itself, it offers little but the ability to consume, and a life centered on consumption will appear and be devoid of meaning. Persons so afflicted will seek sensation as a palliative, and that today's culture offers in abundance...
>
> With the time and energies of so many individuals freed from the harder demands of work, the culture turned to consumerism and entertainment. Technology and its entrepreneurs supplied the

demand with motion pictures, radio, television, and videocassettes, all increasingly featuring sex and violence. Sensations must be steadily intensified if boredom is to be kept at bay.[3]

Technology and Entertainment

Because we have forsaken God, our technology has become a blight upon the landscape. In many ways, we have even surpassed the cities of Sodom and Gomorrah, which were destroyed by fire from heaven for their sins. At least their sins were localized; America, on the other hand, exports its sin by the most sophisticated means, hastening the moral destruction of every nation on earth.

America exports its sin, hastening the MORAL DESTRUCTION of every nation on earth.

For more than thirty years, the television and movie industries have exploited sex, drugs, and violence to turn an unprecedented and indecent profit. As a result, our standards of decency have almost collapsed. While the Christian church stands idly by, films and television shows openly mock and ridicule our God.

Ted Baehr, editor and publisher of *Movie Guide* and a respected movie critic, says that Christians willingly removed themselves from the entertainment industry:

> During the golden age of Hollywood, when Mr. Smith went to Washington, the church was the active instrument in Hollywood through the Protestant Film Office. For thirty-three years from 1933–66, the church was an active influence working with the studios to make sure there was no excessive sex or violence.[4]

In 1966, church mechanisms for influencing Hollywood voluntarily shut down, despite the pleas of studio heads who begged them to remain. Ted Baehr considers that the turning point in American entertainment. "If you remember," he says, "in 1966 you had movies like *The Greatest Story Ever Told*, about Jesus Christ. Probably the worst movie of the year was *Mary Poppins*, and the best was *The Sound of Music*. By the time 1969 came around, you had the first X-rated movie and the first sex and Satanism film."[5]

As the church retreated from a position of responsibility, the philosophies of moral relativism and secular humanism filled the void. Today, American entertainment often glamorizes the worst influences in society. The pornography industry nets its purveyors more than $6 billion every year by graphically displaying the most vile and bizarre sex acts imaginable. Major box office releases mock, ridicule, and bash men and women of God. All too often, these films subtly, and more recently very boldly, propagate humanistic, occultic, and New Age ideologies.

Popular television programs now treat homosexuality as a normal lifestyle choice. Graphic violence overloads our airwaves and cable systems. Most people agree that television has unrivaled efficiency at selling goods, services, culture, music, politics, and fashion. Why is it that the industry claims that the one thing it cannot sell is violence?

Tests of Morality

The decay is insidious, as demonstrated by the example of the sitcom *Ellen*. Initially the producers of the show wrestled over whether the show's main character should "come out of the closet" as a lesbian. At first, loud cries were heard about how disgraceful such a move would be. But within months, not only did the character played by Ellen Degeneres announce that she was a lesbian, the actress did too. That incident tested the public's reaction. When the novelty of the comedienne's "big statement" faded away, viewers lost interest in the show and falling advertising revenues sealed the sitcom's fate. But the damage had been done. Soon few people were bothered by a lesbian heroine in a major network show.

Another test arose when homosexual activists were outraged by a "viewer discretion" warning placed on an episode where Ellen kissed another woman. The activists protested, "What's wrong with two women kissing each other?" But the statement had been made, breaking the ground for even more offensive fare.

Sin always feeds on sin. By indulging our base natures, we crave more sin in every area of life. What was merely tantalizing yesterday becomes necessary today; what is stimulating today becomes tame and unexciting tomorrow. Unless the intensity of the sensual experience is constantly increased and the sin becomes more and more shocking, it quickly becomes boring.

Pornography, as studies have shown, creates an insatiable appetite. It begins with a lustful thought, which eventually leads to soft-core pornography, then hard-core pornography, then often to violence and other social pathologies.

Any pattern of sin is insidious and corrosive and can only be broken by humiliation and repentance before almighty God. And we can say with certainty and with the warrant of Scripture that unless changes come swiftly in our habits of consumption in entertainment, this factor alone may be weighty enough to bring God's final judgment upon America.

Art in Crisis

The largest patron of the arts during the Renaissance era was the Catholic church. This is why we have the great works by Michelangelo, Raphael, Botticelli, Leonardo da Vinci, and so many others which give honor to God and our Lord Jesus Christ.

Michelangelo's art is some of history's best. The story of Creation on the ceiling of the Sistine Chapel in Rome is one of the most awesome achievements in art. The magnificent *Pieta*, chiseled from raw Carrara marble, stands in a protected cove of St. Peter's Basilica at the Vatican. The statue portrays the grief of Mary, clasping the slain body of her son, our Lord Jesus Christ, in her arms. *David*, the statue commissioned as a symbol of Florentine civic virtue, portrays a strong and virile young man as he becomes head of the house of Judah. *The Last Judgment* includes a cameo of Michelangelo himself in intense torment as he faces the reality of his own sin.

To my knowledge, there are no such works in progress today that glorify the Creator or the Savior on such a grandiose scale. Though some nations may produce national works that glorify Him with paintings and icons, America has none.

The masterpieces of the Renaissance were created to glorify God.

The arts of our day, on the other hand, are often used to defame and blaspheme Him. It would have been inconceivable to the great masters that one day their beloved Jesus would be depicted immersed in a jar of the artist's urine! This was Robert Serrano's contribution, paid for by the National Endowment for the Arts with taxpayer money.

The stark reality is that Jesus Christ has been removed from our public square, and our tax money has been used by our artistic leaders to patronize obscenity. The apostle Peter, to whom the Basilica at the Vatican is dedicated, warned of the consequences of such flagrant blasphemy:

> Bold and arrogant, these men are not afraid to slander celestial beings; yet even angels, although they are stronger and more powerful, do not bring slanderous accusations against such beings in the presence of the Lord. But these men blaspheme in matters they do not understand. They are like brute beasts, creatures of instinct, born only to be caught and destroyed, and like beasts they too will perish (2 Peter 2:10–12).

God is serious about destroying those who propagate heresies and lies. Peter concludes:

> If God did not spare angels when they sinned, but sent them to hell, putting them into gloomy dungeons to be held for judgment; if he did not spare the ancient world when he brought the flood on its ungodly people, but protected Noah, a preacher of righteousness, and seven others; if he condemned the cities of Sodom and Gomorrah by burning them to ashes, and made them an example of what is going to happen to the ungodly…then the Lord knows how to rescue godly men from trials and to hold the unrighteous for the day of judgment, while continuing their punishment. This is especially true of those who follow the corrupt desire of the sinful nature and despise authority (2 Peter 2:4–10).

Those who maintain a godly lifestyle in the face of heresy and deceit will be saved. But woe to those who through rebellion perpetrate such destruction on a people and a nation!

False Prophets, False Religions

By allowing sin to flourish, America opened itself to even greater evil. In recent years, we have seen men and women who claim allegiance to God commit acts of terror. Clinton Van Zandt was the lead hostage negotiator for the FBI during the Branch Davidian standoff at Waco, Texas, in 1993. The former FBI officer remembers one particular telephone conversation with cult leader David Koresh:

> He had his Bible, I had mine. We were working through the Scriptures, and David Koresh was trying to tell me by the Scriptures why he had the right to have sexual contact with young girls. I said, "David that's not correct. Look at what the Lord tells us before and after."
>
> "You are totally incorrect."
>
> I said, "David, you are talking about annihilating your whole flock. We read in Scriptures that the Lord will go out for one lost sheep and bring it back again, while you are talking about an entire flock being annihilated." That was the time David Koresh said, "Clint, who do you think I am?" I said, "David, who do you think you are?" [Koresh] said, "I am the christ."

People are not content with a SUPERFICIAL CHRISTIANITY; our natures crave a vital relationship with God.

Van Zandt watched in tears as the Branch Davidian compound burned. He saw adults who proclaimed allegiance to Christianity abdicate their responsibilities as parents, citizens, and adults, dying with their children for cultic beliefs. He says, "It scared me for society as a whole."[6]

People are not content with a superficial Christianity; our natures crave a vital relationship with God. If we are denied the opportunity to interact with our Maker—through prayer, Bible reading, and regular worship—then we fall for any kind of spirituality that promises transcendence. But cults cannot satisfy our souls.

Books on a wide range of spiritual counterfeits now crowd the shelves of local bookstores. We saw earlier how New Age religions are on the rise. Today, television shows glorify angels or the mystical and occult. Science fiction, on television and in the movies, promises mystical insight or paranormal experiences. But these do not satisfy either. The common thread in alternative religions is the promise of power without the personal sacrifice. They claim, "Your eyes shall be opened, and ye shall be as gods, knowing good and evil" (Genesis 3:5, KJV). That is not the road to God, but the road to terror and eternal torment in the lake of fire.

By rejecting faith in Jesus Christ, America has also rejected God's protective hand which, until recently, sheltered this nation from harm. We have invited the devil with all his diabolical and destructive power into our daily lives.

The Breakdown of Law

Have you noticed the blatant disregard for the law and for life in news stories that have blazed across television screens and newspapers in recent months?

- A man arrested in a small New York town for selling crack cocaine confessed he had traded drugs for sex and infected at least a hundred high school girls with the deadly AIDS virus.
- A teenage girl gave birth at her high school prom, then left her baby to die in a garbage can while she danced with her boyfriend to their favorite tunes.
- In Los Angeles, two men in full-body armor robbed a bank in broad daylight. Then they calmly walked outside and engaged in a fire fight with dozens of police officers. In a withering volley of automatic weapons fire, their bullets shattered everyone and everything in sight.
- In Kentucky a boy caught up in the occult opened fire on a group of high school students who were praying in a hallway. He killed three young women.
- In Arkansas, two young boys ambushed classmates with assault rifles during a fire drill.

In three separate cases, juries convicted mothers of drowning, smothering, or beating their children to death. Two Naval Academy cadets were convicted of murdering a sexual rival. People in high government positions, including the President, were accused of lying, having sexual escapades, and obstructing justice. Several cabinet-level administrators have resigned or been indicted for financial impropriety. Business and sports figures make excuses for unruly behavior or criminal acts. These flagrant crimes show the utter disarray of our once-treasured system of law.

Remember the principle of "lex rex" from early in our history? Law used to be firmly based on what Scripture dictated was morally right. Americans treasured the life and the property of others. Nations around the world looked to America and Great Britain as practitioners of model legal systems.

Have you ever wondered why our Founding Fathers did not add more moral rules and regulations to our Constitution? Because they believed that America's deep religious character would provide an enduring moral framework for society. They never imagined that permissiveness and radical individualism would sweep our land.

To date, at least three generations of Americans have been taught that there are no legitimate restraints on personal behavior. As we have slid into moral relativism, our laws have followed suit and increasingly become merely what man says is right in a given situation. We now have "situational" or "sociological" law, which is based on what a certain group thinks is for the good of all the people at that given moment.

With God and the Bible, including the Ten Commandments and the Golden Rule, removed from the foundation of our legal system, our laws no longer carry moral authority. The free-will tyrannies of many judges, the freedom of the individual, and the rights of the minority have become our new standards. We no longer have a way to sustain a just order; consequently, widespread chaos plagues our justice system.

When God's laws are the spirit behind the law, we can measure actions against His higher, eternal moral code. We can judge events with supernatural clarity, and can almost universally figure out what is right and what is wrong, what is forgivable and what must be punished.

Not so in a godless society. With no overarching moral law, all that is left is the letter of man's law. Then specific wording in the law becomes sacred. There is no spirit to the law; there is only exactly what is written on paper. Americans have learned to maneuver their way through the written law to reap huge profits. Lawyers find ways to encourage lawsuits to make millions for themselves.

Separation of Church and State

One hotly contested point of law today is the First Amendment to the Constitution. Over the past fifty years, many have used this amendment as a mechanism for removing the Christian faith from the public arena. By citing the existence of an officially mandated "separation of church and state," anti-Christian forces have worked to overturn the sacred foundations of this nation. But they have no basis whatsoever in law or tradition to separate church and state affairs. Rather, they are instituting what some have called a "new American revolution."

The First Amendment reads, "Congress shall make no laws respecting an establishment of religion, or prohibiting the free exercise thereof." This statement was included to prohibit the establishment of a national church, such as the Church of England, and to prevent the state from interfering with the religious activities of its citizens. The state was not to be partial to any one denomination, but neither was it to be hostile to religious activities. In fact, the First Amendment never mentions "separation," "a wall," or "State." These words were taken from a private letter Thomas Jefferson wrote to the Danbury Baptists.

Over the years, many illustrious men have described the role of religion in government. George Washington said that if he had the faintest idea that this Constitution would in any way diminish the rights of any Christian denomination, he "would never have placed [his] signature to it."[7] Uriah Oakes, who served as president of Harvard College, said in 1673:

> According to the design of our fathers and the frame of things laid by them, the interests of righteousness in the commonwealth and the holiness in the churches are inseparable...to divide what God hath joined is folly in its exaltation. I look upon this as a little model for the glorious Kingdom of Christ on earth. Christ reigns among us in the commonwealth as well as in the church and hath

His glorious interest involved and wrapped up in the good of both societies respectively.[8]

Joseph Story (1779–1845), one of the first Justices of the Supreme Court, said in 1840:

> Probably at the time of the adoption of the Constitution, and of the First Amendment to it, the general, if not universal sentiment in America was that Christianity ought to receive encouragement from the state...Any attempt to level all religions and to make it a matter of policy to hold all in utter indifference would have created universal disapprobation, if not universal indignation.[9]

As late as 1944, Justice William O. Douglas, whom many identify as the most liberal Supreme Court justice to serve on the bench, affirmed, "The First Amendment has a dual aspect. It not only forestalls compulsion by law of the acceptance of any creed or practice of any form of worship, but also safeguards the free exercise of the chosen form of religion."[10]

Today, however, "separation of church and state" has become a weapon to keep God out of the public and political arenas. Writing in *The Liberator*, Matthew Staver explains,

> There is nothing wrong with the way Thomas Jefferson used the "wall of separation between church and state" metaphor. The problem has arisen when the Supreme Court in 1947 erroneously picked up the metaphor and attempted to construct a constitutional principle. While the metaphor understood in its proper context is useful, we might do well to heed the words of the United States Supreme Court Justice William Rehnquist:
>
> The "wall of separation between church and state" is a metaphor based on bad history, a metaphor which has proved useless as a guide to judging. It should be frankly and explicitly abandoned.[11]

D. James Kennedy asks: "Does the separation of church and state mean that God is to have no place in our land? Does it mean that this nation was not founded for the glory of God and the advancement of the Kingdom of our Lord Jesus Christ? Does it mean that our government is to be secularist and humanist in nature? Does it mean that our children are to grow up without any knowledge of the God who brought about the founding of this country? Are we to be neutral?"

Kennedy concludes: "From the history of our country, we realize that all the documents which formed our country, the ideals of those who framed them, the convictions of those who settled this land, all the constitutions of the various states, the inaugurals of all our presidents, the statements on all the monuments, unmistakably testify that this is a nation under God founded for the furtherance of the Gospel and Kingdom of our Lord Jesus Christ."[12]

Though we have been a predominantly Christian nation for most of our history, that legacy is meaningless if it does not influence our thinking and public conduct today. If we view history simply as something to be proud of, some past accomplishment without practical applications to modern life, our heritage is nullified.

> **Our Christian legacy is MEANINGLESS if it does not influence our thinking and public conduct today.**

Outlawing religion from the political arena is not what the Founding Fathers intended when they drafted the First Amendment. We do a grave disservice to our country by removing the influence of religion. If you separate God from the public arena, inevitably you separate good from our government. What a tragedy if we allow those who oppose our God to rob us of our historical mandate to achieve God's purposes through government!

Inevitable Disorder

Because of the breakdown of our law, today professional legal advice is necessary even when entering into the most simple agreements. Where a genuine handshake used to close a business agreement, today nothing is official until every paper is signed and the "legalese" is correct.

Our criminal justice system also suffers tremendously. The critical question in any trial used to be: Did the suspect commit the crime? Today, the questions are: Did he do it? Did the police follow proper procedure exactly? Is there a loophole in the written law which could get the criminal off the hook? Did the judge follow the technicalities precisely during proceedings? Was the jury tainted by the media? And when will the decision be appealed? We have created a legal system of technicalities and confusion which has released hardened criminals onto the streets, and enslaved honest people in mountains of debt and taxes.

The medical community has also been ravaged by modern legal disorder. Thousands of people are making fortunes by waging lawsuits which many hospitals find cheaper to settle out of court. While some cases are certainly legitimate, our legal system has paved the way for opportunists to profit at the nation's expense.

The New Barbarians

C. S. Lewis warned of a time when a far more dangerous variety of criminal will replace the older type of thugs. Organized crime and hooliganism will become less disturbing, he said, as seemingly "decent people" commit more and more crimes. He writes:

> The greatest evil is not now done in those sordid "dens of crime" that Dickens loved to paint. It is not even in concentration and labor camps. In those we see its final result. But it is conceived and ordered (moved, seconded, carried, and minuted) in clean, carpeted, warmed, and well-lighted offices, by quiet men with white collars and cut fingernails and smooth shaven faces who do not need to raise their voices.[13]

Chuck Colson explains the consequences that come from unrestrained liberty:

> Clearly, barbarism is the result of the loss of a transcendent value system where people are taught to love God and to love one another. When you take that away, you reduce us to our basest instincts. Conscience is destroyed. Character is attacked. So we begin to see more and more dreadful things happen...
>
> We are going to see more and more barbarians—not only butchering-killer types, but the subtle barbarians of the boardrooms with the three-piece suits who promulgate values that are destructive of a respect for God, community, and one another.[14]

After all, where did the ideas for Germany's "final solution" originate? Not from within the dreaded concentration camps with their armed guards and brutality, but in pleasant meeting rooms where the Nazi elite contemplated schemes to dominate people everywhere.

This principle is true today. While society managed to defeat human devils like Adolf Hitler, we are shocked to find that we, ourselves, are the greatest risk to peace and the survival of our nation. The reason is that we have licensed and condoned sin and thereby desensitized our moral sensibilities. The first sin we commit or tolerate is troubling; the second a little less so; the third hardly a problem; and by the fourth or fifth occurrence, even serious moral lapses can become acceptable. Eventually, we do not know which evil we should oppose.

One of the worst names to be branded today is "INTOLERANT."

Talk to the man who embezzles from his company. At first, it is just to pay a bill that he cannot meet and he is so guilt-ridden. The second time, he has his excuses thought out. Perhaps he rationalizes, "The company owes me anyway. Look what I do for them and they don't appreciate it." As the months pass without repentance, he more easily shrugs off guilty feelings. Soon he dips into the till whenever he thinks he will not get caught.

Without moral convictions, an entire nation can grow dangerously accustomed to habitual sin. Conscience based on principles of truth becomes passé. Instead, popularly accepted notions are "Whatever feels good," "What's in it for me?" and "What can I get away with?" Those who speak out against corruption or call for repentance and a return to high standards are labeled hate-mongers, extremists, and reactionaries. And one of the worst names to be branded today is "intolerant." Judge Robert Bork writes:

> With each new evidence of deterioration, we lament for a moment, and then become accustomed to it We hear one day of the latest rap song calling for killing policemen or the sexual mutilation of women; the next, of coercive left-wing political indoctrina-

> tion at a prestigious university; then of the latest homicide figure for New York City, Los Angeles, or the District of Columbia; of the collapse of the criminal justice system which displays an inability to punish adequately and, often enough, an inability to even convict the clearly guilty; of the rising rate of illegitimate births; the uninhibited display of sexuality and the popularization of violence in our entertainment; worsening racial tensions; the angry activists of feminism, homosexuality, environmentalism, animal rights—the list could be extended almost indefinitely. So unrelenting is the assault on our sensibilities that many of us grow numb, finding resignation the rational, adaptive response to an environment that is increasingly polluted and apparently beyond our control.[15]

Liberty turned into license threatens our entire way of life. Puritan leader William Penn wrote in a letter to Czar Peter the Great of Russia, "Those who will not be governed by God will be ruled by tyrants."[16] I believe this is what is happening in America today. Having "freed" ourselves from the constraints of morality, we have enslaved ourselves to the rule of government.

LIBERTY turned into LICENSE threatens our entire way of life.

Yet another result of our national march toward destruction has been especially obvious in the last few years. This symptom of a decaying society illustrates the speed of our nation's downward moral spiral. It shows how far we have fallen, and perhaps the end of life as we know it. It all started with a court case called *Roe v. Wade*.

CHAPTER 14

The Culture of Death

A horrible scene recently played out in what should be one of our country's safest places—a school. A young boy just emerging into adolescence smuggled weapons into his high school cafeteria. In a terrifying few moments, he sprayed his helpless classmates with bullets. Two young people died and dozens more were injured. The students who escaped the bullets were wounded too. They are now condemned to finish their high school years under an oppressive cloud of fear.

When the police searched the troubled young man's home, they found the bodies of his mother and father. Before the bodies could be removed, bomb squads had to defuse numerous explosive devices that the teenager had built from instructions he downloaded off the Internet.

This tragic story is just one example of what is going on in communities across our country. Can anyone argue that we do not live in a culture of death? The threat of untimely death reigns in every part of our culture, from the moment of conception to the days of our retirement. How did this all get started?

The Legacy of Abortion

By the 1970s, a new set of cultural priorities was emerging that valued personal freedom above all else. The type of freedom that had been established by our Founding Fathers—freedom that demanded patience, endurance, and self-sacrifice—was replaced by unrestrained license. This new type of liberty came into full bloom by January 1973, when the U.S. Supreme Court declared abortion-on-demand legal in *Roe v. Wade*.

With few exceptions, abortions are a direct result of lust, greed, and selfishness—the same root as materialism. Abortions are fostered by the appetite for self-gratification, and in some cases rebellious lifestyles—making ourselves the center of our own universe. Since the Supreme Court's infamous decision allowing the destruction of infants in the womb, almost forty million babies have been murdered by their mothers. An entire generation of American children will not grow up in "the land of the free" because their parents were licensed to kill them.

The fact that ABORTION persists in modern society reveals that we have LOST RESPECT both for human life and FOR PLEASING GOD.

In an exclusive interview with Robert Bork, he says that abortion coarsened American society and changed our attitudes toward life. He admits that at first many people (himself included) believed that a human embryo was "just sort of a blob of tissue." Our scientific community has now proven that the unborn child is a unique individual from the moment of conception. Bork concludes that the fact that abortion persists in modern society reveals that we have lost respect both for human life and for pleasing God.[1]

As Keith Fournier put it, by making ourselves the center of all things, we fall into the trap of "selfism."[2] It leads to an entirely new view of life. Life itself no longer carries inherent dignity. Neither children nor the elderly, nor any others have worth simply because they are alive.

John Whitehead agrees with Bork that abortion is not merely an attack on the unborn child, but an attack on God Himself:

> It is not simply that modern men hate life, but that they hate the Creator. Every person and every infant in the womb is in the image of God and possesses the resulting dignity given by the Creator. When the abortionist kills an unborn baby, he is in reality killing the image of God.[3]

This chilling idea was expressed by Fyodor Dostoevsky in his great novel, *Crime and Punishment*: "If God is dead, everything is permitted." In a society where nothing is ultimately wrong, including murdering unborn children, anything is possible. The acceptance and practice of abortion has brought about a hardness of heart and an insensitivity to murder. Personal "choice" has become a religion in America. It is valued above everything and every cost. For pro-choice supporters, God-ordained moral limits have no meaning, therefore, all choices are rightfully theirs to make. Consequently, the culture of death has expanded to include ever more bizarre and sickening practices.

Brutal Practices

Two practices that are related to abortion exemplify how abortion results in more brutal procedures: fetal tissue research and partial-birth abortion.

Many Americans, including some leaders in Washington, D.C., favor lifting the ban on federal funding for fetal tissue research. This will open the door for women to become pregnant to harvest fetal tissue from their own pre-born children for medical research. They can sell the children in their wombs as a farmer sells his livestock. Human life in such a case is merely a product or a commodity for sale to the highest bidder. The very idea that we may turn women's bodies into fetal-tissue farms for research or financial gain should send chills of horror down the spines of all Americans.

Partial-birth abortion has been identified as infanticide by experts such as Dr. Bernard Nathanson, co-founder of the National Abortion Rights Action League (NARAL), and former U.S. Surgeon

General Dr. C. Everett Koop. I hesitate to give the details on this gruesome procedure, however, a brief description may help some who do not understand what really happens. Hopefully, it will cause more of us to speak out against this ghastly practice.

This procedure is normally performed well into a pregnancy, often as late as the eighth or ninth month. The doctor turns the baby's body around in the uterus so that it is in the breach position for a feet-first extraction. He then delivers the child as in a normal breach delivery, but stops just short of complete delivery, leaving only the baby's head inside the birth canal. At that point, he plunges a pair of scissors into the base of the baby's skull, inserts a vacuum tube, and suctions out the baby's brain. The baby's head collapses, and the dead baby's body can then be fully delivered. The baby's organs are sometimes sold for use in medical experiments or other consumer product research.

The acceptance of abortion says something profoundly disturbing about where we are as a people, as a nation, and as a culture. What justification can we offer for moral outrage when every day in America children are butchered in legal "abortuaries" that are sanctioned by the highest court in the land? If we can kill our own children and allow others to do the same, are we really any better than the butchers of Auschwitz and other World War II death camps? Are we superior to the promoters of ethnic cleansing in Bosnia or in Asia and Africa? If the nation can justify the murder of an innocent baby just four centimeters from its first breath, should it surprise us to see so many other social pathologies loose in our country? Can we really be astounded when children rape and kill without remorse? Can we feign shock when juvenile crime has become the most persistent and dangerous threat to society? How can anyone claim to be surprised when a young mother like Susan Smith straps her young children in a car and drives them into a lake to drown?

President Lincoln believed that God allowed the Civil War with its loss of over 600,000 soldiers to atone for the nation's sin of slavery. What price must we be expected to pay for the sin of murdering millions of babies?

Dying for a Cause

Not satisfied with the killing of unborn babies, the culture of death is spreading further into our culture through practices such as doctor-assisted suicide and euthanasia. The same arguments used to justify abortion-on-demand—that babies are too embarrassing, too ill, or too inconvenient—are now used for the elderly, terminally ill, or severely handicapped.

To see where the culture of death inevitably leads, we can look at the disaster taking place in the Netherlands. According to a 1990 Dutch government survey, 11,800 patients have been euthanized in Holland. Nearly 6,000 of those killings were performed without the patient's consent. An additional 13,506 were denied critical medical treatment with the specific aim of terminating life—a process the Dutch call "euthanasia by omission." Fully 64 percent of the patients gave no consent to their fate. What is more, 65 percent of Dutch doctors think physicians should suggest euthanasia to their patients who do not voluntarily request it.[4]

Nearly half of the euthanizations in Holland were performed WITHOUT THE PATIENT'S CONSENT.

Would you like to be among the thousands who had no opportunity to give consent? That is a chilling thought.

Former forensic pathologist Jack Kevorkian, nicknamed "Dr. Death," brought assisted suicide to the forefront in America. As of this writing, he has personally assisted in killing many more people than brutal murderers such as Charles Manson, David "Son of Sam" Berkowitz, or John Wayne Gacy.

Articles in dozens of publications describe how death obsesses Kevorkian. Some of his more bizarre paintings of death and dying have been published in national periodicals. In a 1993 article, *Newsweek* magazine reported that in the 1950s, Jack Kevorkian made regular visits to terminally ill patients and "peered deeply into their eyes."[5] He wanted to watch them die, not for any practical application, but, according to Kevorkian, "I was curious, that's

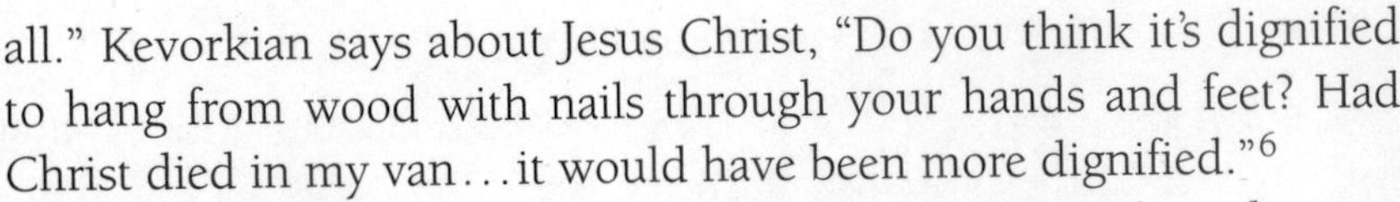

all." Kevorkian says about Jesus Christ, "Do you think it's dignified to hang from wood with nails through your hands and feet? Had Christ died in my van... it would have been more dignified."[6]

One grave danger facing middle-aged adults who advocate these practices today is that they may one day be used on the Baby Boomer generation. As more people become elderly, their existence may strain social programs such as Medicare and Social Security. How easy it would be to assist these elderly in dying to make room for the younger generation. People who argue that euthanasia is good for the elderly now may eventually give their lives for their cause—selfism.

Reaping the Whirlwind

The culture of death resulted in a morbid obsession with death and suicide. As movies, death-metal music, MTV, and daytime TV programming glorify death and violence, Americans become desensitized. For centuries, America was considered a model of individual liberty where each citizen was valued; yet, today, life in America is getting cheaper by the hour. Crime is no longer confined to the inner cities. Drug trafficking, robbery, murder, rape, and other violent crimes have moved into suburban and rural America as well.

Because of violence, people are afraid. These shocking crime facts from the Federal Bureau of Investigation show that they have good reason to fear:

- The U.S. Department of Justice predicts that 83 percent of all Americans will be victims of violent crime at least once in their lives.[7]
- One violent crime occurs every 17 seconds.
- One property crime occurs every 3 seconds.
- One murder occurs every 23 minutes.
- One forcible rape occurs every 5 minutes.
- One robbery is committed every 51 seconds.
- One aggravated assault takes place every 28 seconds.
- One burglary occurs every 12 seconds.

- One larceny-theft occurs every 4 seconds.
- One child in America dies of gunshot wounds every two hours. The typical American child is 15 times more likely to be killed by gunfire than a child born in strife-torn Northern Ireland.
- In 1996, according to the Department of Justice, 538 American children were murdered by their parents, and 308 parents were murdered by their children.[8]

Sheriff Joe Arpaio of Maricopa County, Arizona, is known as America's toughest sheriff. His tent city is a model prison. Arpaio expresses a deep concern that crime has skyrocketed in the course of just one generation. He says:

> When you talk about my generation, when I was a kid, you did not need burglar alarms or bars on the windows, you didn't need to lock your doors. Now, we are all prisoners ourselves, we are prisoners in our own homes, and the bad guys are roaming the streets. The violent crime, especially the juvenile crime, has increased tremendously. When I was a cop on the beat in D.C., if a kid grabbed a purse, he'd grab the purse and run, now they grab the purse and kill.[9]

Consider the example of New Haven, Connecticut, the home of Yale University. In 1960, the city had 6 murders, 4 rapes, and 16 robberies. By 1990, the population had dropped by 14 percent, but there were 31 murders, 168 rapes, and 1,784 robberies.[10] So what changed? Obviously something in the moral fabric of the nation had come unraveled.

When we took prayer and Bible reading out of the schools, we sent America's young people a clear signal that biblical morality and traditional values were irrelevant and out of date. For this reason among others, crime has taken over our streets. In 1960, there were 160 violent crimes per 100,000 Americans. By 1996, violent crime had skyrocketed to 634 per 100,000—a 396 percent increase. Violent crime by juveniles has soared by more than 240 percent since 1970. Today, people under the age of 21 commit almost half of all violent crimes.[11]

Step by step, we have cheapened the value of human life. We have created the very horrors that now threaten our survival as a nation. Radio broadcaster Paul Harvey recently observed, "No generation in American history has ever been terrified by its own offspring—that is, until now."[12] How far we have strayed from the Bible's promise that sons are a heritage from the Lord and children a reward from Him (Psalm 127:3). How far we have wandered from the great purpose and design for which God prepared this land!

The Antidote for Cultural Disease

Any number of government programs have tried to change our nation's problems. They are like putting a Band-Aid on cancer. On the surface, they may seem helpful, but they do not cure what is eating away underneath. The gospel of Jesus Christ offers the only antidote to the ills that plague our society:

For fear, He offers peace.

For worry, He offers confidence and assurance.

For hurt and rejection, He offers forgiveness and affirmation.

For emptiness, He offers meaning in life.

For worthlessness, He offers dignity, value and worth.

For greed and selfishness, He offers a giving spirit with contentment.

For hatred and prejudice, He offers love and acceptance.

For bondage to habits, He offers deliverance and freedom.

For sickness, He offers healing.

For rebellion and stubbornness, He offers submission and servitude.

For self-sufficiency, He offers His power and wisdom to do all things.

For death, He offers eternal life.

How is this possible? Because Jesus Christ has all power over all things—including the bondage of sin. We can use the lessons of history to take the right steps toward healing and growth, or we can ignore the warning signs and incur God's judgment. How much better off we will be if we heed the red-sky warnings!

Yet renewal is difficult. Despite the pain, we should rejoice when the Holy Spirit begins to convict us, exposing our sin. He wants to cleanse, restore, and make us into new persons with a hopeful future. He is the God of the second chance. This can happen when we confess, repent, and forsake our sin, and ask Him to come into our lives and help us. And the good part is that He provides the faith and power for us to do just that.

Sometimes I imagine what would happen if we could change our country's direction through the power of the Holy Spirit. Television would be used to build character along with providing entertainment. The amazing special effects in movies would portray scenes like the crossing of the Red Sea. Think how a director could improve on the scene captured so well in that great classic, *The Ten Commandments*, starring Charlton Heston! The Internet could be used to reach people all over the world for Christ and disciple them in their faith.

Our art would declare the glory of God and that He loves us unconditionally. We could proudly display it all over the world. We would not duplicate horrors like the Waco massacre. Our laws would once again uphold the sanctity of life. Our unborn babies would safely grow in the womb. Our disabled and elderly could rest in the security of knowing that their lives were protected as infinitely valuable to society.

The gospel of Jesus Christ offers THE ONLY ANTIDOTE to the ills that plague our society.

Does that sound like an unreachable dream? It must not be. Our future is right over the horizon. The storms we will endure cannot be avoided. Without doubt, we face that decision right now—to turn back to God or face judgment.

God does not leave us without answers to our moral problems. He wants us to return to Him and to heal our land so we can accomplish the purposes for which He designed us. We all know that His Word provides standards for us as a people to live by. History also gives us numerous examples of what happens when nations make moral—and immoral—choices. In the next chapter, we will look back at other cultures and nations that faced the same moral choice as we do today. What decision did they make? And how did it affect their future?

CHAPTER 15

Nations That Live, Nations That Die

Imagine the executive who is at the top of his career field. He lives in a huge home overlooking a gorgeous lake. His three children do well in school and his wife has a business in graphic design. This executive attends many business functions where he often has a drink or two with his partners or clients. They raise sparkling crystal glasses filled with fragrant wines or shot glasses with strong whiskey. Soon the executive's occasional drink becomes habitual. Over a few years, his alcohol habit undermines his ability to work and he loses his job. About the same time, his wife gets tired of his problems and leaves him, taking his children with her. Soon he loses his home and all the other possessions.

Eventually, he becomes a homeless recluse on the street, wearing tattered clothing, unwashed, with a scraggly beard. Still he clutches his drink, this time a bottle wrapped in a plain brown paper bag. People who once knew him as the up-and-coming executive pass him by on the street and mutter, "How on earth did he get in this condition?"

Can you see similarities between our country and that executive? Are we not right now at the pinnacle of success? But are we not wasting our good fortune with addictions to bad habits and sinful living? Could foreigners say of us, "How could a nation like America get into this condition?"

Pattern of Decay

Pat Robertson offers a profound description of how such a collapse unfolds. It so clearly details what is happening right now in America that it deserves being reprinted at length:

> As the nineties unfold, nothing portrays our world crisis more clearly than man's internal and moral condition. The unmistakable scent of what the Bible calls the antichrist spirit is in the air. It was present at the Tower of Babel and at Sodom and Gomorrah. It was present in the French Revolution and in Nazi Germany. And it is present in Europe and the United States today. The signs of this spirit are clear. They emerge in this fashion: A significant minority, then an actual majority, of the people in a society begin to throw off the restraints of history, then the restraints of written law, then accepted standards of morality, then established religion, and finally, God Himself.
>
> As the rebellion gains momentum, the participants grow bolder. Those practices that once were considered shameful and unlawful move into the open. Soon, the practitioners are aggressive, militant. As each societal standard falls, another comes under attack. The pressure is relentless. Established institutions crumble. Ultimately the struggle that began as a cry for freedom of expression grows into an all-out war against the rights of advocates of traditional morality. The latter are hated, reviled, isolated, and then persecuted.
>
> Honor, decency, honesty, self-control, sexual restraint, family values, and sacrifice are replaced by gluttony, sensuality, bizarre sexual practices, cruelty, profligacy, dishonesty, delinquency, drunkenness, drug-induced euphoria, fraud, waste, debauched currency, and rampant inflation.
>
> The people then search for a deity that will both permit and personify their basest desires. At Babel it was a tower—man's attempt to glorify himself. In ancient Mediterranean cultures, like those of Sodom and Gomorrah, it was a god or goddess of sex. In France, it was the goddess of reason; in Germany, Hitler and the

Nazi party; in Europe and especially in the United States, the god of central government under the religion of secular humanism.

The pattern is always the same. So is the result. No society falling under the grip of the antichrist spirit has survived. First comes a period of lawlessness and virtual anarchy, then an economic collapse followed by a reign of terror. Then comes a strong dictator who plunders society for his personal aggrandizement; he dreams of a worldwide empire and storms into war. Eventually come defeat and collapse.[1]

Where is America in this pattern? How much farther do we have to go before the end?

A Warning and a Promise

In one of the most profound warnings in all Scripture, God lays the choice of survival before ancient Israel:

> I have set before you today life and prosperity, and death and adversity; in that I command you today to love the Lord your God, to walk in His ways and to keep His commandments and His statutes and His judgments, that you may live and multiply, and that the Lord your God may bless you in the land where you are entering…But if your heart turns away and you will not obey, but are drawn away and worship other gods and serve them, I declare to you today that you shall surely perish…I call heaven and earth to witness against you today, that I have set before you life and death, the blessing and the curse. So choose life in order that you may live (Deuteronomy 30:15–19, NASB).

Israel did not heed the warning. Their culture became more and more depraved, until God allowed surrounding nations to take them into captivity. During the time of Jesus, the Jewish people were ruled by the Roman legions. Shortly thereafter, the Jewish temple was razed and the people scattered.

An example of a nation which repented and escaped God's judgment was the wicked city of Nineveh. God sent Jonah to warn Nineveh of its imminent destruction. What followed was the familiar story of Jonah trying to escape God's order to go to Nineveh by fleeing in a ship. A great fish swallowed Jonah. When he finally reached dry land, he obeyed God and went to Nineveh.

The book of Jonah describes what happened:

> The very first day when Jonah entered the city and began to preach, the people repented. Jonah shouted to the crowds gathered around him, "Forty days from now Nineveh will be destroyed!" And they believed him and declared a fast; from the king on down, everyone put on sackcloth—the rough, coarse garments worn at times of mourning (Jonah 3:4,5, TLB).

The king gave the people the following instructions:

> "Let no one, not even the animals, eat anything at all, nor even drink any water. Everyone must wear sackcloth and cry mightily to God, and let everyone turn from his evil ways, from his violence and robbing. Who can tell? Perhaps even yet God will decide to let us live, and will hold back his fierce anger from destroying us" (Jonah 3:7–9, TLB).

Immediate repentance, a passionate desire for forgiveness, and honest confession of sin, along with their sincere commitment to change their ways saved Nineveh from the destruction that threatened them. God came through as He always does when people repent and turn away from their corrupt behavior. "When God saw that they had put a stop to their evil ways, he abandoned his plan to destroy them, and did not carry it through" (v. 10, TLB).

Peter explains God's willingness to forego punishment: "The Lord is not slow in keeping his promise, as some understand slowness. He is patient with you, not wanting anyone to perish, but everyone to come to repentance" (2 Peter 3:9).

The story of Nineveh shows what can happen when a people turn from their wicked ways. I urge you to read the short book of Jonah in the Old Testament. It will increase your hope and faith to believe that it is not too late for America to repent and avoid the judgment of God.

Ten Factors of Decline

Great empires before us have been reduced to rubble by the same forces that prevail in our country today. In his powerful study, *When Nations Die*, Jim Nelson Black identifies ten factors that have appeared in great civilizations of the past and led to their decline and fall. In some cultures, Black observes, as few as three or four of the symptoms of social, cultural, and moral decline would be enough to bring a society to the point of imminent collapse. The list includes:

1. Increase in lawlessness
2. Loss of economic discipline
3. Rising bureaucracy
4. Decline in education
5. Weakening of cultural foundations
6. Loss of respect for traditions
7. Increase in materialism
8. The rise in immorality
9. Decay of religious belief
10. Devaluing of human life

Great empires before us have been REDUCED TO RUBBLE by the same forces that prevail IN OUR COUNTRY TODAY.

Aiding the breakdown of decadent cultures was a philosophy of "change for the sake of change." Dissatisfied with traditional authority, the cultural elites turned their backs on values and traditions as old as the nation itself. Tragically, according to Dr. Black, the United States is the first nation in history where all ten symptoms are present in one society at one time.[2]

In his assessment of the risks to any society that tries to live without God, Chuck Colson writes: "In a society that begins free-floating discussion, certainty evaporates. After a while, nobody is sure of anything. It introduces relativity, so to speak, in human affairs and also eternal affairs. You cannot be sure—there is no such thing as the truth—everything is equivocated—everything is subject to contradiction."[3]

A Greek Tragedy

Some of the greatest empires in history collapsed just as Black described. A good question for us to ask is: What eroded the splendor of Greece?

One historian observes: "In philosophy, in warfare, in the early sciences, in poetry, in grace of manners, in rhetoric, the Greeks excelled all civilizations that preceded it. No other race has ever produced, within a brief period, so many brilliant individuals as did the Greek people at the height of their glory."[4] Aristotle, Socrates, Plato, recognized the world over as sources of wisdom, helped ancient Greece become one of the highest civilizations ever to exist. The early Greeks held to a strict code of purity. Homosexuality was a capital offense. Greek arts and literature, the centerpiece of their society, extolled the virtuous man. Loyalty to the state and neighbors was among the highest callings. Self-sacrifice and examination were the norm. Two ancient maxims were inscribed on the walls of the temple at Delphi: "Know Thyself" and "Nothing in Excess."

The Greeks were noted philosophers and thinkers, yet their failure to come to an understanding of God subverted their success. A decline in virtue and morality swept the culture like wildfire. Absolute truth no longer existed. Greek society began to falter and drift. Despite their knowledge of democracy, a respect for the republican institutions of government, and their complex understanding of the principles of constitutional government, no stable political institutions were ever created in Greek society. Only one city-state ever organized a constitution.

Materialism, sexual immorality, and self-absorption took over Grecian hearts. Homosexuality was glorified. The stage and arts, once the hallmark of the noble Greek character, became lewd and violent. Lacking focus and a consensus of values, the once-great culture became gridlocked in a succession of civil wars. Years later, Greece succumbed to the Roman army. Ultimately, however, Greece was not destroyed by Rome, but by its own moral collapse.

The Collapse of Rome

According to the Greek statesman Polybius, at the time that Rome defeated ancient Carthage, the typical Roman citizen was virtually incorruptible. Polybius says, "Where in other states, a man is rarely found whose hands are pure from public robbery, so among the

Romans, it is no less rare to discover one that is tainted with this crime."[5] The Romans passionately sought great feats of engineering. They were tireless political administrators and organizers of military success. According to Russell Kirk, they were men of law and strong social institutions who gave the world *Pax Romana*, the Roman Peace. Observers said, "All roads lead to Rome."

The strength of Rome lay in her political structures and her strong families. Both were governed by the concept of the "High Old Roman Virtue." Romans believed strongly in being earnest, tenacious, well-disciplined, frugal, and self-sacrificing. Duty, honesty, and honor all complimented the virtue Cicero described as the foundation of all others—piety.

> **The Roman Empire slowly declined as WEALTH, POWER, AND PASSION took first place in the Roman heart.**

"A man was pious," writes Russell Kirk, "who gave the gods their due through worship and sacrifice, who honored his father and mother, and indeed all his ancestors, who stood by his friends, who was ready to die if need be for his country. A pious man submitted himself to things sacred, and believed unflinchingly that it was better to perish than to fail in his sacred duties...A society that is held together by such a cementing belief would offer strong resistance to forces of disintegration."[6]

During the rise of the Roman Empire, Polybius feared that Rome's success would destroy the Roman character. He predicted that arrogance and luxury would infect the Roman people, and then, "being inflamed with rage, and following only the dictates of their passions, they will no longer submit to any control,"[7] the society would destroy itself.

The historian's fears became reality. The nation slowly declined as wealth, power, and passion took first place in the Roman heart. Once again, society became preoccupied with sensuality. Oppressive taxes, combined with moral decadence involving adultery and homosexuality, destroyed Roman families by the thousands.

Roman thinker Sallust observed, "Young men were so depraved by luxury and avarice that no father had a son who could either preserve his own patrimony or keep his hands off other men's."[8] As the bottom fell out of the social order, Roman citizens lost interest in piety and dignity and focused on day-to-day survival and instant gratification.

Consequently, the Romans lost their respect for human life. Bloody spectacles were held daily in the coliseums and amphitheaters. Citizens worshipped the gladiators who fought in these arenas. Originally punishable by death, abortion became common, even encouraged. Violence was epidemic. Gang violence exploded, washing away the last vestiges of order. Soon after, ancient Rome collapsed.

Modern Day Judgment

In my book *The Coming Revival*, I reported on the observations of some in England who believe that America is undergoing a devastating spiritual disintegration at this hour. They connect America's moral decline with similar circumstances that have happened in their own country in recent times. Not long ago, Great Britain was the greatest empire on the face of the earth. England's colonies spanned the globe, and British wealth exceeded any empire in history.

Researcher George Barna says that observers "recall when England was a nation in which the Church was the central institution in society. Moral values, social behavior, cultural activities, family development, lifestyles, and even political decision-making all revolved around the nation's religious perspective and spiritual sensitivity. Ingrained in the nation's thinking was the belief that the highest goal in life is to worship and serve God."[9] England was once the largest missionary-sending nation on earth.

Then secularism steamrolled in and largely destroyed the traditional values upon which the nation had built its greatness. Materialism and modernism replaced a desire for spiritualism, especially Christianity. God no longer played a major role in any of the political, cultural, or societal concerns of the day. Relegated to a Sunday visit in church every now and then, God simply withdrew His blessing from England.

Today, England has been reduced to the status of one small nation on a cold, wet island in the North Sea. The worldwide empire is dead. The grandeur has faded; the power is gone. Though not yet destroyed, England's lampstand has been removed.[10]

Consider also what we have watched unfold in Russia. That nation had a tradition built on more than a thousand years of Christianity. This culture produced rich art, literature, music, and poetry, and had vast resources of oil and precious metals. Then the country was taken over by brutal communists who tried to wipe every mention of God from the Russian culture. The great and wonderful people of Russia were the victims of a cruel system of tyrannical leaders who rejected the truth of what Jesus taught, and led the nation astray. After 72 years of atheistic communism, Russia is today a devastated country, a pathetic basket case—morally, spiritually, economically, and politically.

North and South Korea

In the early 1960s, South Korea was little more than an oxcart economy. Starvation was a serious problem and claimed the lives of thousands. There was a constant threat of invasion from North Korea. At the end of the Korean War, South Korea was a devastated nation. Because of their plight, people prayed, fasted, and cried out to God for help.

Today, South Korea has become a model of Christian success. In less than 30 years, that desperate country became one of the most vital, dynamic, spiritual countries in the world. The followers of Christ grew from less than one million in the 1950s to 11 million in the 1990s. The people of South Korea, who chose Christ, are reaping the reward of a job well done.

North Korea is a contrasting story. Although God blessed North Korea with a great revival at the turn of the 20th century, a self-imposed dictator declared himself "god." The God of the Bible was denied in all circles of society. The nation died spiritually. Consequently, the nation is also dying economically as hundreds of thousands of people are starving from lack of basic foods. What a contrast to South Korea which turned back to God!

The Judgment of America

As we have seen in this section, when a society turns away from God, the inevitable result is chaos and confusion. Society unravels. Those who champion liberating modern society from all forms of authority weaken the foundation of society. They invoke independence and individualism as a means of denying all moral authority and dependence upon God.

Compassion and tolerance, the buzzwords of moral compromise, are merely attempts to disguise society's contempt for divine authority. "Tolerance," as D. James Kennedy said, is the last trait of a totally corrupt society.

> **As America falls victim to ancient vices, we are becoming A NATION ADRIFT.**

Do not be misled. We pay a high price for deceit and sin. Ask the wife who has found out that her husband is seeing another woman. Consider the child who is put in a compromising sexual position by a relative and then threatened if he or she ever tells. Or the adults who continue to suffer from the trauma of a parent's alcoholism.

As America falls victim to ancient vices, we are becoming a nation adrift, doing what is right in our own eyes and ignoring God. Without God's standards, fear and pain occupy the places where the peace of God once reigned. In place of reliable relationships established by God's plan of order, we are left to fend for ourselves and invent new rules as we go.

Because of cultural decay, the United States is being redefined by her sins. The signs of ruin are all around us, and we have reached the point where we must respond passionately to Paul's admonitions to the Romans:

> The wrath of God is being revealed from heaven against all the godlessness and wickedness of men who suppress the truth by their wickedness, since what may be known about God is plain to

> them, because God has made it plain to them. For since the creation of the world God's invisible qualities—his eternal power and divine nature—have been clearly seen, being understood from what has been made, so that men are without excuse.
>
> For although they knew God, they neither glorified him as God nor gave thanks to him, but their thinking became futile and their foolish hearts were darkened. Although they claimed to be wise, they became fools and exchanged the glory of the immortal God for images made to look like mortal man and birds and animals and reptiles.
>
> Therefore, God gave them over in the sinful desires of their hearts to sexual impurity for the degrading of their bodies with one another. They exchanged the truth of God for a lie, and worshiped and served created things rather than the Creator—who is forever praised. Amen.
>
> Because of this, God gave them over to shameful lusts. Even their women exchanged natural relations for unnatural ones. In the same way the men also abandoned natural relations with women and were inflamed with lust for one another. Men committed indecent acts with other men, and received in themselves the due penalty for their perversion.
>
> Furthermore, since they did not think it worthwhile to retain the knowledge of God, he gave them over to a depraved mind, to do what ought not be done. They have become filled with every kind of wickedness, evil, greed, and depravity. They are full of envy, murder, strife, deceit and malice. They are gossips, slanderers, God-haters, insolent, arrogant and boastful; they invent ways of doing evil; they disobey their parents, they are senseless, faithless, heartless, ruthless. Although they know God's righteous decree that those who do such things deserve death, they not only continue to do these very things but also approve of those who practice them (Romans 1:18–32).

Nineteenth-century British historian Thomas Macaulay predicted that the seeds of our demise would come not from outside barbarians, but from excessive devotion to liberty—personal freedom without strong moral boundaries. Just such a moment may have finally arrived. Practically every social institution is in chaos; moral relativism and situational ethics pervade every arena of public life. And any attempt to invoke the authority of Scripture or the lessons of history elicits a cry of, "Don't try to push your view of right and wrong on me; I have my own morality!" We have reached the point of moral deterioration about which the prophets of Israel proclaimed, "Woe to those who call evil good, and good evil; who substitute darkness for light and light for darkness; who substitute bitter for sweet and sweet for bitter! Woe to those who are wise in their own eyes and clever in their own sight! Woe to those who are heroes in drinking wine and valiant men in mixing strong drink, who justify the wicked for a bribe, and take away the rights of the ones who are in the right!" (Isaiah 5:20–23).

The judgment for ungodliness is sure: "Therefore, as a tongue of fire consumes stubble and dry grass collapses into the flame, so their root will become like rot and their blossom blow away as dust; for they have rejected the law of the Lord of hosts and despised the word of the Holy One of Israel. On this account the anger of the Lord has burned against His people, and He has stretched out His hand against them and struck them down. And the mountains quaked, and their corpses lay like refuse in the middle of the streets. For all this His anger is not spent, but His hand is still stretched out" (Isaiah 5:34–25).

The lessons of history cry out to modern America: REPENT or follow us to the grave!

We cannot afford to ignore God's impending judgment. Our Christian roots are rotting away. Hear the deep concern expressed by a group of our spiritual leaders:

> There is not a believer in this nation with any vibrancy in their discernment or sensitivity in their spirit who does not understand that we are in a time of crisis in our land.[11]
>
> *Jack Hayford*
> *Church on the Way*

> You smell the decay, you smell the rotting flesh of Western civilization today, much like you would have smelled the

decay in fourth and fifth century Rome.[12]

Chuck Colson
Prison Fellowship

[People believe that] there is no God that is going to sit in judgment upon the actions of man. This is why we see violence, dishonesty, cheating, stealing, rape, and every kind of immorality imaginable. It is astounding to me that people cannot see that, having forgotten God, we are indeed in the process of destroying ourselves.[13]

Dr. D. James Kennedy
Coral Ridge Ministries

Unless there is a revival, this nation is going to get worse and worse and worse.[14]

Dr. Charles Stanley
In Touch Ministries

America is history. It's over unless there is a broad, sweeping revival of righteousness.[15]

Dr. John Hagee
John Hagee Ministries

The lessons of history cry out to modern America: repent or follow us to the grave! The warning is real. The time is now. Will America live or die? As we know from 2 Chronicles 7:14,15, God is watching and listening to see how we will respond to His urgent plea.

But who can lead us to repentance and a righteous culture? There is only one group of people who have the moral arsenal to combat the forces of evil—the people of God. In our next section, we will discover God's view of our actions and what we can do about them.

PART III

An Appeal to the Church

As the long night of paganism descends on Western nations, we as believers are afforded an even greater opportunity to share the faith that burns within us. Therefore, we must not yield to discouragement, even when everything we cherish appears to be eroding. God is in control, and He can bring triumph out of tragedy.

—Dr. James C. Dobson, founder and president of Focus on the Family

CHAPTER 16

The Crisis in the Church

In the New Testament, followers of Christ are described as the "bride of Christ." What a beautiful picture! Christ, our Bridegroom, is right now preparing a place for us to live with Him for eternity (John 14:1–4). One day soon, He will return to take us to that heavenly home. When we arrive, we will be escorted to a gala banquet in honor of Christ and His bride called the marriage supper of the Lamb. This is how John describes that moment in the book of Revelation:

> Then I heard again what sounded like the shouting of a huge crowd, or like the waves of a hundred oceans crashing on the shore, or like the mighty rolling of great thunder, "Praise the Lord. For the Lord our God, the Almighty, reigns. Let us be glad and rejoice and honor him; for the time has come for the wedding banquet of the Lamb, and his bride has prepared herself. She is permitted to wear the cleanest and whitest and finest of linens." (Fine linen represents the good deeds done by the people of God.)
>
> And the angel dictated this sentence to me: "Blessed are those who are invited to the wedding feast of the Lamb." And he added, "God himself has stated this" (Revelation 19:6–9, TLB).

This glimpse of the future is more than a colorful analogy of a bride and bridegroom; it is a description of our intimate relationship with our Lord. From the foundation of the world, God planned to present a faithful body of believers to Him at the marriage supper of the Lamb. Our part as the Church of Jesus Christ is to be a holy and blameless bride for God's Son. We could not find a better way to honor our Lord's love for us and express our joy to be in His presence!

Scripture tells us that one day, the bride will be revealed before the entire universe. Multitudes of angels and archangels will give glory to God as the bride is by her Bridegroom's side, dressed in her pure linens.

But let me offer, for contrast, a more somber illustration. A young man is standing before the altar with all the joy and anticipation of a groom. He is dressed to perfection for his wedding day, from his perfectly tailored tuxedo to the freshness of the boutonniere on his lapel. As the organ swells with rich chords, the massive doors of the sanctuary swing open.

In stumbles a tattered bride. Her dress is torn and wrinkled, her face and hands caked with dirt. Her hair is a mess; she smells of stale tobacco and alcohol. She looks as if she has spent the night in the gutter.

What a shameful sight for a bride-to-be! Apparently she cares so little for her bridegroom and his promises to her that she has not taken the time to clean herself up for the wedding. The young man is shaken and heartbroken by what he sees. He is justifiably ashamed of his bride.

Could this vignette describe the state of the Church in America today? If we are honest, we have to admit that this analogy is tragically true. As followers of Christ, we have been given the honor to be called the bride of Christ. Yet we often play in the filth of sin and the mire of worldly desires and fail to clean ourselves up to get ready for the marriage supper.

What we are really doing is offering the Bridegroom a half-hearted commitment of fidelity while spending most of our time chasing worldly pleasures or financial gain. Many of us live with unconfessed sin and are ashamed to speak of our Bridegroom in public or to let others know of our blessed hope in Christ. Some of us live in laziness, apathy, and selfishness, yet expect our Lord to receive us warmly and lovingly on that wedding day.

What has happened to the Church? The gospel of Jesus Christ has not lost its power to change lives or to redeem a failing culture. Yet this nation is in chaos and the body of Christ seems impotent to restore godliness. How can this be? Have believers lost their ability to resist the devil's schemes or to bind him while tearing down his evil strongholds? Have we fallen under the influence of evil in the world? For all appearances, our mission as the "shining city on a hill" has dimmed and almost faded.

The questions that arise, then, are: What problems does the Church face in its mission to our country and the world? Why are we so caught up in these issues? How can we become like that spotless bride before the marriage supper of the Lamb? In Part III of this book, we will address these issues.

The World's Seasoning

The Church has not been immune to the problems afflicting our culture. During the last fifty years, the Church has slipped from its former high moral ground. Although there are evidences of revival fires in a few locations, the Church in general is in decline and in desperate need of renewal. While we are struggling with our fast-changing and often adversarial culture, the faith our fathers passed down to us grows frail—and has been largely forgotten.

In the same passage where Jesus speaks of believers being the shining city on a hill, He also describes the Church as salt. "You are the world's seasoning," He teaches, "to make it tolerable. If you lose your flavor, what will happen to the world?" (Matthew 5:13, TLB). The obvious answer is that the world will decay without a generous portion of Christian preservative influence.

Francis Schaeffer expressed a similar concern almost twenty years ago, "Our culture, society, government, and law are in the condition they are in, not because of a conspiracy, but because the Church has forsaken its duty to be the salt of the culture."[1] Because of our laxity, the decay has intensified, yet the Church still has not understood its purpose.

The Church's Responsibility

Who is responsible for our culture's assault on faith? Is it the ACLU? The courts? The schools? Obviously, all of these organizations must bear part of the blame. But I believe the cause is far more disheartening. We have fallen to new moral lows in America because of the absence of a reasonable, responsible, and clearly presented defense of our faith by the body of Christ. In short, you and I have failed to know what we believe, why we believe it, what our rights are under the law, and how to stand our ground against the enemies of Jesus Christ and His Church.

> **It is necessary for us to EXAMINE OURSELVES FIRST before we go on to impact our society.**

When we begin to assess some of the conditions in modern society that have led to the current crises in our social and cultural institutions, then, we must begin with the Church. Peter writes, "The time has come for judgment to begin at the house of God" (1 Peter 4:17).

For that reason, what follows is hard for me to write. Not because stepping up to take the blame is so difficult, but because those of us who make up the body of Christ are bound together in love. The Scripture reminds us that the world will know us by the love we express for one another (John 13:35). Paul urged believers to speak the truth in love (Ephesians 4:15). Real love means sharing honestly and openly. It demands accountability. Tough love means that we hold one another to a higher standard of behavior. Therefore, it is necessary for us to examine ourselves first before we go on to impact our society.

I believe the reason our culture is in an advanced state of decay is largely because the followers of Christ have retreated from their responsibilities to society. There are two reasons why we need to intensify our influence. First, whether secular society recognizes it or not, the Christian Church exerts a major influence on national culture. Whenever the church has been strong and passionate in its allegiance to Christ, the nation has flourished

Second, Christ's return could happen at any moment. Paul urges, "Another reason for right living is this you know how late it is; time is running out. Wake up, for the coming of the Lord is nearer now than when we first believed. The night is far gone, the day of [Christ's] return will soon be here. So quit the evil deeds of darkness and put on the armor of right living, as we who live in the daylight should!" (Romans 13:11–13, TLB). Even today, the Bridegroom may be putting the finishing touches on the home He has prepared for His bride. But by the time the American Church wakes up, it may be too late to ready ourselves to meet Him in white linens.

The Church's Call

Many times now, we have heard about God's purpose for America: to help fulfill the Great Commission. That call has implications beyond obeying the command of our Master to help fulfill His program for the ages. God also warns of the consequences to our own future if we disobey His call to warn others about impending judgment for wickedness.

The Old Testament defines this responsibility as serving as a watchman for God. God commanded Ezekiel to warn his countrymen of the dangers of their rebellion against God:

> "Son of man, I have made you a watchman for the house of Israel; so hear the word I speak and give them warning from me. When I say to the wicked, 'O wicked man, you will surely die,' and you do not speak out to dissuade him from his ways, that wicked man will die for his sin, and I will hold you accountable for his blood. But if you do warn the wicked man to turn from his ways and he does not do so, he will die for his sin, but you will be saved yourself" (Ezekiel 33:7–9).

In the New Testament, Paul considered spreading Christ's message and living a life of righteousness as a top priority for the Christian life. He felt so strongly about this issue that he said, "Let me say plainly that no man's blood can be laid at my door, for I didn't shrink from declaring all God's message to you" (Acts 20:26,27).

Do we have blood on our hands? Have we declared all God's message, or have we shirked our duty and allowed our culture to go on its way without warning? Although some Christians have been faithful to follow our Lord in this responsibility, most have become so wrapped up in the unrighteous lifestyles of our time that they cannot warn others. If we hope to avoid the wrath of God, individually or collectively, we must begin now with a thorough cleansing of the house of God. Before we can hope to reclaim America for Christ, we must get our own house in order.

To begin this process, let us look at three problem areas for the Church. They are the crisis in holiness, the lure of materialism, and the danger of lukewarmness.

The Crisis in Holiness

In a message at the 1996 national fasting and prayer gathering in St. Louis, Nancy Leigh DeMoss asked an important question: "When are we as Christians going to realize that the world is not impressed with a religious version of itself?"[2] The question points out a tragic trend within the Christian Church—our accommodation of the world's attitudes, beliefs, and actions in our effort to gain the world's acceptance.

This accommodation deeply affects those around us. Friedrich Nietzsche, the notorious anti-Christian philosopher who proclaimed, "God is dead, and we have killed him!"[3] spent his adult life fighting the authority of Jesus Christ. He cited many reasons for his bitterness toward the Church, but he once admitted he might be more likely to believe in Jesus as Redeemer if Christians around him looked more redeemed.

In survey after survey, researchers find that the lifestyles of born-again Christians are virtually indistinguishable from those of nonbelievers. The divorce rate among Christians is identical to that of nonbelievers. Christian teens are almost as sexually active as non-Christian teens. Pornography, materialism, gluttony, lust, covetousness, and even disbelief are commonplace in many of our churches. Faith in America, researcher Eric Johnson explains, can be defined as "extremely superficial and convenient rather than obedient and committed." Ours is a "schizophrenic spirituality," and the contemporary Church has almost lost its ability to discern between the secular and spiritual.[4]

Too often our churches act like therapy groups, filled with individuals seeking remedies for their "felt needs." One group of parishioners told their minister, "Make us cry, or make us laugh, but please don't make us change." The Promise Keepers movement is one of the most dynamic and most visible ministries of our day. I believe Promise Keepers has done a lot to help restore America's families, churches, and communities. But a survey conducted during a Promise Keepers rally showed that almost 50 percent of the men at that event struggled with sins of the flesh such as pornography and adultery. That is a frightening statistic.

How can God accomplish His purposes in such unrepentant hearts? Do we imagine that Christ could take delight in an attitude of self-satisfaction and complacency? It is impossible to walk in the Spirit to accomplish supernatural things in the power of the Holy Spirit when we live in sin. We cannot have it both ways.

The lifestyles of born-again Christians are VIRTUALLY INDISTINGUISHABLE from those of nonbelievers.

Righteous living demands personal holiness. God commands us, "I am the Lord your God. You shall therefore consecrate yourselves, and you shall be holy; for I am holy" (Leviticus 11:44). Jesus challenged believers to "be perfect [complete], just as your Father in heaven is perfect" (Matthew 5:48). He knew none of us could meet this high standard of righteousness on our own, so He met the criteria on our behalf that we might become perfect, complete in the righteousness of God through Christ (2 Corinthians 5:21).

A Priority of Holiness

The idea of holiness has four common applications in Scripture.

First, holiness means to be "set apart." In the Old Testament, the implements of sacrifice and worship were set aside as holy objects for God. In the same way, those who served in the temple were reckoned to be holy. Holiness in this use can also mean to be spiritually pure.

Second, holiness is the righteousness we ascribe to saints or other godly people. Although still sinners, their commitment and faithfulness to God's standards and spiritual walk in the power of the Holy Spirit make their lives examples to others.

Third, holiness also applies to aspects of God that may be awesome and inspiring. The handiwork of God in nature and in creation is considered holy. His perfect nature and majesty are beyond our comprehension.

Fourth, holiness refers to being filled with superhuman power and authority. The works of God are holy, righteous, and pure. They are supernatural—that is, beyond nature. Those who call upon the name of God strive for personal holiness, as people who have been set apart for Christ.

When we "seek first the kingdom of God and His righteousness," as Jesus commands in the Sermon on the Mount, we are actually committing ourselves to holiness. But when we live for ourselves and our own sinful indulgences, we show ourselves to be unholy and unfit to pursue the will of God. When we fail to live by God's standards of righteousness, we not only reap the consequences in our lives, but we bring reproach upon the household of faith.

If there was ever a time when the world needed a deeper, more winsome portrait of what the Christian life is like, that time is now. We can take heart from those who went before us and stood up against the evil in their own culture:

- The Pilgrims and Puritans who sacrificed their homelands and even endangered their lives to follow God's standards
- Our Founding Fathers who established our government on

the tenets of faith—against overwhelming odds

- The abolitionists who stood up to the status quo to speak out for freedom and righteousness
- The inventors who were quick to ascribe credit for their accomplishments to God

Each group of people affected their society in profound ways because of their faith and commitment to righteousness. Their priority was God's kingdom, and they were not afraid to proclaim their allegiance.

Holiness can never be hidden. It naturally shines like that city on a hill. It is our statement to the world that God is with us and works in us.

The Lure of Materialism

Although we could address many anti-Christian values in our culture which the Church has embraced, materialism is one of the most insidious. For example, when a Christian commits sexual immorality, the sin is well-defined and obvious to the sinner. But materialism has subtly crept into the Church as part of the dogma and distorted the pure message of the gospel. Many times we do not even recognize its presence.

> **MATERIALISM has subtly crept into the Church as part of the dogma and DISTORTED the pure message of the gospel.**

Jim Bakker, founder of the PTL Television Network and Heritage USA Theme Park, knows as well as anyone that materialism is a dead-end street. His meteoric rise to fame as a television evangelist is matched only by the disgrace he endured when his ministry collapsed in scandal. Bakker lost everything, but today he understands in a new way the dangers represented by material success.

In his heyday, Bakker's ministry focused on financial and material success. In the end, however, his theology, like everything else in his world, utterly collapsed. He lost his wife, his career, his home, and his freedom. After seven long years, he emerged from prison a changed man, with a lesson to share with the church about the dangers of materialism. He described what he learned during his ordeal:

> During my time at FMC Rochester [federal penitentiary], I observed something that seemed to me had gotten nearly every inmate in trouble... Of the 60 percent of inmates who are in prison because of drug-related crimes, most are not there because of an addiction to drugs; they are there because of an addiction to the drug of money.
>
> About the time of my parole hearing, I completed my study of the words of Jesus in the New Testament. To my surprise, after months of studying Jesus, I concluded that He did not have one good thing to say about money. Most of Jesus' statements about riches, wealth, and material gain were in a negative context...
>
> For years I had embraced and espoused a gospel that some skeptics had branded as a "prosperity gospel." I didn't mind the label; on the contrary, I was proud of it. "You're absolutely right!" I'd say to the critics and friends alike. "I preach it and I live it! I believe in a God who wants to bless His people..."
>
> I even got to the point where I was teaching people at PTL, "Don't pray, 'God, Your will be done,' when you are praying for health or wealth. You already know it is God's will for you to have those things... Instead of praying 'Thy will be done' when you want a new car, just claim it. Pray specifically and tell God what kind you want. Be sure to specify what options and what color you want too."
>
> Such arrogance! Such foolishness! Such sin![5]

Jim Bakker now confesses that he helped "propagate an impostor" through PTL. Bakker and others with similar teachings have damaged the cause of Christ, but none of us should point fingers of blame. Each of us has been an accessory. We are consumed with satisfying ourselves, building our own careers, fattening our bank accounts and financial portfolios, driving the latest model car, and buying bigger houses. As each luxury is introduced, it soon becomes a "necessity." Meanwhile, we have lost our compassion for the poor and needy. Our personal debt is so overwhelming that we give less and less to God's causes. In fact, the world cannot distinguish our spending habits from theirs. Why do we need God, they wonder, when God's people live the same selfish lifestyles that we do?

The Dangers of Lukewarmness

The lack of holiness and righteous living infiltrates every part of the life of the Church. They affect how the Church operates in the world.

I believe the most influential people in any community are God's representatives, the pastors. They are the most visible example of God in our midst. In recent years, a few of America's best-known church leaders have fallen into disgrace as scandals destroyed their credibility and ministries. The Church has been deeply hurt by this.

The vast majority of God's servants preach the truth of God's Word, stand up for righteousness, and hold themselves and their flocks to a higher moral standard. If they are true servants of God, faithful to His Word, surrendered to the Lordship of Christ, and filled with the Spirit, we should give them our faithful and complete cooperation, support, and prayer.

These faithful servants, however, are under intense pressure to compromise with sin and the popular culture which infests the lives and thinking of their congregations. I regularly speak to pastors all across America who tell me they are deeply troubled by the apathy in their congregations. The number one frustration is a lack of commitment to ministry by the members of their churches. Most Christians are too busy with family, jobs, businesses, education, or other pursuits to serve faithfully in the local church or give sacrificially. The majority of believers in this country have never shared the gospel with a nonbelieving friend. Few have ever experienced the joy of leading another person to Christ.

Some of our Bible study groups would do better to disband, for all the good they are doing. At the same time, too many churches merely distract believers from the serious challenges facing the Church today. If all our churches do is to make people feel good about themselves or give them an emotional boost over their personal problems, they have failed our Lord and His Great Commission. And if all our pastors do is to pacify the faithful with happy homilies, they become little more than spiritual baby-sitters, shepherding their holy huddles, and waiting for the rapture.

In Revelation, our Lord gives a warning to lukewarm churches:

> I know you well—you are neither hot nor cold; I wish you were the one or the other! But since you are merely lukewarm, I will spit you out of my mouth! You say, "I am rich, with everything I want; I don't need a thing!" And you don't realize that spiritually you are wretched and miserable and poor and blind and naked ...I continually discipline and punish everyone I love; so I must punish you, unless you turn from your indifference and become enthusiastic about the things of God" (Revelation 3:15–19, TLB).

A maxim often heard at Promise Keepers rallies is, "God loves us where we are, but He loves us too much to leave us there." This applies to the Church as well as individual believers. God loves this nation. He cannot allow America to go on conducting immoral business as usual.

During a television interview on the "700 Club" shortly before he died, Francis Schaeffer stated that secular society cannot fix itself. If there is any hope for restoration and renewal in our land, the followers of Christ must be willing to pay the price for confronting a society which holds the Church in disdain. Pride must be put aside as our survival as a nation depends on the willingness of Christians to stand their ground and speak the truth in a credible way.

When asked if he were optimistic about America's chances, Schaeffer always gave a qualified answer. Of all the Western nations in decline, he said, America has the best chance of turning things around. Schaeffer believed that our chances of renewal depended entirely on whether or not the Church was willing to do its job. "If you ask me if we are going to [turn this country around], I say it depends on if the Christians are willing to pay the price."[6]

To pay the price, we must examine ourselves, look beyond the surface, and find the motives that have taken us off course. In the next chapter, we will uncover some of the reasons why the American Church has become bound up in unrighteous living, materialism, and lukewarmness.

CHAPTER 17

A Crisis of Credibility

Becky grew up in a home where her parents sporadically attended church. They rarely attend any services today. Twenty years ago, her brother became a Hindu and embraced Eastern religious beliefs such as reincarnation and karma. Then about ten years ago, Becky was introduced to Jesus Christ and received Him as her Savior and Lord. That decision changed her life, and today she and her husband are living a vibrant Christian life.

In a recent conversation with her father, she mentioned that her brother was not a Christian. "He's *not?*" her father exclaimed, flabbergasted because he had always assumed that everyone born in America was a Christian even though his son is very open about his religious faith.

Becky's father is not alone in his assumptions. In a report on the condition of America's soul in his book, *The Index of Leading Spiritual Indicators*, pollster George Barna concludes, "While traditional—some would say biblical—Christianity is certainly on the decline, most Americans continue to think of themselves as Christian individuals residing in a Christian nation."[1] But considering the degraded condition of society today, that may be the most dangerous assumption we could make. We have retained just enough Christianity to prevent us from seeing how spiritually bankrupt we really are.

What are the underlying causes that have cost us our holiness and propelled us into materialism and lukewarmness? Although not a conclusive list, we would like to examine seven reasons why the American Church and the majority of believers have lost their vibrant faith.

1. We are not really committed to Christ personally.

A few years ago, a major polling organization reported that there were 60 million born-again Christians in America. But a writer for the *Wall Street Journal* took issue with the findings by asking these questions:

> If this is true, why is America ravaged by crime, violence and an epidemic of just about every problem known to man? Are not people of faith supposed to make a difference in society? If it is true that so many Americans are believers in Jesus Christ, then why are we in this pitiful condition? Where is the godly influence of all those people on our morally bankrupt society? Where is their understanding of God's holiness and His command that we be holy too? Has our "salt" lost its effectiveness? Has our "light" gone out in this dark world?

The answer lies partly in the fact that many who call themselves Christians are really not biblical Christians at all. Although they may be religious people who attend church regularly, they have never experienced the new birth and a personal relationship with Jesus Christ. Also, many so-called Christians are living worldly (carnal) lives. Appetites and desires of human nature influence, if not control, their behavior. They have no conception of what holiness means.

The Bible says that our evidence of faith is vital. John writes:

> How can we be sure that we belong to [Christ]? By looking within ourselves: are we really trying to do what He wants us to do? Someone may say, 'I am a Christian; I am on my way to heaven; I belong to Christ.' But if he does not do what Christ tells him to, he is a liar. Those who do what Christ tells them to will learn to love God more and more. That is the way to know whether or

> not you are a Christian. Anyone who says he is a Christian should live as Christ did (1 John 2:3–6, TLB).

Many who claim to be Christians give no evidence of the presence of Christ in their lives. Their lives are not different from those of the unbelieving masses, and the hypocrisy and compromise they exhibit as professing Christians leave a bad taste in the mouth of society. They are just spiritually minded pagans, struggling to survive in a world of sin. This waters down the influence of the Church on our society.

2. We do not respect God.

In my recent book, *The Coming Revival*, I wrote about the condition of the Church in America and the prospects for spiritual awakening. One particular issue I touched on is my concern that so many Christians seem to have lost their fear or respect of God, especially His holiness. I am sure you have heard people call God the "man upstairs," a "buddy," or the great "cosmic force."

These statements show that many people do not understand the nature of our awesome God or His love, grace, wisdom, power, and sovereignty. Some consider God as a genial "grandfather" who would never judge anyone. His job is to pull us out of the messes we get into and stroke us by treating our sins as "mistakes." They trivialize God's justice and abhorrence of sin.

> **Many who claim to be Christians give NO EVIDENCE of the presence of Christ in their lives.**

Other Christians have a view of God as "out there somewhere." They do not realize that God is personable, active, and available to them and that the Bible teaches we can have an intimate relationship with God. These church attenders have only a limited awareness of the riches of knowing our heavenly Father and appropriating His righteousness through Jesus Christ. These people never experience God's presence in their day-to-day events or the joy of seeing His plan unfold in their lives.

Because they do not have an intimate relationship with God, they do not experience the power of His Holy Spirit to teach them God's Word, resist temptation, or live consistent, godly lives. They never witness or become spiritual leaders in their homes or communities.

3. We have changed or ignored biblical truth.

One of our Campus Crusade for Christ staff members relayed his experience while speaking at one of the more than 800 churches here in the greater Orlando area. At the end of his remarks, he went through our tract, *The Four Spiritual Laws*. Afterwards, he simply asked how many in the congregation would like to receive Christ for the first time. Twenty-one people raised their hands. Next he asked how many were trying to live the supernatural life in their own human efforts but would like to be filled with the Holy Spirit. Twenty-six people raised their hands. At the conclusion of the service, sixteen people settled the issue of assurance of salvation. Praise the Lord for this response on the part of those who are sincerely hungry for God. But I ask you: *What is wrong with this picture?* So many Christians in this congregation had no foundation in the basic, practical principles of the New Testament.

Many of our congregations are so lacking in the knowledge of God's Word that they are susceptible to all kinds of errors. Some have strayed so far from the truth that they are not really New Testament believers in their beliefs and practices. As George Barna warns, "Much of American Christianity is nominal in nature. Americans like to have a term to summarize their religiosity, and 'Christian' remains the label of choice, even if their commitment to biblical Christianity is waning."[2]

Os Guinness believes that the level of sincere faith in America is so small that many Christians, for all intents and purposes, are "practical atheists." They claim to believe in Jesus Christ, but He is not a factor in their lives. They use religious language and they still go through the motions, but they have discarded many of the most fundamental tenets of Christianity. Guinness argues, "There are a number of great biblical categories which are negative and vital—

worldliness, sin, judgment, heresy—they have almost all corroded now."[3] Much of this results from a lack of understanding what the Bible says or from misrepresenting God's message.

One of the most serious threats to the authority of believing faith is the new blend of Christianity and humanism that is flooding into many of our churches. This social gospel focuses on man's power, man's authority, man's inner goodness. It bears little resemblance to true biblical Christianity.

Another factor comes from the fact that the pure gospel is not being preached from thousands of pulpits. These pastors do not have an accurate understanding of the depths of God's Word and the dangers of distorting even one word of it. Instead, too many pastors rely on their own intellect instead of simply preaching the infallible, authoritative Word of God. As a result, they propagate a watered-down faith that offers little consolation and few meaningful answers. They tread lightly past the fundamentals, handing out a sugar-coated version of faith to men and women whose souls are in eternal jeopardy. Such preachers are so afraid of appearing dogmatic or legalistic that they compromise the life-saving power of God's Word and rely on entertainment and humor to engage their people. Entertainment and humor from the pulpit are encouraging at times, but will not prepare the Church to engage the secular culture, to clearly defend what they believe and to know why they believe it.

Charles Finney, the great evangelist of the Second Great Awakening, led a revival that touched every region of the nation and helped cleanse the hearts of millions of Americans on the eve of the Civil War. Under Finney's preaching, thousands came to genuine faith in Christ. Finney knew how to spread the gospel, but he also knew how not to spread the gospel. In a brief essay entitled "How to Preach So As to Convert Nobody," Finney offered the following prescription:

> Let your supreme motivation be popularity rather than salvation. Study to please your congregation and to make a reputation rather than to please God. Take up popular, passing, and sensational themes to draw the crowd, and avoid the essential doctrines

> of salvation. Denounce sin in the abstract, but pass lightly over sins that prevail in your congregation. Preach on the loveliness of virtue and the glory of heaven, but not on the sinfulness of sin. Reprove the sins of the absent, but make those present pleased with themselves, so that they will enjoy the sermon and not go away with their feelings hurt. Make the impression on the worldly church members that God is too good to send anyone to hell, even if there is a hell. Preach the universal Fatherhood of God and brotherhood of man so as to show that no second birth is really needed.[4]

How tragic that his prescription, made as an ironic statement, is being taken at face value in many American churches today.

In addition, an entire genre of self-help, weak do-it-yourself books has flooded the Christian market. Emulating the therapy environment of the secular world, they take the focus off God's wisdom and power. These products appeal to those who think that the Word of God and the power of the Holy Spirit are insufficient to cope with the problems of our daily lives and that we need to rely on do-it-yourself psychology. Tragically, psychology may offer insights into human behavior, but it can never break the bondage of sin or provide the wisdom of God's Word.

Psychology can never break the BONDAGE OF SIN or provide the WISDOM of God's Word.

The spreading of weak or misapplied theology has wreaked havoc on what American Christians believe and know. According to one recent survey, 50 percent of the more than one hundred million who attend church on a typical Sunday do not have any assurance of salvation. Ninety-five percent of church-goers say they are not familiar with the person and ministry of the Holy Spirit. Less than two percent of believers in this country ever share their faith in Christ with others.[5] It seems there is no area of biblical truth that has not been neglected.

To give an example of how ideas have drifted away from biblical truth, we can look at what many Americans believe about sin. Sin, says Guinness, is an area where theology, influenced by modern science, has replaced biblical Christianity with what amounts to a counterfeit faith. "We see large parts of the American church for whom sin has been reduced from theology, to crime, to psychology, and it has become a form of low self-esteem. Imagine our Puritan ancestors believing that sin was the hole in the soul of self-esteem. Yet many modern Americans have one of the most trivial, sentimentalized views of sin that the church has seen in 2000 years."[6]

In their efforts not to offend anyone, many of our churches have ceased dealing with sin at all. A majority of Christians have discarded the doctrine of original sin in favor of their man-made faith in the basic goodness of man.

We cannot build a Church that can spread God's message throughout the world if our people do not know that message. We cannot disciple others to live Spirit-filled lives if we do not know how to let Christ's Spirit express Himself fully through our own lives. Our very mission as a nation depends on our commitment to biblical truth.

4. We have misrepresented the Christian life.

In the more than fifty years that I have walked with Christ, I have found that His yoke is easy and His burden light—as long as I walk in the Spirit and not in my flesh. When I daily confess my sins and appropriate by faith the fullness and power of the Holy Spirit, He gives me strength for the journey. I cannot live a victorious, fruitful life in my own strength. Victory is assured only as I abide in Him and His Word abides in me moment by moment (John 15:7).

But this victory does not mean that I do not experience difficult trials and testing. As long as we are on this earth, these ordeals will afflict us. How we handle them proves the Lord's presence in our lives and demonstrates our faith to those who do not believe.

Yet some Christians believe that when a person receives Christ and has enough faith, he will not experience trials and that hardships such as ill health or financial difficulties are a result of insufficient faith. Many preachers oversell the benefits of the Christian life without dealing with the necessary disciplines, the trials, and temptations. They come from the value our culture places upon owning earthly possessions and living the good life. They do not acknowledge the biblical facts about the testing the apostles experienced for their faith. Should we expect anything less?

A belief that Christians are entitled to the "good life" can result in demoralized church members. Expecting the Christian life to be a bed of roses can be very discouraging to a new Christian—and to more mature ones as well—when they are jostled by the storms of life. Billy Graham says:

> No life is without its own set of problems. When I decided to give my life to Christ as a young man, it was not because I believed He would take away all my pain. No, I trusted Him because He promised me eternal life, and I believed He would always be with me and give me the strength to cope with the difficulties of life.
>
> We all have to endure storms in our lives. When any preacher oversells either the material or spiritual benefits of the Christian life, I believe he is contributing to the work of the horseman [of the Apocalypse] who deceives. There is nothing on earth to compare with the new life in Jesus Christ, but it will not always be easy.[7]

Jesus calls us to follow Him regardless of the cost. He never promises that our path will always be smooth. Billy Graham offers a strong warning to those who may be tempted to distort the facts about the hardships of the Christian life:

> When we tell only the stories of victory, we tell only a part of the truth. When we recount only the answered prayers, we oversimplify. When we imply that the Christian faith involves no yoke and no burden, we tell less than the whole truth.[8]

5. We are not consistent in our walk with God.

Christians who are content to live soft, materialistic lives do not have the stamina to walk a consistent Christian life. They take shortcuts to spirituality, neglect the disciplines of their faith, and take the easy way out when temptation strikes. This is reflected in their weak commitment to their churches.

In a recent survey, Barna found that 87 percent of Americans—nearly nine out of ten—say that religious faith is either "important" or "very important" to them. Yet despite the high numbers, church attendance has fallen to the lowest levels in more than a decade. While more than two thirds of Americans claim to be Christians, only 37 percent attend services on a regular basis. Among those, only 31 percent of Baby Boomers (age 31–52) and 34 percent of Baby Busters (age 18–34) attend church in any given week. That is a drop of more than 15 percent since 1981.[9]

In their daily lives, many Christians have become experts at keeping their spiritual lives separate from their secular lives. Young believers go to school and put on their student hats; their parents go to work and don their worker's caps; then they go to church on Sunday and put on their Christian hats. It is dangerous and unscriptural to compartmentalize our lives. I am convinced this is one of the major reasons why America is on the verge of moral and spiritual collapse.

The message of God's Word and the premise of Campus Crusade for Christ is that all believers are called to proclaim Christ boldly in every area of our society. Rather than merely working to add more believers in the various segments of society, we need those who know Christ right now to live consistent, Spirit-filled lives in every sphere of society. One essential part of a consistent spiritual walk is to witness of Christ's love wherever we are. Colossians 1:28 urges, "Everywhere we go we talk about Christ to all who will listen, warning them and teaching them as well as we know how. We want to be able to present each one to God, perfect because of what Christ has done for each of them" (TLB). This verse tells us that we are called to be full-time followers and full-time witnesses of God's love. Paul calls this our ministry of reconciliation: "All this is from God, who reconciled us to himself through Christ and gave us the ministry of reconciliation: that God was reconciling the world to himself in Christ, not counting men's sins against them" (2 Corinthians 5:18,19).

Many Christians have become experts at keeping their SPIRITUAL LIVES SEPARATE from their secular lives.

God put us where we are to serve Him in all things. We cannot section off our lives into God's part and the world's part. We must do our part, no matter where He places us, and no matter how great or how small our gifts and opportunities. We are ministers on the job, in the home, at the church, and on the street.

When we are walking with the Lord daily and living in the Holy Spirit's power, it is not difficult to find the mission fields in our lives. Friends, family, co-workers, employers, neighbors, internationals, or sackers at the grocery store need a Savior. Until believers begin living their Christian lives wherever they go and in whatever they do, we will not have an impact on our society.

6. We do not stand up for our faith.

At various times and places throughout history, God sent special ambassadors to change the world. We recognize some of the more famous names. I think immediately of individuals like Martin Luther, John Knox, John Wesley, William Wilberforce, and George Whitefield, who bore words of passion and renewal. There were some, such as Winston Churchill, who spoke of duty, honor, and country in times of world crisis. Another is Mother Teresa of Calcutta, who spoke for all those who were suffering and could not speak for themselves. But we only see the impact of other faithful Christians through their deeds in small and inconspicuous ways.

Could any of these brave souls have avoided their calling from God? Absolutely. Could the world have continued without them? Probably, but not nearly so well. Can America's mission continue if you and I fail to live up to God's calling upon our lives? That is a question every one of us must answer.

Several years ago, I met two of America's most outstanding educators. They were both believers, both wonderful men. They had known each other for more than twenty-five years. They met frequently at various educators' conferences around the country, but neither knew that the other was a Christian. They were closet Christians. Tragically, there are millions like them in the closets of America.

Distinguished philosopher Edmund Burke reminds us, "The only thing necessary for the triumph of evil is for good men to do nothing."[10] Our modern humanistic system of laws and the corruption of justice in this nation did not just happen without a response from God. I believe that God had people in places of authority who could have halted America's slide into relativism, sin, and national decay; but they turned a deaf ear to the Lord's commands. They did not do their part for the kingdom of God; and the rest, I am sorry to say, is history.

I wonder how many Christian lawyers, placed in positions of influence at important turning points in history, failed to speak up for the truth or to stand up for righteousness when it really mattered? How many congressmen refused to stand up and denounce a bad bill? How many pastors have denied that still, small voice inside their own hearts and refused to speak those words of conviction that might have called a wounded congregation back to repentance? How many men and women will spend eternity in hell because no one had the courage to speak a brief word to them about the love of Jesus?

We used to speak with pride of the so-called "silent majority"—supposedly a vast body of believers who formed the invisible backbone of the nation. Sadly, as we approach the new millennium, we have been silent too long. In our fear of controversy, we allowed those who disagree with our values and the principles of Christian culture to dismantle the proudest and noblest landmarks of our heritage.

Francis Schaeffer questions where the clear voice speaking to the critical issues of the day has gone. Where are the men and women of conviction who have knowledge and skill to offer biblical answers to the problems we are facing? "The last fifty years," he laments, "have given birth to a moral disaster, and what have we done?"

Lukewarmness in the body of Christ is part of the problem. Our responses to what we have seen happening in the culture are generally appalling. Schaeffer says, "With tears we must say that...a large segment of the evangelical world has become seduced by the world spirit of this present age."[11]

As we saw, God looks at the world from the perspective of reconciliation. He could have reconciled man to Himself, but He chose us to share the privilege of reconciling the world to Him. Paul adds, "We are therefore Christ's ambassadors, as though God were making His appeal through us" (2 Corinthians 5:20). Peter reminds us that God is not willing that any should perish, but that all should come to Christ in repentance (2 Peter 3:9).

Most believers are missing the very mission that God has given them. They may be active in the church a couple of days each week, but neglect the needs of those who surround them the other five days. Why do we withhold the matchless offer of salvation Christ has made available through us? We do not stand up for our faith because of embarrassment, lack of knowledge, and our intimidation by the cultural hostility to Christ and His gospel. We have become ambassadors without portfolio, soldiers without a mission, and runners who sit out the race. We are reluctant warriors, unprepared to carry our banner or fight the good fight. And we cannot win the war without fighting a battle!

7. We are not willing to suffer.

So what are we to conclude about the lukewarm faith in America? Jesus told the faithful that they would be hated and abused by the world. He said, "If the world hates you, you know that it hated Me before it hated you." Then he warned, "If you were of the world, the world would love its own. Yet because you are not of the world, but I chose you out of the world, therefore the world hates you" (John 15:18,19, NKJ).

God did not offer us salvation just to take away our trials and give us carefree and happy lives. Joy is the by-product of a one-on-one intimate relationship with Jesus Christ, but happiness and prosperity were never meant to be our primary pursuits. C. S. Lewis makes the point very well when he says, "The Christian religion does not begin in comfort; it begins in dismay. In religion, as in war and everything else, comfort is the one thing you cannot get by looking for it. If you look for truth, you may find comfort in the end. If you look for comfort, you will not get either comfort or truth—only soft soap and wishful thinking to begin with and, in the end, despair."[12]

Jesus Christ died on the cross for our sins. It was a painful, wretched, and humiliating way to die. The Roman soldiers pounded spikes through His wrists and ankles. He was beaten with whips. People spat on Him. His torture was anything but humane, and His death was anything but peaceful. The thieves crucified on either side of Him had robbed and stolen their entire lives, their deaths may have been justifiable. But for the sinless Son of God, crucifixion was the most humiliating, excruciating death imaginable.

How many of us have ever suffered humiliation and torture for the gospel? How many have stood up to jeers and mockery for the cause of Christ? How many have been inconvenienced even a little? Sadly, not many.

Would you be willing to suffer for the truth if it would cost you your savings, pension, or your home? Would you stand by your faith if that meant losing your job or enduring physical pain? I know these are tough questions; but many who went before us suffered and died by those choices. Paul's life was filled with disappointment, pain, suffering, and eventually martyrdom. Our forefathers stood against popular beliefs to serve Christ.

Would you be willing to suffer for the truth IF IT WOULD COST YOU your savings, pension, or your home?

In many places around the world today, Christians are humiliated, beaten, tortured, and murdered for simply attending a church service, carrying a Bible, or speaking about Christ to a person of a non-Christian religion. Are we less able than they are to carry out our mission with a bold faith that is willing to suffer all for Christ? That is the only way we can confront our culture and win!

One researcher writes, "The major change for the church in America is that she has forgotten her identity in relation to the world. We have abandoned our unique identity and have pursued another identity, that of a cultural Christian. When the church loses her identity, she also loses her sense of purpose or destiny; without identity and purpose she has no power."[13] At this critical hour, I believe we are standing on the threshold of the greatest opportunity in 2,000 years to impact our world as well as to help to fulfill the Great Commission. Sadly, at the moment when the world needs us the most, too many Christians are uncommitted, powerless, and caught in the grasp of worldliness and selfishness.

I urge you to examine your part in making the bride of Christ clean and spotless, ready to present herself to the Bridegroom. To begin this journey, the first step is to look at what the Church can do to turn the tide of unrighteousness, materialism, and lukewarmness that is thwarting our ability to confront the culture—and help make this a Christian nation once again.

CHAPTER 18

A Call for Change

We are standing before a new century. Its potentials are unlimited; but the problems are also more than we can imagine. Richard Nixon writes succinctly about our challenge:

> [On January 1, 2001] we will celebrate a day that comes once in a thousand years: the beginning of a new year, a new century, and a new millennium. For the first time on such a historic day, the choice before mankind will not just be whether we make the future better than the past, but whether we will survive to enjoy the future.
>
> In 1999, we will remember the 20th Century as the bloodiest and best in the history of man. One hundred twenty million people have been killed in 130 wars in this century—more than all those killed in war before 1900. But, at the same time, more technological and material progress has been made over the last hundred years than ever before. The twentieth century will be remembered as a century of war and wonder.[1]

These words should make us as believers realize the dire responsibility of our place in history. Will the 21st century be a time or war or wonder? Who will win the moral battle for the souls of

Americans? Can our society survive its moral onslaught before time runs out? As believers, we hold so much in our hands. We have the answers and the power to implement those answers. We cannot fail to answer God's call to repentence and confrontation. But how will we do that?

As a young Christian, I read a book entitled *The Strong Name* by Dr. James Stewart, a New Testament scholar from Edinburgh, Scotland. He said, "If we could but show the world that being committed to Christ is no tame humdrum sheltered monotony, but the most exciting adventure the human spirit could ever know, those who have been standing outside the Church looking with suspicion at Christ, will come crowding in to pay allegiance, and we might well experience the greatest reviving since Pentecost." His words made a lasting impression on me.

Dr. Stewart understood what the Church needs today—to illustrate the love of Christ, the joy of the abundant life, the strength in Christian fellowship, and the hope we have for eternity. The world is waiting. But are we so tied up in our sin, materialistic lifestyles, and complacency that we cannot change? Will we be the spectators in the stands while our nation loses the most important contest in its history?

John and I believe without a doubt that God's power working through the American Church can change our nation and the world for Christ. God spoke and the universe was put into place; He breathed and man became a living creature. Christ conquered sin and death when He died on the cross and rose from the grave. He certainly can change the course of our nation through us.

But change does not come overnight. It takes commitment and hard labor. Let me share with you some ways the Church must change to become salt and light to our culture once more.

Knowing What We Believe

If we could only faithfully transmit the attractiveness of the Christian life to unbelievers, many would gladly turn to Christ. But we cannot expect unbelievers to be satisfied with childish beliefs. We cannot help new Christians develop mature faith if all we feed them is baby food. That is why Paul warns, "Brothers, stop thinking like children. In regard to evil be infants, but in your thinking be adults" (1 Corinthians 14:20). We have a duty to know what we believe and why we believe it so we can state the case for the deity and the authority of Christ in an effective way. To deal with complex problems, we must be nourished on the meat of the Word of God and learn to reason with spiritual depth. The most important step to mature spiritual thinking is immersing ourselves in God's Word—both at home and in our pulpits.

Have you ever considered that owning a copy of the Bible is a privilege many people have never enjoyed? Not until the 16th century did the printing press make it possible for the average family to purchase a copy. Before that time, only the clergy and intellectual elite had access to the holy Book. Soon after Bibles were placed in the hands of the common people, the gospel message became one of the driving factors behind the Reformation and Protestantism.

After the fall of communism in the 1980s, citizens of Russia and other Eastern nations lined up for blocks for an opportunity to receive a copy of the Bible. When gospel meetings were held in these countries, people fought to get their hands on copies of the Bibles which were being distributed.

In America, we have access to the Word as no people in history; yet we TAKE THE BIBLE FOR GRANTED.

In America, we have access to the Word as no people in history; yet we take the Bible for granted. It is estimated that 92 percent of American households own a copy of the Bible, and most have as many as three copies.[2] Americans often discard these Bibles or neglect them in drawers or on bookshelves. Pollster George Barna comments, "Americans revere the Bible—but they don't read it."[3] I have found that even true followers of Christ make a half-hearted commitment to read and learn from God's Word. Most Christians feel they have done God a favor if they skim a few chapters a week. Os Guinness gives the result of this attitude:

> The church today is beset by big problems and big issues, and these must be thought through carefully in light of the Word of God and the situation in our world today. We must renounce simple answers to tough questions and be prepared to pray, think, and work intelligently in order to see where we are and what the Lord would have us do.[4]

As American Christians, we also lack disciplined Bible study. I have found that the typical American believer is defeated, frustrated, and fruitless because he does not feed daily on God's Word. Many who do study the Bible, do not apply its principles to their daily lives or handle contemporary issues according to God's Word.

We also have an obligation to encourage others to study God's Word with us and on their own. Negligent Christians do not need lectures that will further frustrate them and produce more guilt. Instead, they need love, understanding, information, and instructions. To help them gain a passion for the Word, they need to understand who they are in Christ—children of God, the King of Kings, with all the rights and privileges of royalty. Our responsibility is to come alongside our Christian friends, encouraging them to delve deeply into God's Word.

We can start with the basics. All Christians need to know the following about our faith:

- How to surrender to the Lordship of Christ
- How to live by faith in God, trusting and depending on Him for every need
- How to live a consistent, overcoming Christian life
- How to live moment by moment in the power of the Holy Spirit
- How to be trained to share our faith in Christ with others
- How to get rid of the heavy load of self and guilt through repentance and confession
- How the church, as well as our nation, can face this incredible spiritual crisis according to biblical principles

- What we can do to help meet the challenge of fulfilling the Great Commission

In recent years, the Church has often discarded many of its most fundamental biblical principles because it fears looking foolish in the world's eyes. For example, many churches consider it unfashionable to speak about the virgin birth, the cross, the shedding of blood, the resurrection of Jesus, or the Holy Spirit. Paul's explanation why the world will not understand these concepts: "Since in the wisdom of God the world through its wisdom did not know him, God was pleased through the foolishness of what was preached to save those who believe" (1 Corinthians 1:21). But if we ignore the harder truths of Scripture and Christ's atonement, we will not achieve our purpose or honor God.

As a young, happy, pagan businessman, I resented any mention of the cross of Christ and the blood He shed on it. Such reference offended my aesthetic nature. All of this changed when I became a believer in Christ and began walking in the Spirit. As I grew to love the Lord and His Word, I grew to love the harder concepts of God's truth. Now I love to sing hymns such as Robert Lowry's *Nothing But the Blood:*

> What can wash away my sin?
> Nothing but the blood of Jesus;
> What can make me whole again?
> Nothing but the blood of Jesus.
>
> Oh! Precious is the flow
> That makes me white as snow;
> No other fount I know,
> Nothing but the blood of Jesus.

It is foolish not to present the whole gospel, the pleasant as well as the unpleasant. God expects us to be honest with the world about His message to us. We can do no less to win the battle for America's soul.

As the Church recommits itself to the Word, Christians will know how to answer questions about their faith and how to introduce someone to the Lord Jesus Christ. Believers will be less inclined to fall into sin or be led into cults or false religions.

A Commitment to Personal Holiness

As we have seen, the American Church desperately needs a commitment to holiness. But this is not a popular topic today. Whenever Christians speak of moral standards, secular liberals argue that men and women are free to do whatever they wish. When we mention Christ's warning that "narrow is the road that leads to life" or that you must "die to yourself and live to Christ," they talk about freedom of choice, moral relativity, and the perfectibility of the soul. This attitude also permeates the Church.

To serve as an example to a culture which does not have the faintest idea of what holiness is, the Church must once again be "set apart" to God. Theologian Dr. R. C. Sproul believes that the future of the church in America hinges on whether or not we are willing to renew our commitment to personal holiness. He says that sermons stressing the wrath of God no longer seem to fit in the town-hall atmosphere of most local churches. He worries:

> Ours is an upbeat generation with an accent of self improvement and a broad-minded view of sin...Our thinking, goes like this: If there is a God at all, He certainly is not holy. If He is perchance holy, He is not just. Even if He is both holy and just, we need not fear because His love and mercy override His holy justice. If we can stomach His holy and just character, we can rest in one thing: He cannot possess wrath.[5]

Until the Church HUMBLES ITSELF before the holiness and righteousness of God, it remains under the THREAT OF JUDGMENT.

Jonathan Edwards' classic sermon, "Sinners in the Hands of an Angry God," was first preached in 1741. Today, it would not be warmly received in most of our churches because the culture of the Church rejects that message. Until the Church humbles itself before the holiness and righteousness of God, it remains under the threat of judgment. On the other hand, only by accepting God's holiness through His gift of salvation can we partake of the holiness of God.

Personal holiness means living above the world's values, including materialism and lukewarmness toward God. Jesus says, "Do not store up for yourself treasures on earth, where moth and rust destroy, and where thieves break in and steal. But store up for yourselves treasures in heaven, where moth and rust do not destroy, and where thieves do not break in and steal. For where your treasure is, there your heart will be also" (Matthew 6:19–21). He then adds the heart of this message, "No one can serve two masters. Either he will hate the one and love the other, or he will be devoted to one and despise the other. You cannot serve both God and money" (Matthew 6:24). Tragically, the Church today is trying to serve two masters—and succeeding at nothing.

Personal holiness also means giving priority to God's purposes. A pure heart lays aside a desire for money, possessions, and the easy life. The Christian who lives righteously will be offended at the sin he sees around him and will actively fight for righteousness.

Putting on the Armor of God

The enemy has a well-polished arsenal with which to defend their secular world view. They come armed with mountains of scientific evidence. On the surface, their worldview seems more appealing than ours. After all, they avoid the issues of sin and judgment and speak of prosperity, pleasure, liberty, and human dignity. Peter says, "Always be ready to give a defense to everyone who asks you a reason for the hope that is in you" (1 Peter 3:15). To give such a defense, we must put on our spiritual armor.

Modern theology does not prepare us for combat. It produces churches which are more like country clubs than boot camps. Instead of turning out men and women of conviction and resolve, they host dinner groups, coffee klatches, and Bible studies that focus more on gossip and happy-talk than on battle strategy.

Good battle strategy calls for wearing the right uniform. Paul challenged believers to put on the whole armor of God (Ephesians

6:11). The pieces include the belt of truth, breastplate of righteousness, feet fitted with the gospel of peace, the shield of faith, the helmet of salvation, and the sword of the Spirit which is God's Word (Ephesians 6:10–18). This armor enables us to defeat the schemes of Satan. Within our armor are two forces: One is the power of the inspired Word of God. The other is the witness of the Counselor, the Holy Spirit, who teaches us everything Christ said to us (John 14:26).

Be alert! The battle will get fierce. Even if we use intelligent reasoning, we will not be respected by the world. It believes that we are simple-minded for trusting in a God we cannot see. Scripture warns, "The message of the cross is foolishness to those who are perishing, but to us who are being saved it is the power of God" (1 Corinthians 1:18, NKJ). Until a non-Christian opens his heart to the Word, his eyes are covered by scales which prevent him from seeing the truth. Without doubt, the Church will face ridicule and abuse for standing on principle.

Unity in the Spirit

When he introduced the doctrines of Communism, Karl Marx issued the call, "Workers of the world, unite!"[6] His sedition sparked an unrighteous revolution that toppled Eastern Europe and nearly crippled the world. What gave Marxist philosophies such power was the belief that the key to strength was unity. This man who hated God and referred to religion as "the opiate of the people"[7] understood the biblical principle that "a divided house cannot stand" (Matthew 12:25).

Unfortunately, the Church does not always understand this truth. Internal conflicts rips the life from many local churches. Instead of working together for the clearly stated principles of Scripture, factions emerge within the congregation. These are often motivated by selfishness, pride, or expediency. In some cases, scriptural authority ranks second to popular social values and humanistic programs, causing discord and fragmentation in the body of Christ.

Just before his arrest, Jesus prayed, "I pray also for those who will believe in me through their message, that all of them may be one, Father, just as you are in me and I am in you... May they be brought into complete unity to let the world know that you sent me and have loved them even as you have loved me" (John 17:20–22).

Just think what we could accomplish if we were truly united. How powerful our witness would be if we could agree on the basic issues of faith! Chuck Colson writes, "If people could see the unity of the Body of Christ, they would come knocking our doors down. We would not be able to build churches fast enough."[8]

Any move to restore the moral integrity of this nation must begin with a commitment to building biblical unity in the body of Christ. I suggest that this should be a primary focus of the leadership of our churches over the coming months and years. My plea is that the churches of Jesus Christ will receive this wake up call and unite for another great spiritual Awakening to sweep our land. I have seen encouraging movements toward unity in the Church in recent years, but we have a long way to go. I want to recommend one movement which reflects the prayer of our Lord—Mission America. In Chapter 22, I will explain how you can become involved with this exciting strategy.

Confronting the Culture

As I write this, the national media is reporting the recent Southern Baptist Convention's stand on the family. Many reporters ridiculed the idea of biblical submission within marriage. Others were hostile to the statement that a marriage is one man and one woman for a lifetime. Yet the leaders of the Convention had the courage to stand up for biblical truths on the roles of husbands and wives in marriage.

As Christians, we are called to a higher standard. Because it is a biblical standard, it has been largely rejected by the secular culture. But we dare not risk watering down our message. Our responsibility is to warn society that they are on the road to destruction.

At the same time, we must express love for those being devoured by sin. Every aspect of our culture—whether it is business, government, the family, the schools, or the media—is already in an advanced state of decay. People are looking for authenticity, hope, and a way out of their problems. Deep down they want to be free from the bondage of sin. They want to see changes in the lives of people. They want to know a God who has the power to make a difference in their lives. When they see Christ's love in us, they will be drawn to Him to meet their present needs and future challenges.

God is searching for a body of believers who will stand up to the taunts and mockeries of this world. He desires those who love the Lord, who believe His Word, and who will defend its values. Are we up to the challenge? If we lose our confidence in the truth of Scripture or are weak in the way we present it, we will dilute the power of the Christian faith. We must have a deep resolve to confront our culture and spring into action based on the moving of God's Spirit.

Confrontation is never pleasant. It begins with prayer and humility, then moves into areas outside our corners of safety. It means taking risks, becoming unpopular, while loving the sinner. Pastor Jack Hayford explains, "Before we will ever be heard in evangelism, something of the power of God must be manifest in us. The power of God is revealed through the praying church, the love of God by the way we relate to a culture that may very well offend us."[9]

> Many times, we sacrifice our most PRECIOUS BELIEFS so we will not appear INTOLERANT AND JUDGMENTAL.

Jesus demonstrated balance in confronting His culture. He was the sinless Son of God, yet He loved those ensnared by sin and challenged those who excused their sin. Jesus spoke to sinners at the temple, the marketplace, the public well, telling them of God's love and forgiveness. Yet He also fearlessly drove the unscrupulous moneychangers from the temple porch and accused the scribes and Pharisees of hypocrisy. Hayford points out that Jesus seldom spoke in anger to those who were ignorant of their sin; He reserved His wrath for the religious "hardheads" of the day.

What balance does the Church have today? Many times, we sacrifice our most precious beliefs so we will not appear intolerant and judgmental. At the same time, we hammer with rage and hostility against our culture. Hayford says, "There is something about Jesus that has the capacity not to condone immorality or sagging values. He does not condone them for a minute. But still you never pick up any hint of condescension in Him. He had the capacity by His moral power to invite people beyond where they are."[10] We need to adopt His attitude in our confrontations.

Political Involvement

Because of America's moral and spiritual disintegration over the past fifty years, the Church must take immediate action to confront moral decay. But Christians often ask me: "Is it right for Christians to become involved in politics?" Definitely yes! The institution of government was sanctioned by Christ and supported by New Testament writers. (See Matthew 22:21; Romans 13:1; Titus 3:1; 1 Peter 2:13,14.) God does not intend for us to live in a theocracy where the Church is the supreme political authority, but He also does not want us to live as if faith in God were illegal in the political arena. If godly men and women have no voice in the public square, then by default the political life of the nation will remain in the hands of the ungodly.

Charles Finney, who was on the forefront of the abolition movement before the Civil War, considered politics to be very important for followers of Christ: "God will bless or curse this nation according to the course Christians take in politics."[11] But unlike other groups of people who bend the rules and compromise, we have an inviolable standard of truth. We cannot dance around issues. There should never be a question about the boundaries or the ultimate goals.

In the political arena, there is one behavior that hurts our Christian witness—inconsistency. For example, citizens who want to lower taxes, to restore the environment, to end racism, to halt development of nuclear arms, or to pursue any other popular issue must always be alert for one-sidedness in their rhetoric. Those who fight against big government's social and welfare programs must then help church and community programs address these needs. Those who oppose laws and government agencies abetting abortions should also support adoption, youth ministries, and educational programs to help prevent abortions.

We need to be aware that God's standards do not fit neatly into the political agendas of the major parties. This means that on different occasions, we may find ourselves on opposite sides of the political fence. As God's ambassadors, we are not bound by party loyalties; we represent that which is true and honorable according to Scripture.

Joshua, one of Israel's greatest military commanders, commanded the people to choose who they would serve—the gods of this world or the living God of history. That is our choice today. If we choose to serve God, we will face flaming arrows shot from all sides of the political battlefield. If our allegiance to God supersedes our loyalty to all other persons, parties, or philosophies, some will try to discredit us. But our principle still takes precedence over party politics; integrity rules expediency; character is more important than charisma.

Let me give you an example. I may want to lower taxes and someone else may want to raise taxes, so we compromise to achieve our goals. Some issues, however, are not as easily resolved. Abortion and racism are moral issues where we have no room for conciliation. Taking an innocent life is absolutely wrong. The sixth Commandment says, "You shall not murder" (Exodus 20:13). Through the prophet Jeremiah, God commanded, "Do no wrong and do no violence to the stranger, the fatherless, or the widow, nor shed innocent blood" (Jeremiah 22:3). Therefore, we cannot compromise. We have a moral duty to resist any law of any state that violates the law of God and to articulate the moral principles that substantiate our views.

Racism is also always wrong. Peter says, "I now realize how true it is that God does not show favoritism but accepts men from every nation who fear him and do what is right" (Acts 10:34,35). One indictment that nonbelievers make against the Church is that it discriminates along racial lines. This is an affront to God's role as Creator and Savior of the world. As believers we are all brothers and sisters in Christ. In recent years, a message of reconciliation between races has begun in the Church. We need to be on the forefront in showing love to all people.

Let me warn you of a personal danger we all face as we act for our Lord. When we read about certain cultural sins of which we have no part, we may be tempted to say, "I am not like the sinful men and women in our society. I have not committed immorality, taken drugs, or abandoned my children." In our boasting, we forget about our own sinful natures. If we have a proud, arrogant attitude, we will become like the Pharisees in Jesus' parable. He said:

> Two men went up to the temple to pray, one a Pharisee and the other a tax collector. The Pharisee stood up and prayed about himself: "God, I thank you that I am not like other men—robbers, evildoers, adulterers—or even like this tax collector. I fast twice a week and give a tenth of all I get."
>
> But the tax collector stood at a distance. He would not even look up to heaven, but beat his breast and said "God have mercy on me, a sinner."
>
> Jesus added, "I tell you that this man, rather than the other, went home justified before God. For everyone who exalts himself will be humbled, and he who humbles himself will be exalted" (Luke 18:10–14).

The virtuous Christian is not one who claims to be above sin, but one who admits his failings. We must all constantly fight against pride, remembering that we are wretched sinners liberated by the mercy of Jesus Christ. Paul described it so well, "[God] has rescued us out of the darkness and gloom and brought us into the kingdom of his dear Son, who bought our freedom with his blood and forgave us all our sins" (Colossians 1:13,14, TLB).

On the other hand, a follower of Christ who refuses to become involved politically is acting contrary to the will of God. Jesus taught that we are to go into the world (our marketplaces) and make disciples of all men. Social activities are also our mandate. When we care for the poor, the orphans and the widows, when we feed the hungry, or clothe the naked, we are doing a service as unto God Himself and extending the Christian faith within our nation.

Dedicated to Fulfilling the Great Commission

Ron Hutchcraft, a gifted evangelist, has a unique way of sharing his passion with his radio audience. On the program "A Word With You," he recently described the sinking of the *Titanic*. "There's a lot of talk about the *Titanic* right now—TV, blockbuster movie, record-setting Broadway show, museums, etc. Only 700 of the 2,200 passengers on the *Titanic* survived its sinking. Some 1,500 people died in the North Atlantic that night [April 15, 1912, at 2:20 a.m.]. It was an awful scene. But the greatest tragedy may be that many of them didn't have to die!"

A lot of people climbed into the twenty lifeboats, but many were only half full. Hundreds of people were in the cold water with life preservers. Most of them did not die from drowning; they froze to death. The people in the lifeboats heard the cries of those dying people, but they chose not to go back for fear of capsizing. Only one lifeboat returned—after it was too late. Of the hundreds who were in the water, only six people were rescued. *Those who were already saved didn't go after those who were dying.* Then Hutchcraft asked:

> Are we the people in the lifeboat who have already been saved, but we're doing nothing about the dying people around us?...We're surrounded by dying people. If you look at the faces of the people where you work, where you live, where you go to school, where you shop, you will be seeing what people in hell will look like. Those people are all around us. We must ask God to break our hearts for those people. We're their link to Jesus.[12]

This is the Church's greatest agenda—taking the message of God's love to the world. The time is short. For centuries, each generation of Christians has believed that it would see Christ's return. But in the last fifty years, we have seen an incredible buildup of signs that point to the Second Coming of Christ. Prophecies are being fulfilled before our eyes. We need to be ready and working for His kingdom.

Jesus Christ offers answers to the greatest questions in life, especially that ultimate question, "What happens after we die?" Only Christ can give order to a disordered world, peace for times of strife, and love for a culture immersed in anger and hate.

A story is told about a seven-year-old boy who asked his pastor, "Do you know why they call that place where you preach a pulpit?" The pastor replied, "Well, son, I'm not sure of the background of that name." The boy replied, "I know. It's the place where you *pull* people out of their *pit*."

Our mission is not just to confront people with their sin, but to share with them the eternal message of God's Word. Lives need changing; souls need saving from the pit of sin and despair. Then these new believers need to be prepared to witness effectively in their marketplaces and given a passion for world missions outreach.

Training Others in Evangelism

We are not just to evangelize ourselves, but also to train others to share their faith. It took me some time to realize the necessity of having a loving attitude in helping people find a vision for evangelism. In the '40s, I was a zealous new believer and a highly motivated business man, but I saw little emphasis on evangelism and discipleship. I set out to help make some changes in the churches of the Los Angeles area.

> **A PULPIT is the place where you PULL people out of their PIT.**

As a young businessman who was experiencing some considerable success, I was frequently invited to speak to churches and various Christian groups. At the conclusion of my messages, I always challenged believers to witness for Christ. Sometimes because of the emotion of my appeal, a number would pledge to witness for Christ during the coming week and give me a report. I was terribly disappointed that very few followed through. Therefore, I became critical of the church.

I concluded that the churches in Los Angeles were even worse that the churches of Ephesus and Laodicea. I had read in Revelation chapters two and three of how the great church of Ephesus had lost its first love for our Lord and how the church of Laodicea became lukewarm in their faith. God had harsh words for both churches about what was going to happen to them unless they repented. I decided to have nothing further to do with the lukewarm churches I attended. I would simply concentrate on winning others to Christ and put them in discipleship groups to help them grow into New Testament Christians. Frankly, I did not want these new Christians to be exposed to the malady that afflicted older Christians.

After several months, God began to show me that the real problem was me. I was challenging defeated, worldly Christians to witness, but I did not know enough to teach them the source of power, the Holy Spirit, who empowers believers to witness (Acts 1:8).

I remember a brilliant young college student whom I had introduced to Christ. In my ignorance I was always haranguing him to witness for Jesus. I never taught him, however, how to appropriate the power of the Holy Spirit by faith or what to say when talking to people.

> **We need to rethink our strategies as the Church. OUR MISSION remains unfulfilled; OUR DEDICATION is weak.**

One day he became very impatient. "Get off my back," he protested. "You are making my life miserable. I don't want anything more to do with you. Go away; get lost." I was shocked and hurt. But he was absolutely right in not wanting anything to do with me. He needed and wanted help, but I was not mature enough to help him.

As a result I began to realize that many Christians loved the Lord as much as I did and wanted to serve Him. They just needed someone to teach them gently and lovingly how to share their faith. Then I became less judgmental in my attitudes toward other believers.

So many times, the Church does just what I did—makes Christians feel guilty about their failure to witness without coming alongside to help them. We need to show our friends how to discover the joy of introducing men and women to Christ rather than acting out of duty. Fruitless believers need loving encouragement and training, not criticism for their failures.

There is no better time to spread the gospel everywhere than right now! With the incredible advances in science and the mushrooming of the computer industry, we have seen more technological advances in the last hundred years than in all of world history combined. The fulfillment of Bible prophecies concerning the return of our Lord which seemed improbable a decade ago now seem just around the corner. Whether we are near the end of our age or not, something unprecedented is happening in the world today. It is time to do everything possible to finish the task of fulfilling the Great Commission!

Going in the Right Direction

In these desperate times, we need to rethink our strategies as the Church. Our mission remains unfulfilled; our dedication is weak. We do not know where we are going.

This reminds me of the time I visited a strange city in Mexico and found myself driving in the wrong direction on a one-way street. It was very frustrating as well as dangerous. Several people tried to help me by shouting instructions in Spanish, but I did not understand the language. By their gestures, I understood, "You are going the wrong direction." What I really needed was someone to help me get turned around. At this point a kind and helpful policeman assisted me in getting my car turned around. I went on my way gratefully rejoicing.

As the Church, we must change directions, too. Christ wants enthused, power-filled, dedicated churches which teach the whole gospel. Nothing less will do. We know how to change, the path is clear, but will we listen to those who are warning us that we are going in the wrong direction?

There are signs of vitality and victory against the gathering storms. During the forty days before Easter 1998, millions of Christians were mobilized to pray and fast for revival and spiritual awakening in America. Since 1994, many denominational and ministry specialist group leaders have fasted and prayed for forty days each year for our country. Under the banner of ***Pray USA!***, America was bathed in prayer as never before in history. An unprecedented partnership of dozens of denominations, hundreds of parachurch groups and prayer ministries, and thousands of churches, joined to mobilize believers to "Pray America Back To God." This annual ***Mission America*** initiative is part of *Celebrate Jesus 2000*.

Praise God that the burden to fast and pray is not restricted to America. More than three million people in 100 Latin American cities pleaded with God for their troubled region during a day of fasting and prayer on April 6, 1998. Almost 200,000 people in fifty cities gathered in stadiums and churches to ask God to bring spiritual awakening and to commit themselves to prayer, fasting, and evangelization. TV and radio networks broadcast the events across the continent for five hours. About 5,000 churches throughout Latin America participated. In South Africa, more than one million believers committed themselves to forty days of fasting and prayer for revival in their nation.[15] Can we do no less?

Where will we find the kind of laborers and resources we need to complete our mission? Let us seriously take stock and determine the most critical steps as we rapidly approach the end of our time and opportunities. So whether you are a defeated or an on-fire follower of Jesus, I invite you to join with us in fasting, praying, working and believing. Somehow with God's supernatural help, we are going to reverse this tragedy which threatens to destroy our nation and all that we hold sacred and dear. Keep reading, for there is hope—yes, great hope!

CHAPTER 19

A Call for Commitment

There is no question about it. The old ways of solving America's problems no longer work. Humanistic solutions end in emptiness. Socialism has failed. Communism is in retreat. Society's headlong rush into hedonism, narcissism, and sensualism have only heightened emptiness and agony. The appetites that drive secular culture have proven shallow and destructive. During the second half of the 20th century, little moral progress has been made; in fact, our nation has taken many steps backward. While politicians promise a bridge to the 21st century, most Americans are groping in the darkness, praying for a way out of their problems.

The church's response to the sickness of our age has been shamefully inadequate. Christians failed to make room in the boat when the world was drowning in sin. The seeds of destruction and apostasy planted in the early years of the century have been allowed to spread within the Church. Tragically, the world has influenced the Church more than the Church has influenced the world. Perhaps the most dreadful fact of our society's slide into moral chaos is that the immobilized Church has done little to stop the onslaught. With the country being pulled under by the riptide of evil, the Church is paralyzed in apathy, fear, sin, and conformity to worldly standards. Too many of us have given up without a fight to take back our marriages, wayward children, schools, inner-cities, and the religious freedoms we are losing by default.

There are only two possible outcomes to the tragedy of the 20th century. First, we can continue on the road we have traveled for the last fifty years, one that leads inevitably toward more desolation, heartbreak, misery, and eventually destruction. Such was ancient Israel's fate because she turned away from the true God to worship false gods. By all appearances, that is the route most of us have already decided to take. Only a tremendous shakeup or some cataclysmic occurrence in the world will jar some of us awake and into action.

The second alternative, however, offers the only good solution. Given the mercy of God, we have a hope that if we stop now, turn from our wicked ways, and seek His face with all our hearts, He may yet move us toward repentance and revival as He did for the king and citizens of Nineveh. In response to Jonah's preaching, they repented and turned from their sin (Jonah 3:5–10).

Right now our best response is to fall on our knees and cry out, "Forgive us, oh God! Heal our land, and give us another chance to fulfill our mission!" I pray daily that God will give us a spirit of brokenness with a new hunger for the things of God. I want to see His glory come down and sweep throughout all the earth. I pray for myself and all believers to be refreshed in His presence and go forth with a new passion and burden to help change our world.

When enough of us fall on our faces before a holy and sovereign God, asking for and receiving those spiritual blessings, the Church will be revived. Then the saints will live in consistent righteousness, the people of the world will be drawn to the Christ who changes lives and situations, and the whole world will be blessed.

The God of the Second Chance

I truly believe that God will give us a second chance as we renew our covenant with Him and become, as our forefathers expressed it, "stepping stones" for the gospel to the "remote parts of the world."[1] God tells us, "What I have said, that will I bring about. What

I have planned, that will I do" (Isaiah 46:11). God's character is changeless, and His purpose has always been the same: to bring all nations into a full understanding of Himself and into an intimate relationship with His Son, our Lord and Savior Jesus Christ.

This is what God desires. He will do it with or without our cooperation. The question is, *Are we, like our forebears, willing to be used to that end?* If we will return to God, I believe we stand a second chance of seeing an era of renewal in this nation. If our passion and our prayers are sincere, we can yet see our homeland revived and receive the blessing God reserves for those who are faithful to Him.

Will we join hands and work together to restore America, not just to her former glory, but to her *future promise?* I am convinced that you and I have been put here for just such a time as this.

The Measure of Devotion

What God is asking is for the Church to have a much greater measure of devotion than it does now. The first-century Church is our example. Those men and women staked their lives to spread the gospel to the known world. They were incredibly successful, but they also paid a dear price.

> **God is asking for the Church to have a much greater MEASURE OF DEVOTION than it does now.**

The best examples of that selfless devotion to Christ is from the apostles. They walked with Jesus and spoke to Him face to face, yet their personal relationship with Him did not prevent them from suffering greatly. In fact, it guaranteed that they would suffer. Peter and Paul were martyred in Rome around 66 A.D. under the emperor Nero. Peter was crucified; Paul was beheaded. Andrew was crucified in Greece. Thomas was killed by soldiers near Syria. Philip was put to death for converting the wife of a Roman proconsul.

Scholars believe Matthew was stabbed to death in Ethiopia, while Bartholomew was murdered, and James the brother of Jesus was stoned to death. Simon the Zealot was killed after refusing to sacrifice to the sun god. Matthias, who preached with Andrew, was burned to death. The Bible says that James, the son of Zebedee, was executed by Herod. Of the twelve apostles, only John died a natural death while in exile.

Paul described his own selfless commitment to Christ when he wrote, "I have been crucified with Christ and I no longer live, but Christ lives in me. The life I live in the body, I live by faith in the Son of God, who loved me and gave himself for me" (Galatians 2:20). In light of who God is and all He has done for us, dare we have any less devotion? The gospel of Jesus Christ is all-consuming truth, not an alternative truth or an optional theory. God's truth must completely possess each person who claims to be Christ's follower. We must have a passion for our Lord that is radical, sold-out, engaged, and fully dedicated. Anything less is potentially harmful.

Paul says, "You are not your own; you were bought at a price" (1 Corinthians 6:19,20). That price was Christ's own blood shed on the cross for our sins. When we stop to consider the price that Jesus paid to bring us to Himself, we should recognize that "cheap grace" and "easy believism" are a stench to our holy God. True grace, which is the undeserved acceptance of God's love through His Son, should fill us with gratitude overflowing into obedience as we return that love to Him.

Commitment to God comes with a price tag. True believers must be willing to pay the price, however small or great that may be. When we understand the value of the unlimited gift of grace, we respond with abiding faith. Anything less is an insult to our Lord and a rejection of the sacrifices of all those faithful followers of Christ who went before us.

For the Church to experience renewal, millions of believers must realize that, according to God's Word, their lives belong to Christ and that the time we have left on earth is His as well. Only when we have died to self can we truly live for Him.

Whom Shall I Send?

To experience this renewal, the Church must confront the secular culture on a personal level, one by one. Will the Christian nurse risk her job rather than assist in an abortion? Will the Christian businessman take a pay cut rather than sacrifice the principles of his faith on the job? Will the Christian lawyer stand against the secular humanistic legal system even if it costs him clients and cash? Will the politician risk losing the election to publicly stand up for righteousness? Will members of the body of Christ in America be willing to lay aside their reputations, comforts, and worldly successes to "seek first the Kingdom of God and His righteousness" (Matthew 6:33)?

Will our pastors boldly challenge members of their congregations who merely show up to listen to the sermons, absorb the music, and enjoy the fellowship? Will these servants of God confront those who do nothing to share their faith, preserve our culture, or stand up for America's heritage of faith and freedom? Are our teachers and other spiritual leaders so comfortable reciting the same familiar Bible stories and promises for blessings and prosperity that they will not confront sin and apathy in our midst?

And what about you? Is that your heart's cry? Do you want to experience God's renewal and live the abundant supernatural life? Are you concerned enough about our country to change the way you think and live?

What Would Jesus Do?

Followers of Christ today are still challenged by a question posed more than 100 years ago by Charles Sheldon in his classic book, *In His Steps*. The book's premise is that we should conduct our lives, both private and public, by asking the question, "What would Jesus do?"[2] It is a question that allows each of us to put our own morality in perspective. If we can live by Christ's example and maintain a passionate commitment to truth, then we will not make dreadful mistakes that destroy our lives and damage our testimonies.

The future of this nation may rest on the answer we give to Sheldon's question. So let me make it a little more personal. What about you, my friend? What will you do? Do you believe that Christ's example is relevant today? Are you willing to apply Christ's standards in your own life? Will you respond to situations in your life according to what Jesus would do based on His life and teachings?

Are you ready to play "hard ball" in the major leagues? Are you equipped to do battle against the enemy of your soul—and all that is good and decent—in spiritual warfare?

Some time ago, I witnessed to a man who professed to be a Christian. He is a very distinguished man—in fact, twice governor of a great state and a presidential candidate. As our conversation progressed, I challenged him to make his life count for God.

He said with a bit of impatience, "I am a Christian, but I don't wear my religion on my sleeve. It's personal and private for me, and I don't talk about it."

"Please forgive me," I replied. "I do not want to offend you, but did it ever occur to you that in order for you to say that you are a Christian, it cost the Lord Jesus Christ His life? He died on the cross for your sins. It cost all the disciples great persecution and most of them martyrdom. Through the centuries, millions of Christians have died as martyrs, getting this message through to you. Now, let me ask you, do you really think that your Christianity is personal and private and that you should not talk about it?"

Immediately, he responded, "No, sir! I'm wrong. Please tell me what I should do. Help me to make Christ more a part of my life."

If you find yourself falling for the "cheap grace" so fashionable in many churches today, I plead with you to get on your knees before God and repent. If there was ever a time when prayer and fasting were needed to bring us back to God, that time is now.

If America is to be spared the fate of all those fallen empires of the past, the body of Christ will have to wake up, stand up, and speak out for what the Bible teaches. A commitment to the life-changing precepts of our faith must ring out from the pulpits of this land. Believers must get serious about their commitment to Jesus Christ and to the truth of His Word.

Will you do that? Will you seek the face of God and ask Him to show you how you can be a part of this great adventure? In our next section, we will show you practical steps you can take to be part of the solution—and help our country restore its historic Christian roots and its purpose to help fulfill the Great Commission in our lifetime.

PART IV

A Plan for Spiritual Renewal

There are over 70 million of us in the United States alone who claim to be His disciples, who claim a "born again" experience... William Iverson writing in Christianity Today wryly observes, "A pound of meat would surely be affected by a quarter pound of salt. If this is real Christianity, the 'salt of the earth,' where is the effect of which Jesus spoke?"

Imagine a one-pound beef steak (the United States of America). Now, dump one quarter of a pound of salt (evangelical Christians) on that steak. Will the salt make a difference? It should make a significant difference.

—GUY DOUD, 1986 NATIONAL TEACHER OF THE YEAR

CHAPTER 20

The Challenge to Renewal

For approximately fifty years, I have been convinced that the Great Commission will be fulfilled by our generation. There was a time not all that long ago, however, when this goal seemed overly ambitious to most Christians. The logistics were simply too great. But in the last five years, that has changed. Suddenly we have the manpower, the resources, and an unprecedented window of opportunity to help reach the entire world for Christ. He calls us to serve—even to be world-changers—and He has given us His Holy Spirit to empower us to do what He has called us to do.

In my travels, I have seen abundant evidence of how the world looks to the West. Since the fall of communism, the collapse of the Berlin Wall, and the opening of Chinese markets to Western interests, America has enhanced its influence. Borders that had been closed for decades are suddenly open to us, competing for American technology and products. Political and corporate leaders are looking for new ideas and leadership principles. For example, in the 1980s when the Poles and Czechs revolted against communist domination, their leaders read aloud the words of our own Declaration of Independence with tears streaming down their cheeks.

There is no marketplace on the planet where American goods have failed to penetrate. A medical doctor gave her testimony at Intervarsity's Urbana Conference in 1993. She and other physicians had made a mercy trip to northwest China. They flew to the last commercial airport, then boarded a train for a two-day trip to their final destination, a remote village. She recalled how she and the other doctors had walked the streets observing the people and evaluating their living conditions which seemed forty to fifty years behind Western countries.

Through conversations with local Chinese, the Christian doctor learned that few villagers had received medical treatment in their lifetimes, and none had ever heard the name of Jesus Christ. She recalled thinking how tragic that the gospel had never been brought to this part of the earth. Was it too inaccessible? Was the cost too great? Did no one have the desire to come here?

Not long after that moment of reflection, to her great surprise, a Coca Cola truck, with its familiar red and white logo, came down the street and stopped in front of a food store. How tragic, she thought, that a commercial business could overcome the distance problem, pay the necessary expense to establish a business, and invest their product when the Church, which holds the "water of life," had not made the effort.

God intends for us to export, not just goods and services, but THE GOSPEL of His Son.

God intends for us to export, not just goods and services, and not just tennis shoes and sugar water, but the gospel of His Son, Jesus Christ. If we really want to serve Him, we must give them "the real thing"—the truth that satisfies the thirsty soul.

Chuck Colson warns that all too often we have led the world, not to the freedom of Christ, but to the bondage of sin. "The world is looking to the West, but the West is sending a mixed message," Colson says. "On the one hand, there is a rich heritage that has blossomed from the soil of historic Christianity, a heritage of free governments, where power flows from the consent of the governed, not the barrel of a gun. But undercutting it all are newer, compelling images beaming out from movie and television screens—images that glorify the secular, the sexual, and the sensational."[1] We cannot let this be the only America they see!

In 1887 in a message entitled, "National Perils and Opportunities," delivered as president of the Westchester County Bible Society, John Jay, 1st Chief Justice of the U.S. Supreme Court, gave a vision that applies to us and our challenge today:

> It is high time to wake out of sleep! This gathering of citizens from distant parts, representing the millions who hold to the Bible, and cherish the institutions founded upon its inspired truths, shows that the nation is awakening to the perils, foreign and domestic, which threaten the purity of its Christian civilization.[2]

The vision to fulfill America's purpose is within sight. The harvest fields are ripe. How eagerly people around the world respond to the news of Jesus Christ. Are we awakening? Let us be alert and fight the battle before us!

The Day of Salvation

There is much to be excited about. We can find unlimited opportunities to serve the Lord in our world today. Since 1951, as my staff and I have worked with more than a thousand mission groups in helping to train millions of believers from tens of thousands of churches of all denominations, we have helped present the gospel to approximately 3 billion people. As of May 1998, we have sent thousands of teams into villages on every continent to show the *JESUS* film to over 1.2 billion people. Tens, if not hundreds, of millions have expressed their desire to receive Christ. They truly see what the gift of salvation can mean. Compared to the apathy we often see in America, their enthusiasm thrills my heart.

Entire nations such as Russia, Brazil, Argentina, Korea, China, Indonesia, and several in Africa are experiencing different degrees of renewal. For example, I have seen men and women in Russia line up for hours to receive a Bible. Evangelists hold crusades in Africa where they proclaim the gospel freely. Their message of love from God often brings hundreds of thousands of people to their knees as they surrender their hearts and lives to Jesus. In South Africa, more than one million believers committed themselves to forty days of fasting and prayer for revival in their nation. The largest church in the world is not in New York or Los Angeles, but in South Korea, a nation that had barely a million followers of Christ forty years ago. Today their government records more than 11 million believers.

Our Historic Mission

Those who know me know that I am not a "gloom and doom" person. Since Vonette and I received our Lord Jesus Christ many years ago, we have been filled with God's love and joy. We count it a privilege to share that great love with hundreds of million of others around the world. I am nearly always optimistic, hopeful, expectant, and satisfied to be walking by faith and trusting God for every opportunity I have. I truly believe that our "problems" are only God's "opportunities" in disguise.

I believe with all my heart that God can still put this great nation back on track if we will trust and obey Him. With His help and guidance we can complete the task of fulfilling the Great Commission, the mission to which our Founding Fathers were committed.

My dear friends, I ask you to hear my heart as I attempt to speak the truth in love. If the people of this country do not repent and return to God, the days ahead of us will be dark indeed. Now is the time to be loving, serving, obeying, and trusting God. We must lay aside every weight and the sin that ensnares us so that we can run with endurance the race set before us.

But this is the good news! God has made a way of escape for us from our sin. He promises to hear and answer our prayers (Isaiah 59:1) and to heal our land (2 Chronicles 7:14). He will also show us the way that we should go (Isaiah 30:21; Luke 1:79). A day is coming when the time of divine wrath and judgment will be over, and the God of all comfort (2 Corinthians 1:3) will grant final salvation, peace, and blessings evermore to His people (Isaiah 40:1–5).

I readily admit that I do not have all the answers to the problems which grip this nation. Many others have published plans of action over the years, and I subscribe to some of these. A number of pastors, evangelists, prophets, teachers, and spiritual leaders have spoken out forcefully and clearly on the signs of the times. Those warnings notwithstanding, I have no choice at this stage of our national decline except to speak out about what I believe the Holy Spirit is saying to America today.

As President Ronald Reagan stated on various occasions, if the American people would "live closer to the Commandments and the Golden Rule," the problems we face would be solved.[3] If this sounds simplistic, please relate every problem you can list to these biblical commands to see if you agree with Reagan's conclusion.

> **If the people of this country do not REPENT AND RETURN TO GOD, the days ahead of us will be dark indeed.**

Using Our Talents

Jesus used the parable of the talents to teach us an important lesson about the nature of God. The Father expects His children to use His blessings for the good of the kingdom. He expects us to use them efficiently, actively, and immediately. In the parable, Jesus describes a master who embarks on a long journey and entrusts his property to his servants. To one he gives five talents of money, to another He gives two, and to still another He gives one. Two of the men make wise investments and double their funds. However, the third man—the one with only one talent—hid the master's treasure where it would be safe.

One day the master returns to check on his profits. Jesus says, "The man who had received the five talents brought the other five. 'Master,' he said, 'you entrusted me with five talents. See, I have gained five more." His master replied, 'Well done good and faithful servant! You have been faithful with a few things. I will put you in charge of many things. Come and share your master's happiness'" (Matthew 25:20,21). The faithful man who had been entrusted with two talents was also rewarded and entrusted with even greater responsibilities.

But the master's response was far different toward the man who hid his treasure. The master was furious that his servant had not so much as put his money on deposit with the bankers to gain interest. So the master took away the servant's talent and gave it to the man with ten. Then he cast the unfaithful servant into outer darkness where there was weeping and gnashing of teeth. The point of the story is obvious. God demands that we invest our time, talent, and treasure where they can multiply and bring blessings into the kingdom.

I have always found it interesting that the word "talent," which originally stood for a unit of money (some say perhaps a thousand dollars), applies just as well to our skills and abilities. Clearly, God has given Americans unmatched "talents," in both senses of the word. For any of us to fail to use these resources now, or even worse, to use them for our own pleasure, must be an abomination in the eyes of our Lord.

Matthew Henry, the great theologian and Bible expositor of the 18th century, explained the parable this way: "A true Christian is a spiritual tradesman. A tradesman is one who, having made his trade his choice, and taken pains to learn it, makes it his business to follow it, lays out all he has for the advancement of it, makes all other affairs bend to it, and lives upon the gain of it."[4]

The knowledge of Christ is our trade and commission. We have no choice but to use what God has given us for His glory. We are to work tirelessly to further His kingdom while there is still time. But if this is so, why are we doing so little with our treasure?

For example, if you were selling your expensive Porsche, would you be careless in how you described the car? How hard would you work to find the right buyer? How much time would you be willing to spend?

We have a possession that is priceless—our new life in Christ. It includes eternal life, abundant living, joy, peace, and unconditional love. Yet sometimes we treat this gift with much less respect and care than we do our material possessions.

God offers the same gift to anyone who will receive it. This includes our relatives, neighbors, co-workers, friends, and traveling companions. We are His spokesmen to share His message. Unless we tell them, they may never hear and be forever lost.

Tremendous Move of God

History confirms that wonderful things happen when the Church fasts and prays. When believers get right with God, He begins touching lives, softening hearts, changing impossible situations, mending relationships, and visiting His people with His awesome presence.

Already, revivals have been breaking out in churches and communities all across the land. Christian plays and dramas are introducing tens of thousands of unchurched people to Jesus Christ. City-wide evangelistic crusades continue to touch tens of thousands who might never darken the door of a church. Christian radio, television, films, and videos are reaching into the homes and private lives of people who would never attend a traditional church service. Others are hearing the gospel in "contemporary services" of main-line churches.

The Promise Keepers movement has touched a need in the lives of millions of men across America. The fasting and prayer movement is gaining momentum as well, changing lives, homes, churches, and even cities. (For a more detailed discussion of this development, please read my recent books, *The Coming Revival: America's Call to Fast, Pray, and "Seek God's Face,"* and *The Transforming Power of Fasting and Prayer: Personal Accounts of Spiritual Renewal.*) Followers of Christ have become keenly aware of the perils of our nation, and a tremendous move of God has led hundreds of thousands, if not millions, to begin praying and fasting for revival for America. This is an important starting point for the revival of God's Word.

As my good friend Henry Blackaby said, "God is always at work around you. You must make major adjustments in your life to join God in what He is doing. Then you will see results."[5] This is the work of a loving, caring God, revealing Himself to us in ways we cannot ignore. Families are put back together. Bitterness, unforgiveness, and hatred melt. Unhealthy habits fall away.

The appeal of 2 Chronicles 7:14, which calls us to repent and seek the face of God, was not written for the mass of society; rather, it was directed to God's people, the ancient Jews as well as present day followers of Christ. I am convinced that this process has already begun, and it now seems as though God is ready to take His people to the next level. A tangible action plan in the spiritual realm which, if pursued vigorously by believers, can even yet serve as a launching ramp for rebuilding the United States and putting it back on course with its national mission.

"You must make major adjustments in your life to JOIN GOD IN WHAT HE IS DOING."

I challenge you to take this step right now. The next chapter gives a plan for you to begin where we must all start—with personal spiritual renewal. This change will then propel you to the next part of the 2 Chronicles 7:14 process—a renewal of our communities, churches, and government. You have many talents to invest. Join John and me and millions of others in pooling our resources to turn our great ship of state onto a new course!

CHAPTER 21

Personal Spiritual Renewal

In the beginning of our marriage, both Vonette and I were very materialistic. Both of us had been very ambitious and lived selfishly prior to becoming believers. But when the Lord came into our lives, He changed us from the inside out. He gave us a deep and abiding love for Himself and a deep desire to serve Him and others. But a couple of years later, we came to realize that living for Christ and serving Him was our major goal in life. Our Lord Jesus Christ, God the Son, Creator of more than one hundred billion galaxies, left His place of glory in heaven to become a slave for us (Philemon v.16). The God-man, Jesus of Nazareth, died on the cross for our sins, was raised from the dead to demonstrate His deity, and now miracle of miracles, lives in every believer in all of His resurrection power.

In response to Christ's sacrifice, Paul became a slave to his Savior. Paul records his slavery in several passages of Scripture. I was especially captivated by his words in Romans 1:1, "Dear friends in Rome: This letter is from Paul, Jesus Christ's slave, chosen to be a missionary, and sent out to preach God's Good News" (TLB). Following the examples of our Lord Jesus Christ and that of the apostle Paul (Romans 1:1), Vonette and I also chose to become slaves of Jesus Christ. One Sunday afternoon in the spring of 1951, we decided to sign a contract with the Lord. No one suggested we do this, but as a business man I had signed many contracts, so it was only natural that we formalize the surrender of our lives to Christ, to be His slaves, with an official contract.

Vonette went to one room in our home in the Hollywood hills and I went to another. We each made a list of all the things we wanted out of life. When I first proposed to Vonette, we had talked about a honeymoon in Canada and travel in Europe, about securing the finest voice teacher to develop her already beautiful singing voice, and about living in the fabulous Bel Air community in Los Angeles. Had our desires changed?

When we sat down together to go over our lists, we were overjoyed to learn how much our lists were alike. Both lists, although using different wording, included these concepts: 1) to live holy lives, controlled and empowered by the Holy Spirit; 2) to be effective witnesses for Christ; and 3) to help fulfill the Great Commission in our generation. We also wanted to establish a Christian home with two to four children. We thought we should probably have two cars.

On our lists we said that, if it pleased the Lord, we would like to have a nice home. Vonette described it as nice enough to entertain the President of the United States and modest enough that a man from Skid Row would feel comfortable.

That Sunday afternoon, we gave all our hopes and plans to Christ. We surrendered all of our material possessions and ambitions. Then we signed the contract to become slaves of Christ. When we signed our names, we intended this to be a lifetime contract with our Lord. We purposed to always obey Him no matter what He called us to do.

Over the years, the Lord blessed us immensely. God supplied all our needs in great abundance—and we are grateful beyond our ability to express. In return, we desire to use what He gives us to help fulfill the Great Commission.

We have found that we do not need the material wealth we

once desired and worked so hard to earn. Today, we own no property and the honorariums from speaking and royalties from over fifty books and tapes go to Campus Crusade for Christ and other Christian causes. God blessed us with two sons who, with their wives, serve our Lord in Christian ministry. We do not own a car, but God has provided us with transportation through the generosity of a friend who is equally concerned with reaching the world for Christ. Generous individuals gave the ministry a condo for our use, for which we pay rent to Campus Crusade for Christ. It meets the ministry's and our needs very well. Some years ago, we felt led of the Lord to liquidate my $50,000 pension to help start a New Life Training Center at Moscow State University.

In 1996, I was humbled and honored to receive the Templeton Prize for Progress in Religion. Some feel that this award, the world's largest, is more prestigious than the Pulitzer and Nobel Prizes. Vonette and I were flown to London, treated like royalty, and presented the actual award in a private ceremony with Prince Philip at Buckingham Palace. The prize money exceeded one million, fifty thousand dollars. I appointed a committee of godly men to oversee the stewardship of this money to assure that every penny is carefully and wisely used for the special purpose that I feel God has given me: to encourage and facilitate genuine, humble prayer and fasting among followers of Christ worldwide. I truly pray that 2 Chronicles 7:14 becomes a reality in our generation.

A Sense of Urgency

Neither Vonette nor I want to give the impression that we are some kind of super saints, for we are not. Apart from the grace of God, I shudder to consider what our lives would be like. But we decided at the beginning of our married lives to live by the principle of seeking God's will first as expressed by Jesus in Matthew 6:33. Through the years, we have seen that God's will is always better than our own natural desires. The more we have witnessed examples of God's love for us, the more we have come to love, trust, and obey Him.

One of the things that makes that contract so meaningful for me today is that we did it together, as husband and wife. There was no particular emotion involved. It was simply a transaction of the will as the Spirit of God worked in us for His good pleasure. We had no idea what might happen as a result of our commitment, but God did. In less than 48 hours, as I continued with my studies at Fuller Theological Seminary, teaching, deputation work, and business, God's plans began to unfold in the most wonderful way in our lives. A couple of days later, He gave me a vision to help fulfill the Great Commission. That vision later became Campus Crusade for Christ. There is no question in my mind that God would not have given Vonette and me such a wonderful call to serve Him had we not first made the commitment and signed that contract to be His slaves.

There is no higher calling or privilege in life than to KNOW HIM and MAKE HIM KNOWN to others.

I have spent most of my adult life pursuing a closer walk with God, including five 40-day fasts for national and world revival and the fulfillment of the Great Commission. Vonette and I have shared two-and-a-half 40-day fasts together with great blessing. We have learned that there is no higher calling or privilege in life than to know Him and make Him known to others. Our Lord is truly worthy, faithful, and just. He has allowed us to survive certain hardships, to enjoy great pleasure, and to be able to share the gospel with many hundreds of millions of men and women around the world. We could not ask for more. As the passion in our hearts continues to grow, the awareness of the impending judgment upon this nation and upon the Church of Jesus Christ has given us a renewed sense of urgency.

Our goal as believers should be to work for the spiritual and moral restoration of this nation. We can do this personally, tangibly, and dynamically. We can be God's hand extended to needy people around us and throughout the world.

God's vision and purpose always begin in the heart of individuals

—one person, one family, one church, one city at a time. His programs do not begin with nations, but with each person who surrenders his or her life to His control. In this chapter, you will have an opportunity to renew your relationship with Christ and become a contributing member of God's family through ten steps. In the next chapter, you will find a plan to use your gifts and abilities along with others to help turn this nation from its course of self-destruction.

I ask you to please join me in this important mission. Here is what John and I believe must happen for you personally to prepare yourself to join in the great spiritual restoration needed in America.

1. Examine your spiritual condition.

If you have never received Jesus Christ as your personal Lord and Savior, or if you are not sure you have, or if there is no evidence of any real changes in your life since you first prayed for forgiveness, then I urge you to examine your spiritual condition carefully. You can do it now. There is nothing stopping you from asking Jesus to come into your heart, to forgive your sins, and to be the Lord of your life in all things. It is a prayer which you can pray by faith as an act of your will. Through the prophet Ezekiel, God said, "Repent, and turn from all your transgressions, so that iniquity will not be your ruin" (Ezekiel 18:30). Your honest, heartfelt prayer of confession will reach the very throne room of heaven and God will answer (See Psalm 91:15; Isaiah 58:9, 65:24; Luke 11:9; John 15:7).

God will not force Himself on us. Each of us must decide as an act of our free will to move toward God. Do not wait until you get your life in better shape so He will accept you. He will accept you just as you are right now. Do not wait until you better understand the person and ways of God or get things figured out in your mind. None of us understands God fully. Just come to Him in faith and pour your heart and hurts out to Him as you ask for His forgiveness and help.

If you would like to know more about the prayer of salvation, read Appendix B, the text of a small booklet that I first wrote in 1957, presenting what I call the *Four Spiritual Laws*. Over the last 40 years, this booklet has helped millions to come to a new and personal relationship with Jesus Christ. To date, over two billion copies of this booklet have been printed in more than 200 languages. After you have read it, you can pray the prayer printed on page 10 of the booklet. Be assured that "whoever calls on the name of the Lord shall be saved" (Joel 2:32).

2. Ask God to cleanse your heart.

Only God can change our hearts, and He wants to do so; but we must ask Him to come in and do the spiritual housecleaning which needs to be done. King David prayed, "Create in me a clean heart, oh God, and renew a steadfast spirit within me" (Psalm 51:10). That should be our prayer as well. King David, burdened by the sins of adultery and murder, later confessed, "God would not have listened if I had not confessed my sins. But He listened! He heard my prayer! He paid attention to it!" (Psalm 66:18,19, TLB).

> God will not bless WORLDLY CHRISTIANS who continue to walk according to their OLD NATURES.

It is our hope that every believer in this nation will get on his or her knees and pray with a sincere heart: "God, show me the sins of my heart, and as I confess them, rush them away with the blood of Christ shed on the cross for my sins, so that I personally may become the godly man or woman You want me to be." Ask God to cleanse your heart of any known sin, especially the sins of pride and unforgiveness towards others who have mistreated or hurt you in the past.

3. Change the areas of your life that are displeasing to God.

Have the godless culture and humanistic thoughts in our society invaded your life and behavior? We must align our lives by God's biblical standards of truth if we want to be right before Him. He will not bless worldly Christians who continue to walk according to their old natures. The Holy Spirit desires to direct our lives according to our new natures in Christ (Romans 1:1–17). Believers are commanded to "walk (live) in the Spirit and not fulfill (gratify) the works of the flesh (sinful nature)" (Galatians 5:16).

4. Ask God to fill you with His Holy Spirit.

The Bible makes it clear that Jesus Christ sent the Holy Spirit after the resurrection to be our Comforter and Guide. He is also the believer's source of power and boldness to stand up for the truth. He is also called the Helper and the One who comes along beside us to show us how we should live. He comes to guide, strengthen, and teach us so that our lives may glorify God.

Actually, the Spirit-filled life is the Christ-directed life by which Christ lives His life in and through us in the power of the Holy Spirit (John 15). Ephesians 5:18 commands us to be filled with the Spirit. According to this command and the promise in 1 John 5:14,15 to answer our requests, ask God to fill you with His Holy Spirit. Then be assured that He will begin to live His supernatural life through you. (For more information on how to be filled with the Spirit daily, read Appendix C, *Have You Made the Wonderful Discovery of the Spirit-Filled Life?*)

5. Join the prayer and fasting movement.

God is raising up a prayer and fasting movement around the world. You, too, can be a part of it. Fast and pray for personal holiness, for the cleansing of the church, for revival in our nation, the world, and for the fulfillment of the Great Commission. As you begin to fast and pray, keep a daily prayer journal listing His answers to your prayers. Make notes of any changes you observe, great or small, and any scriptural truths that the Holy Spirit lays upon your heart. Remember, when fasting and praying, to make it your priority to seek His *face*, enjoying His presence, and not just His *hand* for what He will give you.

For more biblical teaching on fasting and prayer, see my notes in Appendix D. If possible, join with others in your local church and community who desire to seek God through prayer and fasting. Support your local church and your own denominational prayer efforts. Also participate in prayer events, such as the annual Prayer and Fasting Gathering sponsored by Campus Crusade for Christ and Mission America each year in November. I am also excited about the promotion of prayer in organizations such as ***Pray USA!***, the U.S. Prayer Track, Celebrate Jesus, Mission America, the National Day of Prayer, Concerned Women of America, Concerts of Prayer, Intercessors for America, and the National Association of Evangelicals, among others. For more information and resources on fasting and prayer activities, call 1-888-FASTING.

I believe it would be wrong for us to pray for ourselves, our churches, even the nonbelievers without praying for our community and government servants. They can play key roles in turning our nation around to go in a new direction. The following Prayer List will help you personalize your prayer efforts. Write it in a notebook and list names where appropriate. Personalize the list for your particular situation, then use the list every day, updating it as needed.

Prayer List

Leaders in government:

President
Vice president
Senators
Representatives
Governor
State legislators
Supreme Court justices
Federal and state judges
City government officials
School board

Prayer requests:

My concerns for the federal government
My concerns for the state government
My concerns for the city government
My concerns for my neighborhood
My concerns for my family

6. Pray for and support your pastor and local church.

The local church should be at the heart of evangelism, discipleship, training, world missions, and social concerns. A godly body of believers representing churches of all denominations is the most positive influence for good in any city. Yet most pastors carry very heavy burdens with over-extended work loads. They truly care about you, your needs, and your spiritual growth. Be faithful in your service, responsibilities, and giving to your church. Be in your place of worship or service during church services, Sunday school, missions conventions, vacation Bible school, and other church activities.

7. Participate in and support one or more gospel-preaching ministries and missionaries.

Those who carry the Word of hope and restoration to the ends of the earth can accomplish far more when they are supported by thousands of believers like you and me, giving encouragement, prayers, offerings, volunteer help, and in some cases, applying for full-time missions work. Together we can make a difference!

At Campus Crusade for Christ, we sincerely desire to help win our generations for Christ and then to train them into an army that will also help fulfill the Great Commission. For a list of ministries related to Campus Crusade for Christ, please visit our web site at www.ccci.org.

8. Share your faith with anyone who will listen.

I always assume that if I am placed for a few minutes or more with any person, I am there by divine appointment, arranged by God, to share His love, forgiveness, and eternal life. If the person is not a believer, show them how to receive Christ. The *Four Spiritual Laws* provides a guideline to follow. If the person is already a believer, explain how to be filled with the Holy Spirit. If they are already filled with the Holy Spirit, invite them to join you and us in helping to reclaim America for Christ. For more in-depth instructions, read my book or watch the video, *Reaching Your World through Witnessing Without Fear*. For other tips on witnessing, see "Eight Ways to Share Christ" in Appendix E.

9. Fast and pray for God to reveal a specific plan to you for rebuilding the nation spiritually and morally.

Now comes the critical next step, helping America receive God's blessings by helping complete the Great Commission. Expect to hear from God as you have never heard from Him before. Believe that He wants to show you His will and will enable you to fulfill His plan for you.

I am sure that as you seek God's will and purpose for your life, He will reveal the specific plans and areas for your involvement. They may include things such as rebuilding unity in the body of Christ, reclaiming the American educational system, or making a renewed commitment to helping the poor and needy. You may feel led, in partnership with tens of thousands of churches, to help place the *JESUS* video in every one of the 100 million American homes. Be assured that God will guide you to opportunities based on your gifts and qualifications. While praying for greater leaps of faith into more supernatural exploits, begin with tangible ways of service. Remember that God has a plan for each of us to use, for His Kingdom and His praise, the "talents" He has placed in our hands.

God desires that His people WORK TOGETHER in harmony to accomplish His goal.

10. Commit to following the plan God reveals by joining others in the renewal effort.

God desires that His people work together in harmony to accomplish His goal. Like the Pilgrims, the Puritans, the Founding Fathers, and other godly men and women who have gone before us, we can join hands for a common cause. What better cause to support than the spiritual and moral restoration of our country. As we do, we will display godly unity and do more for His kingdom than we can possibly do alone. In the next chapter, we will offer you a plan of action and call for you to join your plan with ours as together we love, trust, and obey our great God and Savior.

CHAPTER 22

A Vision for the Future

The Bible contains many passages that outline God's vision for the nations. From the first moment that He placed man on this earth and surrounded him with every pleasant thing, God knew what was right for us. He guided our hands and taught us the way in which we should go. There is reason to be encouraged. More and more Christians are joining the battle to choose good rather than evil. They are standing for morality instead of immorality, and desire to reach fellow citizens with the gospel of Jesus Christ.

I receive reports from all over our country of individuals who are joining others to help fulfill the Great Commission. Let me tell you one inspiring story that came into my office.

Robert Desch from East Greenville, Pennsylvania, distributed seventy-one *JESUS* videos to neighbors on his street. That is quite commendable, you might think. However, he did so at great cost. Fourteen years earlier, he fell off a roof leaving him a paraplegic. For the past six months, he had been fighting painful bone cancer.

In spite of his "good excuses," his pain, and inability to go up the steps to any of the homes, he spent about thirty to forty minutes each day distributing the videos. As his grandson climbed the steps and knocked on the doors, Robert sat in his wheelchair on the sidewalk. When someone answered the door, the grandson would offer the video. Seventy-one of Robert's neighbors accepted the gift.

Two weeks after the elderly man gave away the seventy-first video, his exhausted body was laid in a grave. He was in the presence of the Lord, but his work on earth continues in the lives of the men and women he touched with his videos.

With God's help, John Damoose and I, along with many concerned Americans, are personally committed to saving this nation from the chaos and confusion that has exploded in our midst in recent years. We are also personally committed to helping complete the Great Commission. We cannot accomplish either of these worthy objectives on our own. But together with people who have a vision like Robert Desch and through the enabling of the Holy Spirit, we can.

"Behold, NOW is the accepted time; behold, NOW is the day of salvation."

For John and me, and thousands like us around the world, this is the most compelling challenge of our lifetimes. Paul's words ring in our ears: "Behold, now is the accepted time; behold, now is the day of salvation" (2 Corinthians 6:2). Truly, this is our hour for finding ways to bring moral and spiritual renewal to our land. God's purpose for America is that she would be healed and made whole, so that we can be His instruments for the redemption of a fallen world.

After completing your own plan for spiritual renewal and personal involvement, as discussed in the previous chapter, consider partnering with one or more biblical ministries which have plans for reaching America and the world for Christ. These organizations are having a dramatic impact in many communities and countries.

The ministries described below are only examples of the thousands of organizations who are contributing to the renewal of America's will and purpose. They desire to partner with you in sharing your faith, turning America back to God, and reaching the lost throughout the world. Prayerfully read about their activities, write or call them for more information about their work, then put them on your prayer list.

Mission America

Mission America is a cooperative effort with the *AD2000 & Beyond* movement and some seventy denominations, representing approximately 200,000 churches and 150 parachurch groups, including Campus Crusade for Christ. Mission America is the prayerful response of Christian leaders to a prompting of the Holy Spirit to collaborate in united prayer, fasting, revival and spiritual awakening, evangelism, reconciliation, and world outreach. The ministry seeks to facilitate the process of sharing the gospel of Jesus Christ with every man, woman, and child in the United States by the end of the year 2000. I have the privilege of serving with Billy Graham and John Perkins as honorary co-chairmen of Mission America.

Our theme is: What can we do better together than we can do separately to share the love of Christ with our communities? We believe that no single Christian, church, denomination, mission agency, or outreach organization can hope to complete the task of world evangelization alone. Thus, we seek to develop strategic partnerships between ministry networks, churches, denominations, and parachurch ministries across the land. Mission America's plan for helping reach America and impact the world include the following efforts:

- Equipping local leaders to share the gospel of Jesus Christ in 4,000 communities with population of 15,000 or more.
- Training and encouraging 10,000 community facilitators to initiate local collaborative prayer and evangelistic efforts.
- Giving prayerful leadership to national evangelistic initiatives that invite every Christian in America to share the love and grace of Jesus Christ with every person in the United States.
- Forming scores of ministry networks which focus on prayer, fasting, revival, reconciliation and evangelism, and offering ministry resources and assistance to the community outreaches.

Networks focus on multinational ministries to men, women, young people, children, senior adults, Native Americans, artists, Christian educators, persons with disabilities, and the media.

- Facilitating loving and supportive relationships between Christians, regardless of race, gender, or church background. Reconciliation is essential for revival and reformation in Christ's church.
- Establishing church plants in strategic locations around the world (some 1,700 people groups representing 2.2 billion people have been identified) through *The Joshua Project 2000*.
- Promoting the "Heal Our Land" movement to recruit, train, unite, network for reconciliation and community development, and establish prayer support for interactive musical prayer events, "salt-and-light" seminars, prayer, and witnessing.
- Sponsoring *Celebrate JESUS 2000*, an evangelism campaign targeted to reach every person in our nation through prayer, fasting, personal witness, proclamation (revivals, crusades, special evangelistic events, and broadcasts), and preservation (discipleship).

To contact Mission America, call (612) 853-1762.

U.S. Prayer Track

The U.S. Prayer Track is a servant ministry to the other prayer ministries in the United States. Its primary purpose is to mobilize prayer for spiritual awakening by identifying and networking existing prayer ministries. In addition to producing prayer-related books and tapes and conducting seminars and conferences, U.S. Prayer Track sponsors ***PrayUSA!***, a national, forty-day fasting and prayer initiative involving scores of denominations, hundreds of parachurch ministries, prayer networks, and thousands of churches. This annual event mobilizes millions of Christians to fast and pray through a forty-day prayer calendar. Sponsors included the Christian Broadcasting Network, Mission America, and Campus Crusade for Christ International. Dr. Pat Robertson, my wife, Vonette, and I serve as co-chairs.

To contact the U.S. Prayer Track, call (281) 855-1417 or send e-mail to eddiesmith@xc.org.

Campus Crusade for Christ International

The purpose of Campus Crusade for Christ is to help fulfill the Great Commission in this generation through the power of the Holy Spirit according to Matthew 28:18–20. To do this, we have adopted New-***Life*** 2000—our worldwide master strategy for helping fulfill the Great Commission along with our international partners. It encompasses the more than fifty Campus Crusade ministries in the United States and overseas. New***Life*** 2000 has six goals:

1. Help present the gospel to more than 6 billion people using the *JESUS* film and other evangelistic tools.
2. Help introduce 1 billion people to Jesus Christ as their personal Savior.
3. Help establish more than 5 million New***Life*** Groups, which will minister to as many as 200 million new believers.
4. Help provide training through New Life Training Centers in almost 6,000 MPTAs (Million Population Target Areas) and send 10,000 *JESUS* film teams to show the *JESUS* film in 1,000 major languages and dialects.
5. Help start ministries on 8,000 college campuses in strategic metropolitan areas worldwide to present the good news to 60 million university students and their professors.
6. Assist all participating denominations with their church growth goals, resulting in one million new churches.

Meanwhile, I continue to challenge the Campus Crusade for Christ staff of approximately 250,000 full-time and trained volunteers to join me in discipling and mentoring tens of millions of people by teaching them how to:

- Experience the reality of an exalted view of God and His attributes
- Love God with all their heart, soul, and mind

- Surrender totally, completely, and irrevocably to the lordship of Christ
- Be filled with the Holy Spirit and practice spiritual breathing (walking in the power of the Holy Spirit) as a way of life (For more information on the concept of spiritual breathing, read Appendix C, *Have You Made the Wonderful Discovery of the Spirit-Filled Life?*)
- Live obedient lives of holiness before God
- Live lives of great faith
- Live lives characterized by the supernatural
- Receive a God-given vision
- Be courageous and tenacious for Christ
- Be faithful stewards of God's Word
- Be committed to fast and pray for worldwide revival and the fulfillment of the Great Commission
- Be faithful, daily witnesses for our Lord Jesus Christ
- Seek daily seek to help fulfill the Great Commission, generation after generation.

Can we restore our spiritual roots and national purpose before we pass the POINT OF NO RETURN?

I pray that God will lay on your heart one of our more than fifty Campus Crusade ministries. If you feel that God is leading you to participate with a Campus Crusade ministry or the fasting and prayer movement as part of your plan for renewal, please get in touch with us. To receive more information on the kinds of ministries working to help fulfill the Great Commission, visit the Campus Crusade for Christ web site at www.ccci.org. For your convenience we, have included a *Campus Crusade for Christ Response Form* at the back of the book. We will send information on available materials. They will explain how you can get involved with the fasting and prayer movement or how you can contact Campus Crusade for Christ ministries in your area of interest. We look forward to hearing about your decision to commit yourself to helping restore America!

Freedom Ministries of America

Freedom Ministries of America is a newly developed national ministry headquartered in Traverse City, Michigan. It seeks to reignite the faith of the vast body of believers in America, especially those now only nominally involved. Through a host of initiatives designed to penetrate mainstream America with the gospel of Jesus Christ, Freedom Ministries hopes to join hands with fellow believers from every denomination to help evangelize America. Additionally, American believers can join with other countries and national churches to help evangelize the world.

Freedom Ministries is headed by John B. Damoose, former vice-president of marketing for the Chrysler Corporation. He was listed by Automotive News as one of the world's top twenty auto executives when at age 46 and near the top of his career, he left it all behind to answer the call of Jesus Christ on his life. He said, "Jesus Christ stepped into my life and said, 'Drop your nets, John, and follow me.'"

New approaches are needed to answer the following question: At this most critical time in the life of our nation, can we restore our spiritual roots and national purpose before we pass the point of no return? Americans can only be reached if we develop new platforms and initiatives in the years to come, uniting Christians in taking the gospel of Jesus Christ to people through unique and dynamic ways. The ultimate mission of Freedom Ministries is to "join hands to help evangelize America and equip Americans to help evangelize the world." To help accomplish this mission, Freedom Ministries' goals center around three specific objectives:

1. To "re-ignite" the vast body of nominal Christians in America to the gospel and provide a nation of "seekers" after the saving knowledge of Jesus Christ. Thus,"*to win their hearts to Christ.*"
2. To "educate" young and old about America's covenant with

God and how we have departed from the faith of our Founding Fathers and pulled away from God. Now we face a serious crisis and need to restore our duty as Christians. Thus, *"to win their minds to Christ."*

3. To "equip" and "mobilize" Christians to participate in the Great Commission at home and around the world. Thus, *"to enlist their work for Christ."*

To meet these objectives and incorporate the premises, a four-step action plan will guide the movement's activities over the next several years:

Step 1: Tell the Story

In 1997, Freedom Ministries joined hands with the Christian Broadcasting Network to tell the story of America in the original documentary, *Victory in Spite of All Terror.* The goal was to reveal God's hand moving to shape the United States into a nation uniquely prepared to touch the world with the gospel of Jesus Christ. The project featured original interviews with a broad coalition of prominent Christian leaders from every denomination and walk of life.

In 1998, Freedom Ministries joined hands with Campus Crusade for Christ to co-author *Red Sky in the Morning* and to co-produce the video documentary and study guide which accompany this book. These materials are available for church, Sunday school, group Bible studies, radio, and television broadcasts.

Step 2: Build a Grand Coalition

Freedom Ministries seeks to develop a "Grand Coalition" of 100,000 believers from all walks of life who will commit their hearts, minds, and work to the task of reigniting America for Christ. Rooted in prayer and fasting, the Grand Coalition will represent a new unity for the body of Christ in America.

The Grand Coalition will include individuals, business and professional leaders, private institutions, and ministries. They will join hands to create enduring initiatives to reignite a fervor for the gospel in the hearts and minds of the vast body of Christians in America. The Grand Coalition will also equip and mobilize followers of Christ to evangelize. The group will then execute the plan systematically and support the efforts of believers from every denomination to help change America and expand her witness to the world.

Step 3: Launch a Unified Initiative

The next step will be to issue a "Holy Summons" to Christian leaders from every facet of society to come together to develop a systematic plan to reclaim America for Jesus Christ. This organization, along with a grassroots "army" of 100,000 men and women called forth by God, will concentrate on executing the plan to restore America and her national mission of world evangelism.

Operating on local, state, and national levels, the plan will present a tangible series of steps. With the Holy Spirit's help, these steps will radically reshape our character and provide a new focus as to who we are as a people. Then, we will go forth to do what we should do as a nation. The plan will maximize the various revelations received by believers throughout the nation who have joined our fight for righteousness.

The second unified initiative will show what can happen when we work together to help bring biblical Christianity back into mainstream America. This project is known as "The Great Freedom Train"—a twenty-four-car traveling exposition which will embark on a five-year, 250-city journey throughout America starting near the turn of the millennium. The train will take the gospel of Jesus back to the people in a profound initiative driven by an unprecedented coalition of ministry, spiritual, business, and cultural leaders.

Relating to a simpler time in our history, this train is reminiscent of the 1976 Bicentennial Freedom Train which crisscrossed the country and drew forty million Americans. The ultimate mission of the Freedom Train is to unite the body of Christ around an innovative and enduring project focused on the gospel of Jesus Christ and restoring our spiritual roots and purpose. It will offer Americans the opportunity to experience freedom found only in Jesus Christ.

Step 4: Leave a Legacy

The train will leave a living legacy in its wake through a nationwide network of "Freedom Centers." They will be built as upscale gathering places with a friendly, inviting atmosphere. They will create a Christian presence in a prime, central location of many communities. No less than a Christian "embassy," they will provide an exciting, interactive, resource center for believers of all denominations. These staging centers will offer programs and initiatives reflecting the activism and unity of the Great Freedom Train project that originally birthed them. Funds generated by the Freedom Train will help support the centers.

While reflecting regional, local, and ethnic differences and compositions, each center will share a myopic focus on Jesus Christ and the Great Commission and include many of the following:

- Community Bible studies
- Education and information centers
- Training for believers on how to witness to and disciple others
- Interactive networking to national and international ministries
- Missions conferences and ministry seminars
- Resource libraries
- Charitable outreach
- Local preaching and church resource centers
- Community choir concerts
- Christian entertainment
- Youth activities
- Resources for public school teachers, Christian schools, and home-schoolers.

Freedom Centers can become the hub of Christian activity within a community, continuing to unite believers and churches, discipling them and equipping them to participate in the Great Commission. Present plans call for at least two Freedom Centers strategically placed in each state. Thus a Freedom Center will be within driving distance of 98% of all Americans.

If you choose to join with us, sign the commitment card on the *Freedom Ministries Response Form* printed at the back of this book and mail or fax it to us. Later, you will receive instructions on how to share the plans you have received from God. After we receive your response form, we will keep you informed as to the Freedom Movement's activities, prayer requests, and opportunities for you to meet with other Christians who share your burden for America and reaching nonbelievers for Christ.

Restoring America

This book was never intended to be read in your spare time, then put on the shelf to gather dust. After reading this book, you may merely agree with what I have said in these pages and say to yourself, *"Yes, that was interesting."* But if you do nothing to help bring the gospel back into the American culture, we have accomplished nothing.

John and I wrote this book to be the first in a series of efforts to help reignite the flame of the gospel of Jesus Christ to burn brightly once again in America's soul. Therefore, we would like to invite you to pray about our challenge and ask God to guide you on these matters. Then, if you feel God wants you to become involved, we trust you will join the Grand Coalition to restore America. This coalition will work to continue the process you have already begun by reading this book.

If you commit yourself to helping to restore America, you will be joining many ordinary people who are becoming extraordinary through the power of God—and who are already giving of themselves to do their part. For example, John Gaither, a member of a singing group called the Convertibles, was able to do the impossible—share the gospel with public high school students in the public school during a public school assembly! This was an audience of kids wearing T-shirts with strange logos and wild hairdos. He also had a chance to explain the importance of virginity and sexual purity. In fact, he shared at fourteen different assemblies at different schools, and no one stood up to object. Even more exciting, 7,000 high school students heard the gospel message.

A woman in Massachusetts had a one-to-one Bible study with her sister who is a recovering alcoholic of nineteen years. The sister went on to share the Bible study concepts with her family as well as two friends. The woman also witnessed to a doctor and his wife who had lost all their material possessions. They in turn discipled their children who shared the same material with their children. The woman is also studying with her husband and son, and these two have plans to share the material with someone, too.

Dr. Bob Cosby, the *JESUS* Video Project Director for the state of Alabama, and his team had placed, as of Easter Sunday 1998, a copy of the *JESUS* video in approximately 1.7 million homes in Alabama. Tapes were distributed to 758 post offices across the state. Some 9,300 churches have received letters asking for their participation in follow-up ministry. Based on prior responses to the video showings, hundreds of thousands of people in Alabama will receive Christ as Savior.

Whether America survives or not is IN OUR HANDS. There is a choice to be made. It may well be our FINAL CHOICE.

My dear friends, unless a great army like the ordinary believers in these examples is willing to commit to restoring America, I am convinced we shall not survive. But as the church of Jesus Christ, we are not helpless victims. We can be the intercessory force and front-line leaders who turn this nation around! Like many national Christian leaders, I believe God will give America another chance as He did for Nineveh, if we truly repent.

There is cause for hope, but it is a conditional hope. God will only move when His people take Him at His word and act boldly and courageously out of faith and obedience. Whether America survives or not is in our hands. There is a choice to be made. It may well be our final choice.

CHAPTER 23

Hope for the Future

Allow me to end this book with a positive story. A few days ago I received word from our director in the tragic war-torn country of Rwanda. As you know, Rwanda has been devastated by tribal warfare between the Hutus and the Tutsis, who are killing each other by the hundreds of thousands. Millions are homeless, hundreds of thousands live in refugee camps.

Our Campus Crusade for Christ director in Rwanda received a copy of my book, *The Coming Revival*, which had been translated into French. He took it to the pastor of his church of twenty-five-hundred members. Moved by the book, the pastor called his people to join him for forty days of fasting and praying for their country. Five hundred volunteered immediately, and night after night as they gathered in the church to continue their fast and to pray for each other, hundreds more joined them until the whole church was experiencing revival. Pastors and members of other churches came to have their hearts warmed, and revival spread throughout the capital city of Rwanda. As the revival spread, members of the warring tribes began to reach out in reconciliation, asking each other for forgiveness and to make peace. The dramatic results of their fasting and prayer spread across their land and to other countries.

Leaders in the Rwandan government began to inquire what the church was doing that changed the lives of warring tribal members. This was something the government and its powerful military forces had not been able to accomplish.

Similar reports are coming to us from other parts of the world. For example, more than one million Christians in Latin America are fasting and praying for forty days in their respective countries. Revival has already begun.

We know that nothing is impossible with our great Lord and Savior who is always faithful to His promises. He wants to transform our beloved country too. The same unlimited measure of God's power is available to us. When God moves in our midst to revive us, as He has already begun to do and as He did in Rwanda, people will acknowledge the mighty works of God. Our neighbors, employers, and government leaders will take notice as God works in our midst to renew our spirits, make us more righteous, and spread His love and forgiveness to others.

Our ULTIMATE VICTORY must not blind us to the realities of the present. Important battles need to be WON NOW!

We are engaged in spiritual warfare for the minds and souls of men, women, young people, and children. We know our enemy; his tricks and schemes are not new. However, he is a defeated foe and the cause of righteousness will triumph in the end. But our ultimate victory must not blind us to the realities of the present. Important battles need to be won now!

Moving Forward

Indeed, hard times require hard solutions. We readily admit that good parents need to deal firmly with rebellious children. They do this both for the sake of their child as well as for their own benefit. In the same way, God often deals strongly with His children for their sakes and the sake of His kingdom here on earth. When challenged by our past and present failures, we should not be offended or defensive by the strong words intended to help us.

It is true that we have written a powerful challenge in this book, but we trust you recognize the spirit of love and compassion behind everything we have said. We care very much for this nation and for the cause of Christ in the world, and yet we realize that we have little time to help our churches see the imminent dangers. The red sky is looming and the gathering storms are upon us. We trust that this book will help interpret the times in which we live according to God's Word. We will not escape the Lord's discipline if we do not repent. Therefore, we must speak the truth in a spirit of love. The book of Hebrews beautifully describes how we are to react under God's discipline:

> Endure hardship as discipline; God is treating you as sons. For what son is not disciplined by his father?...We have all had human fathers who disciplined us and we respected them for it. How much more should we submit to the Father of our spirits and live! Our fathers disciplined us for a little while as they thought best; but God disciplines us for our good, that we may share in His holiness. No discipline seems pleasant at the time, but painful. Later on, however, it produces a harvest of righteousness and peace for those who have been trained by it (Hebrews 12:7–11).

Our goal is not to make you feel better, but to help us all be better and do better. Neither do we want to make anyone feel discouraged or hopeless. We believe there is great hope for our nation and its people, but only through spiritual cleansing and renewal. As so many of my peers have said, the only hope for America is a sweeping spiritual renewal. It must start at the grass roots and ascend to the highest pinnacle of leadership in our country.

Our prayer is that the warning contained in this book, which we believe is in line with God's message to our nation, may be one more instrument in His plan for sparking revival in this land. From that turning point, we can march on to finish the work of world evangelism which Christ left for us, His followers, to complete in each generation.

Take heart! When we are on God's side, we simply cannot fail. Bound together in Christian love, let us move forward to do what must be done. If this book has struck a cord with your concern for America, the church, and our children, please let us hear from you.

I leave you with this sure word from almighty God:

> *But despite all this, overwhelming victory is ours through Christ who loved us enough to die for us. For I am convinced that nothing can ever separate us from his love. Death can't, and life can't. The angels won't, and all the powers of hell itself cannot keep God's love away. Our fears for today, our worries about tomorrow, or where we are—high above the sky, or in the deepest ocean—nothing will ever be able to separate us from the love of God demonstrated by our Lord Jesus Christ when he died for us* (Romans 8:37–39, TLB).

Appendices

Many conditions around us seem so bad. In reality, however, we are living in a most exciting time to be alive…People worldwide seem to have a greater spiritual hunger today than at any time in history, and they are responding to the gospel message in numbers hard to believe…The great question we face is this: Will we submit to God's refining fire so He can make us clean vessels through which He can work to redeem a lost world? We pray that your answer will be yes!

—Henry T. Blackaby and Claude V. King,
Fresh Encounter

APPENDIX A

Begin at My Sanctuary

A Call to Repentance in the Church

By Nancy Leigh DeMoss

We have come together to cry out to God on behalf of our nation. In setting aside these days, we are acknowledging that there are no human solutions to the tidal wave of evil in our land, and that nothing short of divine intervention can overcome the darkness and the lostness of our world. But I believe we need to remind ourselves at the outset of this gathering that there are some prayers God will not hear; there are some solemn assemblies He will not attend; there are some fasts that are not pleasing to Him.

When the children of Israel came to fast and pray with unclean hands and hearts, God said, "Though they shout in My ears, I will not listen to them...Though ye make many prayers, I will not hear" (Ezekiel 8:18; Isaiah 1:15). In fact, the Scripture goes so far as to say that our prayers and our fasts are actually an abomination to Him if they are not accompanied by humility and repentance.

We would all be quick to agree about the need for repentance outside these walls. But are we as quick to recognize our own need for repentance? We can readily identify the sins of the White House. But have we become blind to the corruption in our own house? We decry the sin of our world. But have we not tolerated virtually all the same sins in the Church?

Tonight we face a danger of feeling that the problem is somewhere "out there"—in Washington, San Francisco, or Hollywood, on our college campuses, or among nominal church members. But as we read the Scripture, we see that the sternest words of reproof were issued, not to the pagan world, but to the people of God. The prophet Isaiah calls out, "Hear, oh heavens, and give ear, oh earth, for the Lord hath spoken: I have nourished and brought up children, and they have rebelled against Me...They have forsaken the Lord; they have provoked the Holy One of Israel unto anger; they are gone away backward...The whole head is sick, and the whole heart faint. From the sole of the foot even unto the head, there is no soundness in it; but wounds, and bruises, and putrifying sores ...How is the faithful city become an harlot!" (Isaiah 1:2,5,6,21).

Throughout the Old Testament, the Father/Husband heart of God grieved over the waywardness of His chosen people. Time after time, He begged them to repent. And when they refused, the Hound of Heaven pursued their stubborn, sinning hearts with painful discipline.

In the New Testament, we hear Jesus' indictment against the spiritual leaders of His day—men who were renowned for their much fasting and praying: "These people honor me with their lips," He said, "but their hearts are far from me." The opening words of Jesus' ministry here on earth were not, "Fast and Pray!" but "Repent!"

And when the ascended Lord Jesus looked down from His throne in heaven, His final message to the churches was not, "Go and preach the gospel," but, "Repent!" For an unrepenting church has neither the motivation nor the capacity to fulfill the Great Commission of our Lord. To the first of the seven churches, He said, "You have committed spiritual adultery...You have left your first love...Repent!" To another, "You have a reputation for being alive, but you are really dead...Repent!" And to the comfortable, complacent church at Laodicea, He said, "You don't think you have any needs, but the fact is, you are wretched, naked, miserable, blind, and poor...Repent!"

And still tonight, the Lord Jesus pleads with His beloved Bride: "Be zealous, and repent, or else I will come and remove your light from its place."

Over and over again, I have been gripped by the account in Ezekiel 8 and 9, where God takes His servant in a vision to the temple in Jerusalem. No less than ten times in the 8th chapter, God says to Ezekiel: "Look! See! Do you see what's going on in there? Look at the detestable things taking place right in the middle of My temple!"

I have been asking God to help me see what He sees when His all-knowing eyes examine the church in America. The picture is not a pretty one, and the truth is painful to admit. But we have got to get honest, if we ever hope to get God's attention. The truth is, we have not only flirted, but actually fornicated with the world. When it comes to how we live, how we think, how we look, how we sound, and how we "do ministry," we have become virtually indistinguishable from the world outside the church.

Recent Barna research indicates, for example, that, for the first time in our nation, the divorce rate in the church is actually higher than outside the church. We have bought into the world's philosophies and practices. Whereas the church used to tell the world how to live, now the world is telling the church how to live. We have accommodated to the culture, rather than calling the culture to accommodate to Christ. Thus, church and ministry have become big business. We are more familiar with management and marketing principles than with the principles of humility, purity, faith, and prayer. Many pastors and Christian leaders have become CEO's rather than spiritual shepherds.

We have utilized nearly every worldly method conceivable to attract the lost, and, in many cases, have lost both our distinctiveness and our effectiveness. We have built our ministries on pragmatism—"whatever works"—without stopping to evaluate if the means we are using are in accordance with the ways and Word of God.

In an effort to convince the world that Christianity is fun, we have entertained and amused ourselves to death. Why do Christian celebrities and comedians perform to sell out crowds while scarcely a few attend the prayer meetings? Why do we feel we can't reach people today without rock bands, hip talk, and worldly dress? Whatever happened to the power of God? Have we become more dependent on methods, techniques, strategies, and programs, than on prayer and the Holy Spirit?

Have we lost confidence in the power of the Word to convict, the gospel to convert, and the Spirit to draw men to Christ? We have seen what human effort, ingenuity, creativity, and technology can do; we know what money, organization, and promotion can do; but we have yet to see what God can do!

We care more about public relations—how our constituents view us—than about how God views us; we are more concerned about our reputation than His. In our seeker-driven mindset, we are more worried about offending visitors than offending God. We are more concerned about people "feeling good" than about their "being right." We want people to leave feeling good about church, about us, and about themselves—never mind that they have grossly offended a holy God and are under His condemnation and wrath!

We are so afraid of seeming intolerant or unloving that we tiptoe around crucial issues of the Word of God. Our cowardice in standing with God on such matters as divorce and remarriage has made us accessories to the carnage of millions of Christian families. In fact, we have placed ourselves in the precarious position of justifying and defending what God says He hates!

We have commercialized and merchandised the gospel of Christ for the sake of financial gain and worldly acceptance. In many instances, we have pursued unity at the expense of purity. Today, anyone who dares to call sin by name, or to point out doctrinal error is likely to be branded as divisive, unloving, or "legalistic." In an effort to make Christianity palatable to our soft, self-centered generation, we have preached a diluted message that sidesteps the issue of sin, eliminates the demands of the cross, and overlooks the need for conviction and repentance.

In an effort to make our message "relevant," we have ended up preaching "another gospel" that is no gospel at all. We have preached Christianity as a way to find fulfillment, rather than a calling to take up the cross and follow Jesus.

In many cases, we are more concerned about additions and statistics than actual converts, or the quality of those converts. Never before in the history of the church have there been so many millions of people on the church rolls who profess to be Christians, who can even pinpoint the time and place of their "conversion," but whose lives give no credible evidence of a saving relationship with Christ.

Inside the church itself, in far more ways than we care to admit, we have failed to live by the Scripture. Like King Saul, we say we have obeyed the Word of God; but how do we explain all the evidence to the contrary? For example, we are a community of the forgiven who refuse to forgive. We live with unresolved conflicts—in our homes, among church and ministry staff, and in the pew.

Further, we have ignored or rejected biblical standards for spiritual leadership. Instead, we exalt giftedness over godliness and elevate men whose lives and homes are far from conforming to the standard of Scripture. We brush known sin under the carpet. Why do so few churches practice biblical church discipline? And why are professing believers who refuse to repent allowed to continue as members in good standing?

The Bride has forgotten how to blush. We sin without shame; we have lost our ability to mourn and grieve and weep over sin. Even our language betrays our theology of irresponsibility: We speak of leaders "falling" into sin, rather than acknowledging that these men and women have chosen a pathway of compromise and gratifying the lusts of the flesh.

In keeping with the times in which we live, we as Christian women have tossed aside such outmoded notions as virtue, modesty, femininity, and submission. We have exchanged the adorning of a meek and quiet spirit for an angry, demanding, controlling spirit. Abandoning our God-created role as helpers, we have insisted on taking up the reins in the home and in the church.

In our casual brand of Christianity there is little sense of the fear of the Lord. How else could millions of churchgoers sit under the preaching of the Word week after week and leave unchanged, unmoved? How else could so-called believers who claim to believe in holiness, sit in their living rooms or hotel rooms, watching television and laughing at ungodly jokes, lifestyles, and philosophies? When is the last time you saw God's people "tremble at the Word of the Lord"? When is the last time we trembled at the Word of the Lord?

Should it come as any surprise that the watching world should reject our message, when our lives bear so little witness to its truth and power?

At the heart of our problem is that subtle, deadly sin of pride—insidious, cancerous, blinding pride. We are proud of our doctrinal correctness, proud of our spiritual accomplishments, proud of our statistics, proud of our stand on moral issues, proud of our reputation and our level of sacrifice.

Pride causes us to be self-righteous, self-congratulatory and self-sufficient. It blinds us to our true condition and our great need. It causes us to fear men rather than God. Pride causes us to compare ourselves to others and breeds a competitive, critical spirit. Our pride is strangling the life of Jesus right out of the church.

Yet, even as we list these sins, some of us may feel that we have not rejected the ways and the Word of God. Then could I ask you some questions God has been asking me in recent days?

If we are so close to God, where is the passion? Where is the compulsion, the unction, the fire? Where are the tears? Where is the mourning, the grieving, the weeping? Why are our eyes dry and our hearts dull? Where is the groaning, the crying out in soul travail? Where are those who cry out with David, "It is time for you, oh God, to act, for they have trampled Your law"?

Where are the Isaiahs who stir up themselves to take hold of God, praying fervently, "Oh, that Thou wouldest rend the heavens, that Thou wouldest come down?" Where are those who plead with the psalmist, "Turn us again, O Lord God of hosts, cause Thy face to shine?" Where are those who abhor sin, whether in the world, in the church, or in their own breast, who cry out, "Horror hath taken hold upon me because of the wicked that forsake Thy law?"

Where are the Jeremiahs whose hearts are in anguish, and whose eyes overflow with tears for the desolation of God's people?

Where are the prophets who are willing to risk their reputation, their retirement funds, and their acceptance within the Christian community, in order to say what needs to be said to our generation? Where are the men who are sounding the alarm to waken the church out of her sleep and lethargy?

Is not God's Word like a fire, and like a hammer that breaks the rock in pieces? Then where is the preaching with conviction, confrontation, divine fire, and Holy Spirit anointing? Where is the urgency, the solemnity, when we talk to men about eternity and the condition of their souls? Where are the intensity and terror when we speak of the judgment and the wrath of God? Where, for that matter, are the tenderness and passion when we speak of the loveliness, the beauty, and the grace of our Lord Jesus? Have our minds been engaged without our hearts being ravished?

Where are the hot hearts, SET AFLAME by the coal from the altar of the Lord?

Where are the hot hearts, set aflame by the coal from the altar of the Lord? Where are the men who have been with God, who have tarried in His presence until they have heard His Word, and then descended from the mount with the glory of God radiating from their faces and the power of God reverberating from their hearts? Where are those who refuse to be satisfied with explainable, status quo ministry, but who expect to see Hell shattered at the feet of Jesus when they go forth in His name?

Having shown Ezekiel the abominations taking place in the inner court of the temple, God sends forth into the holy city a man with a marking pen. He is told: "Go throughout the city of Jerusalem and put a mark on the foreheads of those who grieve and lament over all the detestable things that are done in it." Then executioners are sent into the city with instructions to slaughter all who do not have the intercessor's mark on their forehead. And, says the Lord, *"Begin at My sanctuary."*

In that passage, as in this auditorium tonight, there are only two groups of people: Those who are the cause of the problem, and those who grieve and mourn with repentant hearts. There is no middle ground.

We know for sure of One who carries this burden on His heart tonight. What grief must the Savior feel as He beholds His adulterous Bride in her tattered, stained, threadbare wedding garments?

He who became sin for us that we might become the righteousness of God in Him—He who shed His precious blood to purchase for Himself a holy Bride without spot and without blemish. What must He think, what must He feel as He sees His Beloved One seduced, infatuated, and defiled by the world?

If our hearts are not broken over what breaks the heart of God, if we are not part of the remnant that sighs and laments and groans within over the detestable things that are going on in the temple of God, then we are part of the multitude that is in danger of His chastisement and in desperate need of repentance. So tonight, God calls us to repent: To be afflicted and mourn and weep—first over our sin. For He will not hear or heed our prayers for our nation, as sincere as they may be, until we have first humbled ourselves and repented of our wicked ways. "The time is come that judgment must begin at the house of God!"

In a few moments, I am going to suggest that we go to our knees and humble ourselves in the presence of the Lord—each of us asking God to search our own heart. During that time, would you join me in praying: "Oh God, it's not my brother, not my sister, not my pastor, not the deacons; it's not the church or the ministry down the street—but it's me, oh God...Please shine the light of Your holiness into the innermost parts of my heart. Show me how I have sinned against You; how I have been a part of the problem, rather than a part of the solution. Show me where I need to repent."

As the Holy Spirit brings conviction to our hearts, let's humble ourselves, confess our wicked ways, and plead with God for mercy and forgiveness. "Let us search and try our ways;" let us "turn to Him with all our hearts, with fasting, with weeping, and with mourning."

APPENDIX B

The Four Spiritual Laws

By Bill Bright

Just as there are physical laws that govern the physical universe, so are there spiritual laws that govern your relationship with God.

LAW 1: *God **loves** you and offers a wonderful **plan** for your life.*

God's Love
"God so loved the world that He gave His one and only Son, that whoever believes in Him shall not perish but have eternal life" (John 3:16, NIV).

God's Plan
[Christ speaking] "I came that they might have life, and might have it abundantly" [that it might be full and meaningful] (John 10:10).

Why is it that most people are not experiencing the abundant life? Because...

LAW 2: *Man is **sinful** and **separated** from God. Therefore, he cannot know and experience God's love and plan for his life.*

Man Is Sinful
"All have sinned and fall short of the glory of God" (Romans 3:23).

Man was created to have fellowship with God; but, because of his own stubborn self-will, he chose to go his own independent way and fellowship with God was broken. This self-will, characterized by an attitude of active rebellion or passive indifference, is an evidence of what the Bible calls sin.

Man Is Separated

"The wages of sin is death" [spiritual separation from God] (Romans 6:23).

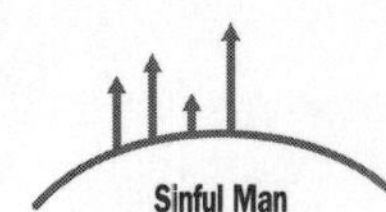

This diagram illustrates that God is holy and man is sinful. A great gulf separates the two. The arrows illustrate that man is continually trying to reach God and the abundant life through his own efforts, such as a good life, philosophy, or religion—but he inevitably fails.

The third law explains the only way to bridge this gulf…

LAW 3: *Jesus Christ is God's **only** provision for man's sin. Through Him you can know and experience God's love and plan for your life.*

He Died In Our Place

"God demonstrates His own love toward us, in that while we were yet sinners, Christ died for us" (Romans 5:8).

He Is the Only Way to God

"Jesus said to him, 'I am the way, and the truth, and the life; no one comes to the Father but through Me'" (John 14:6).

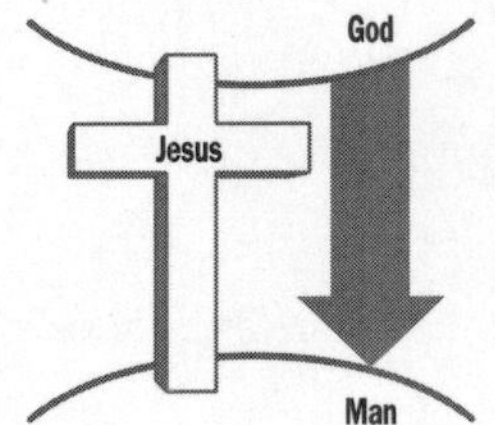

This diagram illustrates that God has bridged the gulf that separates us from Him by sending His Son, Jesus Christ, to die on the cross in our place to pay the penalty for our sins.

It is not enough just to know these three laws…

LAW 4: *We must individually **receive** Jesus Christ as Savior and Lord; then we can know and experience God's love and plan for our lives.*

We Must Receive Christ

"As many as received Him, to them He gave the right to become children of God, even to those who believe in His name" (John 1:12).

We Receive Christ Through Faith

"By grace you have been saved through faith; and that not of yourselves, it is the gift of God; not as a result of works that no one should boast" (Ephesians 2:8,9).

When We Receive Christ, We Experience a New Birth

(Read John 3:1–8.)

We Receive Christ Through Personal Invitation

[Christ speaking] "Behold, I stand at the door and knock; if any one hears My voice and opens the door, I will come in to him" (Revelation 3:20).

Receiving Christ involves turning to God from self (repentance) and trusting Christ to come into our lives to forgive our sins and to make us what He wants us to be. Just to agree intellectually that Jesus Christ is the Son of God and that He died on the cross for our sins is not enough. Nor is it enough to have an emotional experience. We receive Jesus Christ by faith, as an act of the will.

These two circles represent two kinds of lives:

Self-Directed Life
S – Self is on the throne
† – Christ is outside the life
• – Interests are directed by self, often resulting in discord and frustration

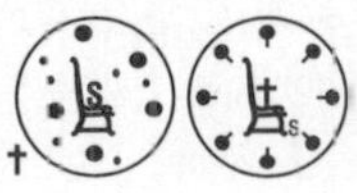

Christ-Directed Life
† – Christ is in the life and on the throne
S – Self is yielding to Christ
• – Interests are directed by Christ, resulting in harmony with God's plan

Which circle best represents your life?
Which circle would you like to have represent your life?

The following explains how you can receive Christ:

You Can Receive Christ Right Now by Faith Through Prayer

(Prayer is talking with God)

God knows your heart and is not so concerned with your words as He is with the attitude of your heart. The following is a suggested prayer:

> *Lord Jesus, I need You. Thank You for dying on the cross for my sins. I open the door of my life and receive You as my Savior and Lord. Thank You for forgiving my sins and giving me eternal life. Take control of the throne of my life. Make me the kind of person You want me to be.*

Does this prayer express the desire of your heart?

If it does, I invite you to pray this prayer right now, and Christ will come into your life, as He promised.

How to Know That Christ Is in Your Life

Did you receive Christ into your life? According to His promise in Revelation 3:20, where is Christ right now in relation to you? Christ said that He would come into your life. Would He mislead you? On what authority do you know that God has answered your prayer? (The trustworthiness of God Himself and His Word.)

The Bible Promises Eternal Life to All Who Receive Christ

"God has given us eternal life, and this life is in His Son. He who has the Son has the life; he who does not have the Son of God does not have the life" (1 John 5:11–13).

Thank God often that Christ is in your life and that He will never leave you (Hebrews 13:5). You can know on the basis of His promise that Christ lives in you and that you have eternal life from the very moment you invite Him in. He will not deceive you.

An important reminder…

Do Not Depend on Feelings

The promise of God's Word, the Bible—not our feelings—is our authority. The Christian lives by faith (trust) in the trustworthiness of God Himself and His Word. This train diagram illustrates the relationship among fact (God and His Word), faith (our trust in God and His Word), and feeling (the result of our faith and obedience). (Read John 14:21.)

The train will run with or without the caboose. However, it would be useless to attempt to pull the train by the caboose. In the same way, as Christians we do not depend on feelings or emotions, but we place our faith (trust) in the trustworthiness of God and the promises of His Word.

Now That You Have Received Christ

The moment you received Christ by faith, as an act of the will, many things happened, including the following:

- Christ came into your life (Revelation 3:20; Colossians 1:27).
- Your sins were forgiven (Colossians 1:14).
- You became a child of God (John 1:12).
- You received eternal life (John 5:24).
- You began the great adventure for which God created you (John 10:10).

Can you think of anything more wonderful that could happen to you than receiving Christ? Would you like to thank God in prayer right now for what He has done for you? By thanking God, you demonstrate your faith.

To enjoy your new life to the fullest…

Suggestions for Christian Growth

Spiritual growth results from trusting Jesus Christ. A life of faith will enable you to trust God increasingly with every detail of your life, and to practice the following:

G *Go* to God in prayer daily (John 15:7).

R *Read* God's Word daily (Acts 17:11); begin with the Gospel of John.

O *Obey* God moment by moment (John 14:21).

W *Witness* for Christ by your life and words (Matthew 4:19; John 15:8).

T *Trust* God for every detail of your life (1 Peter 5:7).

H *Holy Spirit*—allow Him to control and empower your daily life and witness (Galatians 5:16,17; Acts 1:8; Ephesians 5:18).

Fellowship in a Good Church

God's Word instructs us not to forsake "the assembling of ourselves together" (Hebrews 10:25). If you do not belong to a church, do not wait to be invited. Take the initiative; call the pastor of a nearby church where Christ is honored and His Word is preached. Start this week, and make plans to attend regularly.

APPENDIX C

Have You Made the Wonderful Discovery of

The Spirit-Filled Life

By Bill Bright

Every day can be an exciting adventure for the Christian who knows the reality of being filled with the Holy Spirit and who lives constantly, moment by moment, under His gracious direction.

The Bible tells us that there are three kinds of people:

1. **Natural Man:** One who has not received Christ.

   "A natural man does not accept the things of the Spirit of God; for they are foolishness to him, and he cannot understand them, because they are spiritually appraised" (1 Corinthians 2:14, NASB).

Self-Directed Life
S - Self is on the throne
† - Christ is outside the life
• - Interests are directed by self, often resulting in discord and frustration

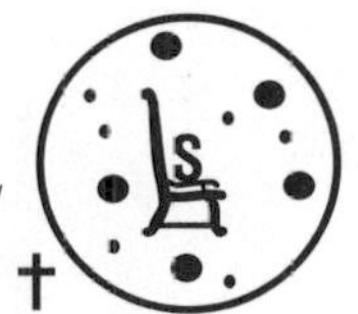

2. **Spiritual Man:** One who is directed and empowered by the Holy Spirit.

   "He who is spiritual appraises all things" (1 Corinthians 2:15, NASB).

Christ-Directed Life
S - Christ is in the life and on the throne
† - Self is yielding to Christ
• - Interests are directed by Christ, resulting in harmony with God's plan

3. **Carnal Man:** One who has received Christ, but who lives in defeat because he trusts in his own efforts to live the Christian life.

"I, brethren, could not speak to you as to spiritual people but as to carnal, as to babes in Christ. I fed you with milk and not with solid food; for until now you were not able to receive it, and even now you are still not able; for you are still carnal. For when there are envy, strife, and divisions among you, are you not carnal and behaving like mere men?" (1 Corinthians 3:1–3).

Self Directed Life
S – Self is on the throne
† – Christ dethroned and not allowed to direct the life
• – Interests are directed by self, often resulting in discord and frustration

The following are four principles for living the Spirit-filled life:

1 God has provided for us an abundant and fruitful Christian life.

"Jesus said, 'I have come that they may have life, and that they may have it more abundantly'" (John 10:10, NKJ).

"The fruit of the Spirit is love, joy, peace, patience, kindness, goodness, faithfulness, gentleness, self-control; against such things there is no law" (Galatians 5:22,23).

Read John 15:5 and Acts 1:8.

The following are some personal traits of the spiritual man that result from trusting God:

- Love
- Joy
- Peace
- Patience
- Kindness
- Faithfulness
- Goodness

- Life is Christ-centered
- Empowered by Holy Spirit
- Introduces others to Christ
- Has effective prayer life
- Understands God's Word
- Trusts God
- Obeys God

The degree to which these traits are manifested in the life depends on the extent to which the Christian trusts the Lord with every detail of his life, and on his maturity in Christ. One who is only beginning to understand the ministry of the Holy Spirit should not be discouraged if he is not as fruitful as more mature Christians who have known and experienced this truth for a longer period.

Why is it that most Christians are not experiencing the abundant life?

2 Carnal Christians cannot experience the abundant and fruitful Christian life.

The carnal man trusts in his own efforts to live the Christian life:

- He is either uninformed about, or has forgotten, God's love, forgiveness, and power (Romans 5:8–10; Hebrews 10:1–25; 1 John 1; 2:1–3; 2 Peter 1:9).
- He has an up-and-down spiritual experience.
- He wants to do what is right, but cannot.
- He fails to draw on the power of the Holy Spirit to live the Christian life (1 Corinthians 3:1–3; Romans 7:15–24; 8:7; Galatians 5:16–18).

Some or all of the following traits may characterize the carnal man—the Christian who does not fully trust God:

- Legalistic attitude
- Impure thoughts
- Jealousy
- Guilt
- Worry
- Discouragement
- Critical spirit
- Frustration

- Aimlessness
- Fear
- Ignorance of his spiritual heritage
- Unbelief
- Disobedience
- Loss of love for God and for others
- Poor prayer life
- No desire for Bible study

(The individual who professes to be a Christian but who continues to practice sin should realize that he may not be a Christian at all, according to 1 John 2:3; 3:6–9; and Ephesians 5:5.)

The third truth gives us the only solution to this problem…

3 Jesus promised the abundant and fruitful life as the result of being filled (directed and empowered) by the Holy Spirit.

The Spirit-filled life is the Christ-directed life by which Christ lives His life in and through us in the power of the Holy Spirit (John 15).

- One becomes a Christian through the ministry of the Holy Spirit (John 3:1–8.) From the moment of spiritual birth, the Christian is indwelt by the Holy Spirit at all times (John 1:12; Colossians 2:9,10; John 14:16,17).

  All Christians are indwelt by the Holy Spirit, but not all Christians are filled (directed, controlled, and empowered) by the Holy Spirit on an ongoing basis.

- The Holy Spirit is the source of the overflowing life (John 7:37–39).
- In His last command before His ascension, Christ promised the power of the Holy Spirit to enable us to be witnesses for Him (Acts 1:1–9).

How, then, can one be filled with the Holy Spirit?

4 We are filled (directed and empowered) by the Holy Spirit by faith; then we can experience the abundant and fruitful life that Christ promised to each Christian.

You can appropriate the filling of the Holy Spirit right now if you:

- Sincerely desire to be directed and empowered by the Holy Spirit (Matthew 5:6; John 7:37–39).
- Confess your sins. By faith, thank God that He has forgiven all of your sins—past, present, and future—because Christ died for you (Colossians 2:13–15).
- Present every area of your life to God (Romans 12:1,2).
- By faith claim the fullness of the Holy Spirit, according to:

  His command: Be filled with the Spirit. "Do not get drunk on wine, which leads to debauchery. Instead, be filled with the Spirit" (Ephesians 5:18).

  His promise: He will always answer when we pray according to His will. "This is the confidence we have in approaching God: that if we ask anything according to his will, he hears us. And if we know that He hears us—whatever we ask—we know that we have what we asked of Him" (1 John 5:14,15).

How to Pray in Faith to be Filled With the Holy Spirit

We are filled with the Holy Spirit by faith alone. However, true prayer is one way of expressing your faith. The following is a suggested prayer:

> Dear Father, I need You. I acknowledge that I have been directing my own life and that, as a result, I have sinned against You. I thank You that You have forgiven my sins through Christ's death on the cross for me. I now invite Christ to again take His place on the throne of my life. Fill me with the Holy Spirit as You commanded me to be filled, and as You promised in Your Word that You would do if I asked in faith. I pray this in the name of Jesus. As an expression of my faith, I now thank You for directing my life and for filling me with the Holy Spirit.

Does this prayer express the desire of your heart? If so, bow in prayer and trust God to fill you with the Holy Spirit right now.

APPENDIX D

Fasting & Prayer Notes

Fasting

How Does Fasting Help?

- Fasting is a primary means of restoration. Humbling ourselves by fasting takes us into a deeper life in Christ and gives us a greater awareness of God's reality and presence in our lives, bringing personal revival.
- Fasting reduces the power of self so that the Holy Spirit can do a more intense work within us. As a result, He can accomplish His will in us and do "superabundantly" more for us than we could ever imagine.
- Fasting brings a yieldedness, even a holy brokenness, resulting in inner calm and self-control. It eliminates some of the physical distractions in our lives, such as preparing and eating food, and can lead to a slower, more peaceful pace of life.
- Fasting renews spiritual vision. When we feel our life is out of control or have lost our first love for the Lord, fasting can help us focus once again on God's plan for our lives.
- Fasting inspires determination to follow God's revealed plan for our life. Fasting can help strengthen your resolve and keep you on track.

- Fasting can bring revival to a nation. God promises to hear from heaven, forgive our sins, and heal our land.
- Fasting and prayer are powerful means for causing the fire of God to fall again in a person's life. This fire produces the fruit of the Spirit. Fasting prepares us to receive the Holy Spirit's power over the lusts of the flesh, the pride of life, and the lies of the enemy. This fire from the Holy Spirit also provides the power to witness boldly for the Lord and His saving gospel, and to pray more intensely for ourselves and others.

Fasting Is Safe

When done properly, fasting is safe. However, therapeutic fasting (no food intake) should be done only under medical supervision and limited to a few meals. Persons with medical problems or on medication should consult a medical doctor before beginning a fast.

7 Steps to Successful Fasting and Prayer

1. Set your objectives.
2. Ask the Holy Spirit to reveal the kind of fast God wants you to undertake.
3. Prepare yourself spiritually.
4. Prepare yourself physically.
5. Put yourself on a schedule.
6. End your fast gradually.
7. Expect results.

How to Lead Your Congregation in a Fast

1. Prepare your congregation for a fast.
2. Set a specific time for corporate fasting.
3. Give your congregation clear instructions.
4. Focus on prayer.
5. Set up a temporary hotline.
6. Do not expect everyone to attend every day.
7. Teach your people to expect results.

Prayer

What is Prayer?

Prayer is communicating with God.

Who Can Pray?

Anyone can pray, but only those who walk in faith and obedience to Christ can expect to receive answers to their prayers.

Why Are We to Pray?

God commands us to pray and we need to stay in constant communication with God.

To Whom Do We Pray?

We pray to the Father in the name of the Lord Jesus Christ who accepts our prayers, which are interpreted to God the Father by the Holy Spirit.

When Should We Pray?

God commands us to "Pray continually" (1 Thessalonians 5:17).

ACTS Acrostic Outline

- Adoration: Worshiping and praising God, exalting Him with your lips and in your heart and mind. Read John 4:23, 24; Hebrews 12:28; Psalm 103.
- Confession: Agreeing with God concerning any sins He brings to mind in order to restore fellowship with Him. Review 1 John 1:5–9.
- Thanksgiving: Rendering thanksgiving to God with a prayer expressing gratitude. Read 1 Thessalonians 5:18; Ephesians 5:20; Psalm 50:23.
- Supplication: Presenting needs to God, for yourself and others. Read Philippians 4:6,7; Psalm 116:1,2.

PRAY Acrostic Outline

Praise
Repent
Ask for Someone Else
Your own needs

Encouraging Individuals to Pray Continuously

1. Remember that God commands us to pray without ceasing (1 Thessalonians 5:17)
2. Recognize that God is present wherever you go and that He is always ready to answer prayer. Practice the presence of God as a way of life.
3. Thank God for everything He allows into your life. (1Thess. 5:18), from a beautiful day to a flat tire.
4. Talk to God whenever you feel a need any time of the day or night.
5. Use your time more wisely by developing a habit of praying during daily activities that do not require total concentration, such as showering, driving, walking, or gardening.

How to Establish a Fasting & Prayer Movement Within Your Church

1. Give prayer priority in the church. (Isaiah 56:7)
2. The pastor and church staff must have a vision for the involvement of their members in a vital prayer ministry. (Ephesians 4:11–13)
3. Establish a prayer ministry in your church.
4. Challenge a prayer group to commit themselves to make training and personal involvement in prayer a top priority.

APPENDIX E

Eight Ways to Share Christ

1. **Pray the "3-Open Prayer" (Col. 4:3,4)**: "Lord, *open a door* for me to talk to a lost person I know; *open the heart* of that lost person to hear about Christ; and *open my mouth* when You open the door." You are not the persuader, just the presenter.
2. **Be there for them in their bad times (Rom. 12:15b)**. Be there with them when they are sick, grieving, in a crisis or emergency.
3. **Be there for them in their good times (Rom. 12:15a)**. Be at the wedding, baby shower, house warming, or do something special for a birthday or anniversary. You are winning the right to be heard.
4. **Pray with them**. Promise them you will talk to God about their burden. Then ask if they would mind if you did it right there. Explain your personal relationship with God.
5. **Write a thank you letter to them**. In the course of thanking them, tell them about your relationship with Jesus Christ and your desire that they share that relationship with you, because you care so much about them.
6. **Be ready with customized testimonies**. Have a lot of personal testimonies ready to come in through a different direc-

tion: What difference Jesus makes as a parent or spouse; in depressing, lonely or stressed out times; as a single person; or in the seasons of life.

7. **Lend them a Christian cassette, video, CD, book**. Why? Because you want them to give it back so you can ask them what they thought about what they read or heard. Then tell them how the message changed your life.
8. **Invite them to an outreach**: A concert, seminar, social evening, etc., geared to lost people where Christ will be presented. Invite them over for dinner first or for dessert after the event so you can talk about what was heard, and how the Jesus they heard about there has changed your life.

Two imperatives when sharing Christ with someone:

1. **Stick to Jesus**. Don't get into lifestyles, habits, religion, denominations, churches, or "hypocrites"—its all about Jesus.
2. **Present a relationship**. The One we were created to have, the One we don't have because we run our lives instead of our Creator running our lives, the One we can have because of what Jesus did on the cross, and the One we must choose.

APPENDIX F

Rules to Live By

The Ten Commandments

1. You shall have no other gods before me.
2. You shall not make for yourself an idol in the form of anything in heaven above or on the earth beneath or in the waters below. You shall not bow down to them or worship them; for I, the Lord your God, am a jealous God, punishing the children for the sin of the fathers to the third and fourth generation of those who hate me, but showing love to a thousand generations of those who love me and keep my commandments.
3. You shall not misuse the name of the Lord your God, for the Lord will not hold anyone guiltless who misuses his name.
4. Remember the Sabbath day by keeping it holy. Six days you shall labor and do all your work, but the seventh day is a Sabbath to the Lord your God. On it you shall not do any work, neither you, nor your son or daughter, nor your manservant or maidservant, nor your animals, nor the alien within your gates. For in six days the Lord made the heavens and the earth, the sea, and all that is in them, but he rested on the seventh day. Therefore the Lord blessed the Sabbath day and made it holy.

5. Honor your father and your mother, so that you may live long in the land the Lord your God is giving you.
6. You shall not murder.
7. You shall not commit adultery.
8. You shall not steal.
9. You shall not give false testimony against your neighbor.
10. You shall not covet your neighbor's house. You shall not covet your neighbor's wife, or his manservant or maidservant, his ox or donkey, or anything that belongs to your neighbor.

The Golden Rule

"So then whatever you desire that others would do to and for you, even so do you also to and for them, for this sums up the Law and the prophets" (Matthew 7:12, *Amplified*).

Pledges of Allegiance

Pledge to the United States Flag

I pledge allegiance to the flag of the United States of America, and to the Republic for which it stands, one Nation under God, indivisible, with liberty and justice for all.

Pledge to the Christian Flag

I pledge allegiance to the Christian flag, and to the Savior for whose kingdom it stands, one brotherhood uniting all Christians in service and in love.

Pledge to the Bible

I pledge allegiance to the Bible, God's Holy Word, and will make it a lamp unto my feet, a light unto my path, and hide its words in my heart that I may not sin against God

Source Notes

They Spoke of Their Faith

1. George Washington's personal prayer book in his own handwriting. W. Herbert Burk, B.D , *Washington's Prayers*, (Norristown, PA: Published for the benefit of the Washington Memorial Chapel, 1907), pp. 87-95.
2. Henry Halley, *Halley's Bible Handbook*, (Grand Rapids, MI: Zondervan, 1927, 1965), p.18.
3. September 19, 1796, in his Farewell Address. James D. Richardson, *A Compilation of the Messages and Papers of the Presidents, 1789–1897*, (Published by Authority of Congress, 1899), Vol. I, p. 220.
4. Steve C. Dawson, *God's Providence in America's History*, (Rancho Cordova, CA: Steve C. Dawson, 1988), Vol. I, p. 5.
5. Merrill D. Peterson, ed., *Jefferson Writings*, (New York: Literary Classics of the United States, Inc., 1984), p. 289. From Jefferson's Notes on the State of Virginia Query XVIII, 1781.
6. Charles E. Kistler, *This Nation Under God*, (Boston: Richard G. Badger, The Gorham Press, 1924), p. 83.
7. October 11, 1798, in his address as President to the Military. Charles Francis Adams, ed., *The Works of John Adams—Second President of the United States*, (Boston: Little, Brown, & Co., 1854), Vol. IX, p. 229.
8. November 9,1772, in writing to William Bradford. William T. Hutchinson, ed., *The Papers of James Madison*, (Chicago: University of Chicago Press, 1962), Vol. I, p. 75.
9. March 4, 1815. James D. Richardson, *A Compilation of the Messages and Papers of the Presidents, 1789–1897*, (Published by Authority of Congress, 1899), Vol. I, p. 561.
10. *Journals of Congress* (1823), Vol. III, p. 85, October 12, 1778.
11. Samuel Adams, July 16, 1776, to the Earl of Carlisle and others. Harry Alonzo Cushing, ed., *The Writings of Samuel Adams*, (New York: G. P. Putnam's Sons, 1904), Vol. IV, p. 38.
12. Samuel Adams, *By the Governor. A Proclamation for a Day of Public Fasting, Humiliation, and Prayer*, (Printed at the State Press: Adams and Larkin, 1795).
13. To the Committee of the Corporation of the City of New York on June 29, 1826. William Jay, *The Life of John Jay: With Selections From His Correspondence and Miscellaneous Papers*, (New York: J & J Harper, 1833), Vol. I, pp. 457,458.
14. October 12, 1816. *The Correspondence and Public Papers of John Jay*, Henry P. Johnston, ed., (New York: Burt Franklin, 1970), Vol. IV, p. 393.
15. To Elias Boudinot on July 9, 1788. Benjamin Rush, *Letters of Benjamin Rush*, L.H. Butterfield, ed., (Princeton, NJ: American Philosophical Society, 1951), Vol. I, p. 475.
16. To James McHenry on November 4, 1800. Bernard C. Steiner, *The Life and Correspondence of James McHenry*, (Cleveland: The Burrows Brothers, 1907), p. 475.
17. Peter Marshall and David Manuel, *The Glory of America*, (Bloomington, MN: Garborg's Heart N' Home, Inc., 1991), 12.7.
18. 1828, in the preface to his *American Dictionary of the English Language* (reprinted San

Francisco: Foundation for American Christian Education, 1967), Preface, p. 12. Quoted in David Barton, *The Myth of Separation*, (Aledo, TX: WallBuilder Press, 1991), pp. 126,251.

19. May 17, 1776, in a speech at Princeton (The College of New Jersey). *The Works of the Rev. John Witherspoon*, (Philadelphia: William W. Woodward, 1802), Vol. III, p. 46.
20. Alfred Armand Montapert, *Distilled Wisdom*, (Englewood Cliffs, NJ: Prentice Hall, Inc., 1965), p. 36.
21. Congress of the United States of America. May 1854. A Resolution passed in the House. Benjamin Franklin Morris, *The Christian Life and Character of the Civil Institutions of the United States*, (Philadelphia: George W. Childs, 1864), p. 328.
22. March 30, 1863, in a Proclamation of a National Day of Humiliation, Fasting and Prayer. James D. Richardson, *A Compilation of the Messages and Papers of the Presidents, 1789–1897*, (Washington, D.C.: U.S. Government Printing Office, 1897, 1899), Vol. VI, p. 164,165.
23. Richardson, *Compilation*, p. 164,165.
24. February 29, 1892. Justice Josiah Brewer, *Church of the Holy Trinity v. United States*, 143 U.S. 457-458,465-471, 36 L ed 226.

Foreword

1. John Adams, *The Works of John Adams, Second President of the United States*, Charles Francis Adams, ed. (Boston: Little, Brown, 1854), Vol. IX, p. 229, October 11, 1798.

Chapter 1: A Red Sky Is Rising

1. George Barna, *The Leading Indicators of Spiritual Indicators*, (Dallas: Word Publishing, 1996), p. 77.

Chapter 2: The Next American Century

1. George Mason, August 22, 1787, in an address to the Continental Congress. James Madison, *Notes of Debates in the Federal Convention of 1787*, (1787, reprinted New York: W. W. Norton Co., 1987), p. 504.
2. George Washington. In writing to the Hebrew Congregations of the City of Savannah, GA. William Barclay Allen, ed., *George Washington—A Collection,* (Indianapolis: Liberty Classics, Liberty Fund, Inc., 1988).
3. Verna Hall, *The Christian History of the American Revolution*, (San Francisco: Foundation for American Christian Education, 1976), p. 48.
4. W. Herbert Burk, *Washington's Papers*, (Norristown, PA: Published for the benefit of the Washington Memorial Chapel, 1907), pp. 87–95.
5. Chuck Colson, *Burden of Truth: Defending Truth in an Age of Unbelief*, (Wheaton, IL: Tyndale Publishers, 1997), p. 88.
6. John Eidsmoe, *God and Caesar: Christian Faith and Political Action*, (Westchester, IL: Crossway Books, 1984), p. 215.
7. David Barton, *America's Godly Heritage,* (Aledo, TX: WallBuilders Press, 1993), p. 9.
8. Josh McDowell, *A Ready Defense*, (San Bernardino, CA: Here's Life Publishers, 1990), p. 454.
9. Daniel Webster, *The Words of Daniel Webster,* (Boston: Little, Brown and Company, 1853), Vol. I, p. 48.
10. Roy Basler, ed., *Abraham Lincoln: His Speeches and Writing*, (Cleveland: DeCapro Press, 1946), pp. 77,78.
11. Keith Fournier, *Life, Liberty, and Family Foundational Documents*, (Washington, D.C.: Life, Liberty, and Family Foundation, 1997), p. 4.

12. From Patrick Henry's "Give Me Liberty or Give Me Death" speech to the Virginia Convention on March 23, 1775. Quoted in Catherine Millard, *Great American Statesmen and Heroes*, (Camp Hill, PA: Horizon Books, 1995), p. 129.

Chapter 3: Roots of the Republic

1. Peter Marshall interview by John N. Damoose in 1996 at Virginia Beach, Virginia.
2. Christopher Columbus from his personal diary, *Book of Prophecies*. Quoted in Washington Irving, *Life and Voyages of Christopher Columbus*, (New York: The Cooperative Publication Society, Inc., 1892), p. 41.
3. Queen Isabella's Commission to Christopher Columbus, circa 1490–1492. *Letter From Plymouth Rock*, (Marlborough, NH: The Plymouth Rock Foundation), p. 1.
4. Christopher Columbus. In a letter from Queen Isabella to the Pope. Cecil Jane, trans. and ed., *The Voyages of Christopher Columbus*, (London: Argonaut Press, 1930), p. 146.
5. Bjorn Landstrom, *Columbus*, (New York: The MacMillan Co., 1966), p. 66–75.
6. Irving, *Life and Voyages*, p. 41.
7. Russell Kirk, *The Roots of American Order*, (Washington, D.C.: Regnery Gateway, 1991), p. 230.
8. Kirk, *American Order*, p. 231.
9. 1606, granted by King James I. Gary DeMar, *God and Government—A Biblical and Historical Study*, (Atlanta, GA: American Vision Press, 1984), p. 127.
10. "The Mayflower Compact," November 11, 1620, as recorded in William Bradford's *The History of Plymouth Plantation*, 1608–1650, (Boston: Massachusetts Historical Society, 1856), from original manuscript, Library of Congress, Rare Book Collection, Washington, D.C.
11. Bradford, *Plymouth Plantation*.
12. Bradford, *Plymouth Plantation*.
13. John Winthrop, *Model of Christian Charity, 1630*, (Boston: Massachusetts Historical Society, 1931), Vol. II, pp. 292–295.
14. Winthrop, *Model of Christian Charity*, p. 292–295.

Chapter 4: Birth of a Nation

1. Peter J. Marshall and David Manuel, *The Light and the Glory*, (Grand Rapids, MI: Fleming H. Revell Co., 1977), p. 248.
2. Benjamin Franklin, 1781, *The Autobiography of Benjamin Franklin*, (New York: Books, Inc., 1791), p. 146. Quoted in Carl Van Dorn, *Franklin's Autobiographical Writings*, (New York: Viking Press, 1945), p. 624.
3. Isaiah Thomas, ed., *The Works of President Edwards*, Vol. III, (Worchester, MA: Isaiah Thomas, 1808–1809), pp. 14–19.
4. Dr. Paul Johnson, *History of Christianity*, (Atheneum, NY: Atheneum, 1976). p. 422.
5. Dr. D. James Kennedy interview by John N. Damoose in Ft. Lauderdale, Florida, in 1996.
6. Daniel Webster, *The Works of Daniel Webster*, (Boston: Little, Brown and Company, 1853), Vol. I, p. 22.
7. *The Code of 1650, Being a Compilation of the Earliest Laws and Orders of the General Court of Connecticut* (Hartford: Silas Andrus, 1822), p. 92,93.
8. *New England Primer, 1691*. Quoted in John Bartlett, ed., *Bartlett's Familiar Quotations*, (Boston: Little, Brown and Company, 1980), p. 320.
9. Thomas Dilworth, *New Guide to the English Tongue*, 1740. Quoted in H. R. Warfel, *Noah Webster: Schoolmaster to America*, (New York: Octagon Press, 1966), pp. 11–13.
10. *The Constitution of the United States of America With the Latest Amendments*, (Trenton:

Moore and Lake, 1813), p. 364, "An Ordinance of the Territory of the United States Northwest of the River Ohio," Article III.

11. Rosalie J. Slater, ed. *Teaching and Learning America's Christian History*, (San Francisco: Foundation for Christian Education, 1980), p. vii.
12. 1692. Original Charter of the College of William and Mary, Williamsburg, Virginia, Rare Books Collection, Swem Library. John Fiske, *The Beginnings of New England* (Boston: Houghton, Mifflin and Company, 1898), pp. 127,128,136.
13. 1701. Peter G. Mode, *Sourcebook and Bibliographical Guide for American Church History*, (Menasha, WI: George Banta Publishing Co., 1921), pp. 109,110.
14. 1701, as stated by the founders. William C. Ringenberg, *The Christian College: A History of Protestant Higher Education in America*, (Grand Rapids, MI: William B. Eerdmans Publishing Company, 1984), p. 38.
15. Richard Hofstader and Wilson Smith, eds., *American Higher Education: A Documentary History*, (Chicago: University of Chicago Press, 1961), p. 1.
16. Steve McDowell and Mark Beliles, *America's Providential History* (Charlottesville, VA: Providence Press, 1989), p. 100.
17. McDowell and Beliles, *America's Providential History*, p. 109.
18. Donald S. Lutz and Charles S. Hyneman, "The Relative Influence of European Writers on Law: Eighteenth Century Political Thought," *American Political Science Review*, 1984, pp. 189–197.
19. William Blackstone, *Commentary on the Laws of England*, (Oxford, England: Clarendon Press, 1769). Reprinted in *Commentary on the Laws of England*, Vol. I, (Philadelphia: J.B. Lippincott and Co., 1879), pp. 39,41,42.
20. John Eidsmoe, *Christianity and the Constitution*, (MI: Baker Book House, 1987), pp. 51,53.
21. Baron Charles Montesquieu, *The Spirit of the Laws*, 1748, Anne Cohler, trans. (reprinted Cambridge: Cambridge University Press, 1989), p. 157.
22. 1773, in a unanimous declaration by the men of Marlborough, Massachusetts. Charles E. Kistler, *This Nation Under God* (Boston: Richard G. Badger, The Gorman Press, 1924), p. 56.
23. 1774. George Bancroft, *Bancroft's History of the United States*, (Boston: Charles C. Little & James Brown, 1838), Vol. VII, p. 229.
24. Jonathan Mayhew, 1765 sermon in Boston. Quoted in Clinton Rossiter, *Seedtime of the Republic*, (New York: Harcourt, Brace, and World, Inc., 1953), p. 241.
25. Peter J. Marshall interview by John N. Damoose in Virginia Beach, Virginia, in 1996.
26. 1774, colonial motto issued through the Committees of Correspondence from Boston, Massachusetts.
27. Rus Walton, *They Signed for Us*, (Plymouth Rock Foundation, P.O. Box 577, Marlborough, NH 03455).
28. Charles E. Kistler, *This Nation Under God*, (Boston: Richard G. Badger, The Gorham Press, 1924), p. 71.
29. John Adams, July 3, 1776, in a letter to his wife Abigail. Quoted in L. H. Butterfield, ed., *Adams Family Correspondence*, (Cambridge, MA: Harvard University Press, 1963), Vol. II, pp. 28–31.
30. Marshall, *The Light and the Glory*, pp. 313,314.
31. Lutz, "The Relative Influence," pp. 189–197.
32. John Adams in a letter to his wife sent from Philadelphia on September 7, 1774. Charles Francis Adams, ed., *Letters of John Adams—Addressed to His Wife*, (Boston: Charles C. Little and James Brown, 1841), pp. 23,24.
33. Thomas Y. Rhoads, *The Battlefields of the Revolution* (Philadelphia: J. W. Bradley,

1860), pp. 36,37.
34. Charles Francis Adams, *Letters of John Adams*, pp. 23,24.
35. W. Herbert Burk, B.D., *Washington's Papers*, (Norristown, PA: Published for the benefit of the Washington Memorial Chapel, 1907), pp. 87–95. Quoted in LaHaye, *Faith*, pp. 111–113.
36. M. E. Bradford, *Religion & the Framers: The Biographical Evidence*, (Marlborough, NH: The Plymouth Rock Foundation, 1991), p. 8.
37. Norene Dickson Campbell, *Patrick Henry: Patriot and Statesman*, (Greenwich, Connecticut: Devin-Adair Co., 1969), p. 428.
38. From his *Will*. Stephen Abbott Northrup, D.D., *A Cloud of Witnesses*, (Portland, Oregon: American Heritage Ministries, 1987), p. 5.
39. David Barton, *Original Intent: The Courts, the Constitution, & Religion*, (Aledo, TX: WallBuilder Press, 1997), 134.
40. From an autographed letter written by Charles Carroll to Charles W. Wharton, Esq., on September 27, 1825, from Doughoragen, Maryland. Quoted in Barton, *Original Intent*, p. 137.
41. David Barton, WallBuilders, Inc., 1998.
42. David Barton, "The Founding Fathers and Deism," article available on Internet.
43. March 9, 1790, in a letter to Ezra Stiles, President of Yale University. John Bigelow, *Complete Words of Benjamin Franklin*. Quoted in Northrup, *A Cloud of Witnesses*, p. 159.
44. James Madison, *Notes of Debates in the Federal Convention of 1787*, (New York: W. W. Norton and Co., 1987), pp. 209,210.
45. January 9, 1816, in a letter to Charles Thomson. Henry S. Randall, *The Life of Thomas Jefferson* (NY: Derby and Jackson, 1958), Vol. 3, p. 451.
46. April 21, 1803, in a letter to Dr. Benjamin Rush. *The Writings of Thomas Jefferson*, Vol. X, p. 379.
47. Gary DeMar, *God and Government: A Biblical and Historical Study*, (Atlanta, GA: American Vision Press, 1982), pp. 137,138.
48. John Adams, February 22, 1756, in a diary entry. L.H. Butterfield, ed., *Diary and Autobiography of John Adams*, (Cambridge, MA: Belknap Press of Harvard Press, 1961), Vol. III, p. 9.
49. John Quincy Adams, July 4, 1821. John Wingate Thornton, *The Pulpit of the American Revolution 1860*, (reprinted NY: Burt Franklin, 1860, 1970), p. XXIX.

Chapter 5: God's Purpose for America

1. John Quincy Adams, July 4, 1837. *An Oration Delivered Before the Inhabitants of the Town of Newburyport at their Request on the Sixty-First Anniversary of the Declaration of Independence*, (Newburyport: Charles Whipple, 1837), pp. 5,6.
2. Daniel J. Boorstin, *The Americans: The Democratic Experience*, (New York: Vintage Books, 1983), p. 559.
3. *Victory in Spite of All Terror* (video), (Traverse City, MI: Freedom Ministries of America, Inc. and Christian Broadcasting Network, Inc., 1997).
4. Constitution of the New England Confederation, May 19, 1643. Benjamin Franklin Morris, *The Christian Life and Character of the Civil Institutions of the United States*, (Philadelphia: George W. Childs, 1864), p. 56.
5. Charles Bancroft, "The Footprints of Time," 1879. Quoted in Rosalie J. Slater and Verna Hall, *The Christian History of the United States of America*, (San Francisco: Foundation for American Christian Education 1966), p. 9.

Chapter 6: Purification and Preparation

1. Alexis de Tocqueville, *Democracy in America*, (New York: Vintage Books, 1945), p. 319.
2. Russell Kirk, *The Roots of American Order*, (Washington, D.C.: Regnery Gateway, 1991), p. 406.
3. Dr. Paul Johnson, *A History of Christianity*, (New York: Atheneum, 1983), pp. 436,437.
4. Robert E. Lee in a letter to his wife dated December 27, 1856. Quoted in Catherine Millard, *The Rewriting of America's History*, (Camp Hill, PA: Horizon House Publishers, 1991), p. 184.
5. James M. McPherson, *Battle Cry of Freedom*, (New York: Oxford University Press, 1988), p. 8.
6. McPherson, *Battle Cry*, p. 544.
7. President Abraham Lincoln, Second Inaugural Address, March 4, 1865.
8. March 30, 1863, in a Proclamation of a National Day of Humiliation, Fasting and Prayer. James D. Richardson, ed., *A Compilation of the Messages and Papers of the Presidents, 1789–1897,* (Washington, D.C.: U.S. Government Printing Office, 1897), Vol. VI, p. 164,165.
9. December 1, 1862, in his Second Annual Message to Congress. John Bartlett, *Bartlett's Familiar Quotations,* (Boston: Little, Brown and Company, 1855, 1980), pp. 520–524.
10. Peter J. Marshall, Jr., and David Manuel, *The Glory of America*, (Bloomington, MN: Garborg's Heart and Home, Inc., 1991), p. 4.
11. President Abraham Lincoln, Second Inaugural Address, March 4, 1865.
12. Theodore Roosevelt in a speech delivered April 10, 1899. Quoted in William Safire, ed., *Lend Me Your Ears: Great Speeches in History*, (New York: W. W. Norton and Company, 1992), p. 480.
13. 1844. *Webster's Family Encyclopedia*, (NY: Ottenheimer Publishers, Inc., 1988), Vol. 8, p. 1763.
14. Daniel Boorstin, *The Americans: The Democratic Experience*, (New York: Vintage Books, 1973), p. 3.
15. These inscribed words came from an original poem, "The New Colossus," written by Emma Lazarus in 1883.
16. George Grant, ed., *The Patriot's Handbook*, (Elkton, Maryland: Highland Books, 1996) p. 13.
17. George Marlin, Richard Rabatin, Heather Higgins, eds., *The Quotable Paul Johnson*, (New York: Noonday Press, 1994), p. 9.
18. Joseph Stowell, *Proclaim* Radio Program, (Moody Broadcasting Network, May 1998).

Chapter 7: The Battle for America's Soul

1. Sherwood Eddy, *Pathfinders of the World Missionary Crusade*, (New York: Abingdon–Cokesbury, 1945), p. 5,6. Quoted in Ruth A. Tucker, *From Jerusalem to Irian Jaya*, (Grand Rapids, MI: Zondervan Publishing House, 1983), p. 263.
2. Elisabeth Elliot, *Through Gates of Splendor*, (New York: Harper & Row, 1958), p. 176. Quoted in Tucker, *From Jerusalem*, p. 290.
3. J. Herbert Kane, *A Concise History of the Christian World Mission*, (Grand Rapids, MI: Baker, 1978), p. 102. Quoted in Tucker, *From Jerusalem*, p. 290.
4. C. S. Lewis, *Mere Christianity*, (New York: The MacMillan Co., 1952), p. 180.

5. Francis Schaeffer, *The Great Evangelical Disaster*, (Wheaton, IL: Crossway Books, 1984), p. 25.
6. William Federer, *America's God and Country: Encyclopedia of Quotations*, (Coppell, TX: FAME Publishing, Inc., 1994), p. 205.
7. *Scopes v. State*; 289 S.W. 363 (Sup.Ct. Tenn. 1927). James Kennedy, *The Gates of Hell Shall Not Prevail*, (Nashville: Thomas Nelson, 1996), p. 117.
8. Ralph Reed, *Politically Correct*, (Dallas: Word, Inc., 1994), p. 53.
9. Margaret Sanger from her personal writings. Quoted in *Victory in Spite of All Terror* (video), (Traverse City, MI: Freedom Ministries, Inc., and the Christian Broadcasting Network, Inc., 1997).
10. From Jean-Paul Sartre, *Existentialism*, 1947. Quoted in George Seldes, ed., *The Great Thoughts*, (New York: Ballantine Books, 1996), p. 408.
11. Sigmund Freud, *The Future of an Illusion*. Quoted in Seldes, *The Great Thoughts*, p. 161.
12. Dr. Paul Johnson, *Modern Times: The World From the Twenties to the Nineties*, (New York: Harper Collins, 1992), p. 11.
13. Aldous Huxley, *Time Must Have a Stop*, 1944. Quoted in Seldes, *The Great Thoughts*, p. 219.
14. Aldous Huxley, quoted by Dr. Os Guinness in *Victory in Spite of All Terror* (video).
15. Johnson, *Modern Times*, p. 784.
16. President Ronald Reagan, Address to the Library of Congress, November 20, 1981.

Chapter 8: The Darker Side of Life

1. Harvard Sitkoff, *Fifty Years Later: The New Deal Evaluated*, (Philadelphia: Temple University Press, 1985), pp. 3,4.
2. Sitkoff, *The New Deal*, pp. 3,4.
3. *1998 Information Please Almanac*, (Boston: Information Please LLC, 1997), p. 140.
4. Sitkoff, *The New Deal*, pp. 3,4.
5. Larry Burkett, *Whatever Happened to the American Dream?*, (Chicago: Moody Press, 1993), p. 22.
6. Burkett, *American Dream*, p. 66
7. Winston Churchill, speech to the House of Commons after Britain signed the Munich Pact in 1938. Francis Schaeffer, *How Should We Then Live?*, (Wheaton, IL: Crossway Books, 1976), p. 251.
8. Walter Hooper, ed., *God in the Dock: Essays on Theology and Ethics*, (Grand Rapids, MI: Eerdmans, 1970), p. 312.
9. D. James Kennedy, *Character and Destiny*, (Grand Rapids, MI: Zondervan, 1994), p. 14.
10. Kennedy, *Character and Destiny*, p. 142.
11. Charles Malik, "Hope for a World in Crisis," *Collegiate Challenge* 7:2 (1968). Quoted in Josh McDowell, *A Ready Defense*, (San Bernardino, CA: Here's Life Publishers, Inc., 1990), p. 454.
12. November 11, 1948, in an address on Armistice Day. John Bartlett, *Bartlett's Familiar Quotations*, (Boston: Little, Brown and Company, 1855, 1980), p. 825.
13. Bartlett, *Bartlett's Familiar Quotations*, p. 825.
14. William Safire, ed., *Lend Me Your Ears: Great Speeches in History*, (New York: W. W. Norton, 1992), p. 55.
15. *Vidal v. Girard's Executors* 43 U.S. (2 How.) 127 (1844).
16. *Church of the Holy Trinity v. United States* 143 U.S. 457 (1892).
17. *United States v. Macintosh* 283 U.S. 605 (1931).
18. *Everson v. Board of Education* 330 U.S. 1 (1947).

19. *Florey v. Sioux Falls School District*; 464 F. Supp. 911 (U.S.D.C., SD 1979), cert. Denied, 449 U.S. 987 (1980).
20. *Grove v. Mead School District* 753 F. 2d 1528 (1985), cert. denied, 474 U.S. 826.
21. *Vidal v. Girard's Executors*, 43 U.S. 126, 132 (1844) pp. 198, 205-206.
22. Benjamin Rush, July 9, 1788, in a letter to Elias Boudinot. *Letters of Benjamin Rush*, L. H. Butterfield, ed., (Princeton, NJ: American Philosophical Society, 1951), Vol. I, p. 475.

Chapter 9: Torn Apart at the Seams

1. Alexis de Tocqueville, *Democracy in America*. Quoted in Jim Nelson Black, *When Nations Die*, (Wheaton, IL: Tyndale House, 1994), p. vii.
2. Dr. Os Guinness interview by John N. Damoose in Fairfax, Virginia, in 1996.
3. Guinness interview.
4. Judge Robert H. Bork interview by John N. Damoose in Virginia Beach, Virginia, in 1996.
5. Bork interview.
6. Ravi Zacharias, *Deliver Us From All Evil*, (Dallas: Word Publishing, 1996), p. 8.
7. Francis Schaeffer, *How Should We Then Live?*, (Wheaton, IL: Crossway Books, 1976), p. 205.
8. Bork interview.
9. Pastor Greg Laurie interview by John N. Damoose in Virginia Beach, Virginia, in 1996.
10. Kennedy, *Character and Destiny*, p. 149.
11. *Humanist Manifestos I and II*, (New York: Prometheus Books, 1973), portions reprinted in Marty Pay and Hal Donaldson, *Downfall: The Secularization of a Christian Nation*, (Green Forest, AR: New Leaf Press, 1991), p. 220.
12. *Humanist Manifestos*, p. 221.
13. Marty Pay and Hal Donaldson, *Downfall: The Secularization of a Christian Nation*, (Green City, AR: New Leaf Press, 1991), p. 220.
14. Pay, *Downfall*, p. 221.
15. Francis Schaeffer, *A Christian Manifesto*, (Wheaton, IL: Crossway Books, 1981), p. 26.
16. Dr. Paul Johnson, *Modern Times: The World From the Twenties to the Nineties*, (New York: Harper Collins, 1992), p. 5.
17. Michael Denton, *Evolution: A Theory in Crisis*, (Bethesda, MD: Adler & Adler, 1985), p. 67.
18. Charles Darwin, *Origin of Species*, (London: J. M. Dent & Sons, 1971), p. 167.
19. Darwin, *Origin*, pp. 292,293.
20. H.S. Lipson, "A Physicist Looks at Evolution," *Physics Bulletin*, Vol. 31, 1980, p. 138.
21. Charles Darwin, 1858, in a letter to a colleague regarding his *Origin of Species*. Quoted in "John Lofton's Journal," *The Washington Times*, February 8, 1984.
22. G. W. Harper, "Darwinism and Indoctrination," *School Science Review*, December 1977, pp. 258,265.
23. W. R. Bird, *The Origin of Species Revisited,* (NY: Philosophical Library, 1989), Vol. 1, p. 9.
24. Dr. Michael Walker, "To Have Evolved or To Have Not? That Is the Question," *Quadrant*, October 1981, p. 45.
25. T. Rosazak, *Unfinished Animal,* 1975, pp. 101,102.
26. Francis Schaeffer interview by John N. Damoose in Virginia Beach, Virginia, in 1996.
27. Schaeffer interview.
28. Schaeffer interview.
29. Kay Coles James interview by John N. Damoose in Virginia Beach, Virginia, in 1996.

Source Notes

Chapter 10: A Relative Disaster

1. D. James Kennedy, *Character and Destiny*, (Grand Rapids, MI: Zondervan, 1994), p. 155.
2. Dr. Paul Johnson, *Modern Times: The World From the Twenties to the Nineties*, (New York: Harper Collins, 1992), p. 4.
3. Kennedy, *Character and Destiny*, p. 61.
4. Dr. Os Guinness interview by John N. Damoose in Fairfax, Virginia, in 1996.
5. Dr. Alan Keyes interview by John N. Damoose in Virginia Beach, Virginia, in 1996.
6. Eric Johnson, *Say You Want a Revolution*, (Debary, FL: Longwood Communications, 1994), p. 90.
7. Wade Clark Roof, *A Generation of Seekers*, (San Francisco: Harper Collins, 1993), p. 41.
8. Roof, *Seekers*, p. 41.
9. Charles Colson interview by John N. Damoose in Virginia Beach, Virginia, in 1996.
10. *Herald Star*, Steubenville, Ohio, 1984. Stephen K. McDowell and Mark A. Beliles, *America's Providential History*, (Charlottesville, VA: Providence Press, 1988), p. 79.

Chapter 11: The Golden Touch

1. Marty Pay and Hal Donaldson, *Downfall: The Secularization of a Christian Nation*, (Green City, AR: New Leaf Press, 1991), pp. 181,182.
2. Cotton Mather, *Christi Americana*, 1702. Quoted in Peter J. Marshall, Jr., and David Manuel, *The Light and the Glory* (Grand Rapids, MI: Fleming H. Revell Co., 1977), p. 216.
3. F. Lagard Smith, *When Choice Becomes God*, (Eugene, OR: Harvest House, 1990), p. 26.
4. Smith, *When Choice*, p. 26.
5. Smith, *When Choice*, p. 26.
6. Larry Burkett, *Whatever Happened to the American Dream?*, (Chicago: Moody Press, 1993), p. 33.
7. Burkett, *American Dream*, p. 34.
8. Burkett, *American Dream*, p. 34.

Chapter 12: Broken Hearts, Broken Homes

1. Bishop T.D. Jakes interview by John N. Damoose in Virginia Beach, Virginia, in 1996.
2. George Gallup, Jr., interview by John N. Damoose in Virginia Beach, Virginia, in 1996.
3. Gallup interview.
4. Statistics by the Family Research Council, "The 700 Club: Crisis of Confusion Special," aired in January 1997.
5. Dr. Alan Keyes interview by John N. Damoose in Virginia Beach, Virginia, in 1996.
6. Keyes interview.
7. Keyes interview.
8. Keith Fournier interview by John N. Damoose in Virginia Beach, Virginia, in 1996.
9. Fournier interview.
10. Dr. Paul Johnson, *Modern Times: The World From the Twenties to the Nineties*, (New York: Harper Collins, 1992), p. 781.
11. Johnson, *Modern Times*, p. 781.
12. George Barna, *Generation Next*, (Glendale, CA: Barna Research Group, 1995), pp. 41,42.
13. Nicky Cruz, *Code Blue: Urgent Care for the American Youth Emergency*, (Ann Arbor, MI: Vine Books, 1995), p. 13.
14. Eric Johnson, *Say You Want a Revolution*, (Debary, FL: Longwood Communications, 1994), p. 13.
15. George Barna, *Generation Next*, (Ventura, CA: Regal Books, 1995), p. 98–100.

16. Johnson, *Revolution*, p. 291.
17. Kennedy interview.
18. Johnson, *Revolution*, p. 62.
19. United States Supreme Court, *Stone v. Graham* 449 U.S. 39 (1980).
20. From an Internet article by Lynne Cheney, "President Clinton's Mandate for Fuzzy Math," *On the Issues*, (Washington, D.C.: American Enterprise for Public Policy Research, 1997).
21. Josephson Institute of Ethics, 1993.
22. Chuck Colson, *Burden of Truth: Defending Truth in an Age of Unbelief*, (Wheaton, IL: Tyndale Publishers, 1997), p. 13,14.
23. "The 700 Club," CBN News, January 15, 1997.
24. Heritage Foundation study reported by CBN News, January 15, 1997.
25. Family Research Council statistics quoted by CBN News, January 15, 1997.
26. Barna, *Generation Next*, pp. 56–65.
27. James C. Dobson and Gary L. Bauer, "Stop and Listen, America" *USA Today*, April 7, 1990, p. 12A.

Chapter 13: Backward Advances

1. Robert H. Bork, *Slouching Toward Gomorrah*, (New York: Harper Collins, 1996), p. 9.
2. Daniel Boorstin quoted by Dr. Os Guinness in interview by John N. Damoose in Fairfax, Virginia, in 1996.
3. Bork, *Slouching Toward Gomorrah*, p. 9.
4. Ted Baehr interview by John N. Damoose in Virginia Beach, Virginia, in 1996.
5. Baehr interview.
6. Clinton Van Zandt interview by John N. Damoose in Virginia Beach, Virginia, in 1996.
7. May 10, 1789, in addressing the General Committee of the United Baptist Churches of Virginia. Jared Sparks, ed., *The Writings of George Washington*, (Boston: American Stationer's Company, 1837), Vol. XII, p. 154.
8. Dr. Paul Johnson, *History of Christianity*, (Atheneum, NY: Atheneum, 1976), p. 422.
9. Joseph Story, *Commentaries on the Constitution*, Vol. III, 1833, (reprinted New York: DaCapro Press, 1970), p. 726.
10. Francis Schaeffer, *A Christian Manifesto*, (Wheaton, IL: Crossway Books, 1981), p. 35.
11. Matthew D. Shaver, *The Liberator*, Vol. 9 No. 4, April 1998, p. 4.
12. D. James Kennedy, from the sermon "Church and State," (Coral Ridge Presbyterian Church, Fort Lauderdale, FL: Coral Ridge Ministries, 1979).
13. C. S. Lewis, *The Screwtape Letters*, (New York: The MacMillan Co., 1982), p. x.
14. Charles Colson interview by John N. Damoose in Virginia Beach, Virginia, in 1996.
15. Robert Bork, *Slouching Toward Gomorrah*, (New York: Harper Collins, 1996), pp. 2,3.
16. Hildegarde Dolson, *William Penn: Quaker Hero*, (New York: Random House, 1961), p. 155.

Chapter 14: The Culture of Death

1. Judge Robert H. Bork interview by John N. Damoose in Virginia Beach, Virginia, in 1996.
2. Keith Fournier interview by John N. Damoose in Virginia Beach, Virginia, in 1996.
3. John Whitehead, *The Stealing of America*, (Westchester, IL: Crossway Books, 1983), p. 44.
4. Statistics quoted on "The 700 Club," January 15, 1997.
5. *Newsweek*, December 6, 1993, Vol. 122, p. 28.
6. Deborah Zabarenko, Reuters News Service, July 29, 1996.
7. Joe Arpaio, *America's Toughest Sheriff*, (Arlington, TX: Summit Publishers, 1996), p.

xviii.

8. Patrick Fagan and Robert Moffit, *Issues '96: The Candidate's Briefing Book*, (Washington, D.C.: The Heritage Foundaiton, 1996), pp. 2–5.
9. Sheriff Joe Arpaio interview by John N. Damoose in Virginia Beach, Virginia, in 1996.
10. Arpaio, *Toughest Sheriff*, p. xviii.
11. Bureau of Justice Statistics, (FBI Uniform Crime Reports), 1997.
12. Eric Johnson, *Say You Want a Revolution*, (DeBary, FL: Longwood Communications, 1994), p. 224.

Chapter 15: Nations That Live, Nations That Die

1. David J. Gyertson, ed., *Salt and Light: A Christian Response to Current Issues*, (Dallas: Word Publishing, 1993), pp. 24,25.
2. Jim Nelson Black, *When Nations Die*, (Wheaton, IL: Tyndale House, 1994), p. 18.
3. Chuck Colson interview by John N. Damoose in Virginia Beach, Virginia, in 1996.
4. Russell Kirk, *The Roots of American Order*, (Washington, D.C.: Regnery Gateway, 1991), pp. 51,52.
5. Kirk, *The Roots of American Order*, pp. 99,100.
6. Kirk, *The Roots of American Order*, p. 103.
7. Kirk, *The Roots of American Order*, p. 102.
8. Kirk, *The Roots of American Order*, p. 102.
9. George Barna, *The Frog in the Kettle*, (Ventura, CA: Regal Books, 1990), pp. 22,23.
10. Excerpts from Bill Bright, *The Coming Revival*, (Orlando, FL: NewLife Publications, 1995), pp. 66–75.
11. Dr. Jack Hayford interview by John N. Damoose in Virginia Beach, Virginia, in 1996.
12. Charles Colson intervew by John N. Damoose in Virginia Beach, Virginia, in 1996.
13. Dr. D. James Kennedy interview by John N. Damoose in Ft. Lauderdale, Florida, in 1996.
14. Dr. Charles Stanley interview by John N. Damoose in Virginia Beach, Virginia, in 1996.
15. Dr. John Hagee interview by John N. Damoose in Virginia Beach, Virginia, in 1996.

Chapter 16: The Crisis in the Church

1. Francis Schaeffer, *A Christian Manifesto*, (Wheaton, IL: Crossway Books, 1981), p. 56.
2. Nancy Leigh DeMoss, "Begin at My Sanctuary: A Call to Repentance in the Church," presented at Fasting & Prayer '96, St. Louis, MO, November 14, 1996.
3. Friedrich Nietzsche, *The Gay Science*, translated by Walter Kaufman, (New York: Random House, 1974), section 125.
4. Eric Johnson, *Say You Want a Revolution*, (DeBary, FL: Longwood Communications, 1994), p. 338.
5. Jim Bakker, *I Was Wrong*, (Nashville: Thomas Nelson, 1996), pp. 531–534.
6. Interview with Francis Schaeffer on "The 700 Club," January 1984.

Chapter 17: A Crisis of Credibility

1. George Barna, *The Index of Leading Spiritual Indicators*, (Dallas: Word Publishing, 1996), p. 118.
2. Barna, *Index of Leading Spiritual Indicators*, p. 4.
3. Dr. Os Guinness interview by John N. Damoose in Fairfax, Virginia, in 1996.
4. Louis Parkhurst, Jr., ed., *Principles of Victory*, (Minneapolis: Bethany House, 1981) p. 13.
5. Bill Bright, *The Coming Revival*, (Orlando, FL: NewLife Publications, 1995), p. 65.
6. Guinness interview.
7. Dr. Billy Graham, *Storm Warning*, (Dallas: Word Publishing, 1992), p. 28.

8. Graham, *Storm Warning*, p. 28.
9. Barna, *Index of Leading Spiritual Indicators*, p. 1.
10. Edmund Burke, quoted in John Bartlett, ed., *Bartlett's Familiar Quotations*, (Boston: Little, Brown and Company, 1980), p. 332.
11. Francis Schaeffer, *The Great Evangelical Disaster*, (Wheaton, IL: Crossway Books, 1984), p. 141.
12. C. S. Lewis, *Mere Christianity*, (New York; Macmillan, 1952) p. 39.
13. Johnson, *Revolution*, p. 339.

Chapter 18: A Call for Change

1. Richard M. Nixon, *1999: Victory Without War*, (New York: Simon and Schuster, 1988), p. 13.
2. George Barna, *The Index of Leading Spiritual Indicators*, (Dallas: Word Publishing, 1996), p. 55.
3. Barna, *Leading Spiritual Indicators*, (Dallas: Word Publishing, 1996), p. 57.
4. Dr. Os Guinness, *The Devil's Gauntlet*. Quoted in David J. Gyertson, ed., *Salt and Light: A Christian Response to Current Issues*, (Dallas: Word Publishing, 1993), p. 31.
5. R. C. Sproul, *The Holiness of God*, (Wheaton, IL: Tyndale House Publishers, 1985), p. 264.
6. Karl Marx and Freidrich Engels, *The Communist Manifesto*, (New York: PocketBooks, 1964), p. 116.
7. Karl Marx, *A Contribution to the Critique of Hegel's Philosophy of Right*, (1844), Preface.
8. Bill Bright, *The Coming Revival: America's Call to Fast, Pray, and "Seek God's Face,"* (Orlando, FL: NewLife Publications, 1995), p. 70.
9. Dr. Jack Hayford interview by John N. Damoose in Virginia Beach, Virginia, in 1996.
10. Hayford interview.
11. Charles Finney, *Revival Lectures*, (Old Tappan, NJ: Fleming Revell Co., 1970), pp. 336,337.
12. Ron Hutchcraft Radio Program, "A Word With You," (Ron Hutchcraft Ministries, 1998).

Chapter 19: A Call for Commitment

1. William Bradford, *Of Plymouth Plantation 1650*, rendered into modern English by Harold Paget and retitled *Bradford's History of the Plymouth Settlement 1608–1650*, (Portland, OR: American Heritage Ministries, [1909], 1988), p. 21.
2. Charles M. Sheldon, *In His Steps,* (Grand Rapids, MI: Spire Books, 1984), p. 5.

Chapter 20: The Challenge to Renewal

1. Chuck Colson, *Burden of Truth: Defending Truth in an Age of Unbelief*, (Wheaton, IL: Tyndale Publishers, 1997), p. 89.
2. John Jay, 1887, in "National Perils and Opportunities," pp. 8,9. Quoted in Stephen Abbott Northrup, D.D., *A Cloud of Witnesses,* (Portland, OR: American Heritage Ministries, 1987), p. 250.
3. Gales Quotations CD-ROM (Detroit, MI: Gale Research Inc, 1995).
4. Matthew Henry, *Matthew Henry's Commentaries on the Whole Bible, Vol. V*, (Peabody, MA: Hendrickson Publishers, 1991), p.302
5. Henry T. Blackaby and Claude V. King, *Experiencing God,* (Nashville: Lifeway Press, 1990), p. 20.

Index

Index

Index

Index

Acknowledgments

Within minutes of the quickly arranged meeting at the Orlando airport in the Spring of 1997, I sensed the powerful potential for helping to bring our great land of America back to God. I listened with intense excitement as John B. Damoose, former Marketing Director at Chrysler and Ford Motor Company, and his son, John N. Damoose, described their plan to help reach America for Christ. Our hearts resonated in harmony with godly assurance that this meeting was a divine appointment and what was to follow was truly from God. This book and related video are among the first steps in the cooperative efforts of our two ministries, Campus Crusade for Christ International and Freedom Ministries of America.

I would like to acknowledge the efforts of all who contributed to this book. First, my heart-felt appreciation goes to my co-author, John N. Damoose and his dear wife, Margo. He did an excellent piece of work on researching and writing the historical chapters on America and the church, as well as contributing to the other chapters.

Along with John, many more people were involved in this effort. My special heartfelt thanks to my dear friend, Chuck Colson, a giant among men for God who wrote the Foreword, to researcher Dr. Don Highlander and writer Dr. Jim Nelson Black whose wordsmith gifts helped to sharpen the manuscript. My continual gratitude goes to the New*Life* Publications staff: Dr. Joe Kilpatrick, Executive Director, who took the idea for this book and nurtured it along to a finished product; Joette Whims, editing, and Michelle Treiber, cover and printing. My gratitude also goes to Lynn Copeland of Genesis Publications for her help with the writing and research.

My special thanks to Sid Wright, my Chief of Staff, who with his lovely wife, Ann, have helped lighten immeasureably my load with this book and our fasting, prayer and revival efforts. My deep gratitude also to all those who reviewed, critiqued and commented on the rough draft, and to my many friends who read and sent in endorsements to encourage others to read and follow this book's proposed plan to help recapture America for Christ and return it to its original national purpose.

Finally, I save my dearest expressions of love and appreciation for my beloved wife of 50 years, Vonette, who has encouraged me through five forty-day fasts in the last five years as I have sought God's face for revival for America, the world, and the fulfillment of the Great Commission. She has joined me in the last two and a half forty-day fasts with great blessings and joy, but primarily, she shares with me an awesome burden for America and for the spiritual revival in the churches of America.

Bill Bright
Orlando, Florida
June 1998

Campus Crusade Response Form

☐ I have received Jesus Christ as my Savior and Lord as a result of reading this book.

☐ As a new Christian I want to know Christ better and experience the abundant Christian life.

☐ I want to be one of the two million people who will join Dr. Bright in forty days of prayer and fasting for revival for America, the world, and the fulfillment of the Great Commission.

☐ Please send me *free* information on staff and ministry opportunities with Campus Crusade for Christ International.

☐ Please send me *free* information about the more than 50 other books, booklets, audio cassettes, and videos by Bill and Vonette Bright.

____
NAME (please print)

____
ADDRESS

____
CITY STATE ZIP

____
COUNTRY E-MAIL

Please check the appropriate box(es), clip, and mail this form in an envelope to:

Dr. Bill Bright
Campus Crusade for Christ
P.O. Box 593684
Orlando, FL 32859-3684 U.S.A.

You may also fax your response to (407) 826-2149, or send E-mail to newlifepubs@ccci.org. Visit our website at www.newlifepubs.com.

Freedom Ministries Response Form

☐ Please send me *free* information about Freedom Ministries of America.

☐ Please send me more information about how the "Grand Coalition" will help save America.

☐ Please send me more information about the "Great Freedom Train" and "Freedom Centers."

☐ I want to join the efforts to recapture America's national purpose and make the following **Personal Commitment:**

I hereby commit myself to the task of proclaiming and sharing the Gospel of Jesus Christ throughout the United States of America and the world. I recognize that America is in serious trouble as we begin a new millennium. As a nation, we now risk the disgrace of failing to complete our national mission to help fulfill the Great Commission. As a result, we stand on the brink of national disaster.

I hereby pledge my support to this cause. Enlist me in the struggle to help save America and complete the Great Commission. I understand that this is not a club to join, but a working body of believers which will actively seek to reverse the trend of decadence and despair afflicting our nation. I am ready for the task, and in the power of Jesus Christ, I will do my part as God reveals Himself and His directions to me.

SIGNATURE

NAME (please print)

ADDRESS

CITY STATE ZIP

COUNTRY

PHONE NUMBER E-MAIL

Please check the appropriate box(es), clip and mail this form in an envelope to:

Mr. John N. Damoose
Freedom Ministries of America
P.O. Box 48
Traverse City, MI 49686-0048

You may also fax your response to (616) 947-3490 or send E-mail to fma@pentel.net.